THE HANDBOOK

of the Middle East

MICHAEL G. KORT

Twenty-First Century Books
Brookfield, Connecticut

For Carol, Eleza, and Tamara

Photographs courtesy of SuperStock: pp. 8, 12, 24, 256 (top), 257, 259 (top),
266; AP/Wide World Photos: pp. 19, 245, 254, 258, 259 (bottom), 260, 262
(bottom), 268, 269 (bottom), 272, 274 (top), 281, 283 (top); Gamma Presse:
pp. 37 (© Keystone), 51 (© Keystone), 196, 246 (top © Merillon Georges), 251
(© Merillon Georges), 269 (top © Eslami Rad), 270 (© Aunos-Stevens), 274
(bottom © Keystone); Christine Osborne/Middle East Pictures: pp. 57 (© M.
Crame), 106 (© Caray Hauri), 113 (© L. Mitchell), 188 (© M. Dutton), 207,
213, 246 (bottom), 264, 284 (bottom © Christine Osborne); Panos Pictures:
pp. 65 (© Guy Mansfield), 89 (© Giacomo Pirozzi), 127 (© Caroline Penn), 136
(© Caroline Penn), 158 (© Morris Carpenter); © Cory Langley: pp. 97, 115, 154,
180; Corbis: pp. 141 (© Adam Woolfitt), 280 (© Reuters NewMedia, Inc), 286
(© S.I.N.); Archive Photos: pp. 252 (© Jack Dabaghian), 253 (bottom/Hulton
Getty), 255 (© Ricardo Watson), 256 (bottom/Hulton Getty), 267, 273 (CNP),
275 (© Reuters/David Silverman), 277 (© SAGA/Frank Capri), 282 (top,
bottom © Reuters/Aziz Taher), 283 (bottom/Hulton Getty), 284
(top © Reuters/Frederic Neema), 285 (© William Philpott); Magnum
Photos, Inc.: pp. 253 (top © 2000 Abbas), 262 (top © 1998 Abbas)

Published by Twenty-First Century Books
A Division of The Millbrook Press, Inc.
2 Old New Milford Road
Brookfield, CT   06804
www.millbrookpress.com

Library of Congress Cataloging-in-Publication Data

Kort, Michael, 1944-
The handbook of the Middle East / Michael G. Kort.
p. cm.
Includes bibliographical references and index.
Summary: Examines the past, present, and future of all the
countries in the Middle East, discussing their history and culture.
ISBN 0-7613-1611-6 (lib. bdg.)
1. Middle East—Handbooks, manuals, etc.—Juvenile literature.
[1. Middle East.] I. Title.
DS44 .K67 2002   956—dc21   2001037330

Contents

PREFACE 5

CHAPTER 1 7 What Is the Middle East?

CHAPTER 2 21 North Africa: Egypt and Libya

CHAPTER 3 55 Israel, the Palestine Authority, and Jordan

CHAPTER 4 104 Lebanon, Syria, and Iraq

CHAPTER 5 138 The Northern Tier: Turkey and Iran

CHAPTER 6 184 The Arabian Peninsula: Saudi Arabia, Yemen, Oman, Kuwait, United Arab Emirates, Qatar, Bahrain

221 MAPS AND FLAGS

230 CHRONOLOGY

245 ENCYCLOPEDIA

291 NOTES

293 INDEX

Preface

On January 20, 1957, three maps appeared in *The New York Times*, a leading newspaper in the United States. All three supposedly showed the "Middle East." Yet these maps were quite different from each other. All three included Egypt, Israel, Lebanon, Syria, Iraq, Iran, Saudi Arabia, and Libya. Yet each map added a different list of countries to that core group. The map reflecting the British government's definition added Sudan in Africa and Cyprus, a Mediterranean island nation that generally is considered part of Europe. The map based on the viewpoint of then U.S. secretary of state John Foster Dulles added Sudan and Ethiopia in Africa and Afghanistan, Pakistan, and Turkey in Asia, but excluded Cypress. The map consistent with a mid-1950s dictionary definition stretched 1,000 miles (1,600 kilometers) eastward in Asia to India and beyond, and westward in North Africa to Tunisia. Other definitions of the Middle East, some old and others new, eliminate everything east of Iran and south of Egypt but include Algeria, Tunisia, and Morocco in North Africa; include Afghanistan but eliminate Sudan; or include or eliminate other combinations of nations.

Obviously, the definition of what countries belong to the Middle East has changed over time; nor is there a consensus even today. The actual term "Middle East" dates from 1902. It was used that year by American military strategist Alfred Thayer Mahan to designate a region between Europe and the "Far East," the eastern part of Asia that includes countries such as China and Japan. This book uses two broad criteria to define the Middle East: geographic proximity to the Fertile Crescent and the Persian Gulf and a survey of current text-book definitions. According to these admittedly imprecise criteria, the Middle East includes sixteen countries: Bahrain, Egypt, Iran, Iraq, Israel, Jordan, Kuwait, Lebanon, Libya, Oman, Qatar, Saudi Arabia, Syria, Turkey, the United Arab Emirates, and Yemen, as well as territory controlled by the semi-independent Palestinian Authority. You may find that other books you consult include in the Middle East parts of North Africa or Central Asia not discussed here, or exclude one or more of the countries included in this volume.

Whatever its precise boundaries, aside from its long his-tory and contributions to civilization, the Middle East is important to Americans for several reasons. It contains the largest oil resources in the world, fully two-thirds of the world's total reserves. What happens in the Middle East therefore can affect whether Americans will have the fuel they need to drive their cars, run their electric power plants, and heat their homes. And a lot is happening. The Middle East is riven by serious and long-standing disputes that have led to numerous wars since the end of World War II, includ-ing the 1991 Gulf War in which American soldiers fought and died. Nowhere in the world is there a greater threat that countries considered dangerous by the United States might acquire nuclear weapons or other weapons of mass destruc-tion. The Middle Eastern countries that most worry the United States in this regard are Iran, Iraq, Libya, and Syria, all of which are listed by the U.S. State Department as pow-ers that promote international terrorism. For these and other reasons, events in the Middle East are important enough to make the front pages of our newspapers regularly, which is why each of us should be informed about that pivotal region of the world.

CHAPTER 1

What Is the Middle East?

No part of the world is more central to the story of human civilization than the Middle East. As a region it is geographically unique, the only place on Earth where three continents—Europe, Asia, and Africa—meet and, in a historical and cultural sense, converge. It is appropriate that the shores of the world's geographic and historical "middle land" are washed by its "middle sea," the Mediterranean (from the Latin *medius* for "middle" and *terra* for "land"), which is encircled by Europe, Asia, and Africa and since prehistoric times has connected the inhabitants of those three continents. The Middle East's location has made it the oldest and most important crossroads in human history.

The Middle East was the original cradle of civilization. Between 10,000 and 11,000 years ago people living near the present-day city of Jericho near the Dead Sea probably were the first human beings to practice agriculture. Jericho itself became the world's first city about 8000 B.C., complete with a wall that surrounded an area of about 10 acres (4 hectares). Signs of equally ancient town life have been found at a place called Catal Huyuk in Turkey. Catal Huyuk may also have been the place where people first practiced irrigation and domesticated animals. The first civilization with a system of writing arose in the Middle East between the Tigris and Euphrates rivers around 3500 B.C. Since writing enabled people to keep records of what they did, it can be said that humanity's prehistory ended and its history began in the Middle East. The Sumerians, the ancient people who developed the world's first writing system, also are the first people known to have used the wheel. Their system of mathematics, based on multiples of sixty, gave us our system of measuring time with 60 seconds to a minute and 60 minutes to an hour, as well as our practice of dividing a circle into 360 degrees. Shortly after the beginning of Sumerian civilization, another civilization developed in the Nile River valley in Egypt. When Egypt was united about 3100 B.C., the world had its first political unit large enough to be called a country. When King Sargon of Akkad conquered the surrounding city states of Mesopotamia about seven hundred years later, the world had its first empire.

The Middle East, the birthplace of monotheism (the belief in only one God), is arguably the world's most influen-

The Nile River offers visual relief, a narrow band of blue in a sea of sand in Egypt.

tial religious epicenter. Judaism, the world's first genuinely monotheistic religion, was born in the Middle East among the ancient Israelites almost 4,000 years ago. The world's other two great monotheistic religions, Christianity and Islam, also were founded in the Middle East, respectively about 2,000 and 1,400 years ago. Today they are the two most widespread religions in the world. Monotheistic ideas also appeared at other times and places in the Middle East. They were part of a short-lived movement associated with the Egyptian pharaoh Akhenaton in the fourteenth century B.C. The Zoroastrian faith of ancient Persia, which probably originated in the seventh century B.C. and was the dominant religion there until the Arab conquest fourteen centuries later, envisioned a good, ethical deity engaged in a constant struggle with the forces of evil. Another monotheistic religion, the Baha'i faith, began in Persia (present-day Iran) in the mid-nineteenth century. Severely persecuted in Iran today, the Baha'is have their world headquarters in Israel.

Two of the Middle East's sixteen countries, Egypt and Libya, are in North Africa. The rest are in Asia, although Turkey includes a small chunk of Europe. Some Middle Eastern countries, such as Saudi Arabia and Kuwait, are extremely wealthy because of enormous oil resources; others, such as Egypt and Yemen, are very poor. All of the region's countries except three—Turkey, Iran, and Israel— have a majority Arab population, and all except Israel are primarily Islamic in religion. Only Israel has a modern industrial economy. All of the countries in the Middle East, from the largest, Saudi Arabia, to the smallest, Bahrain, are going through rapid and often difficult changes that put enormous strains on their social structures.

The Middle East is a region of political turmoil. Only one country, Israel, is an established functioning democracy that guarantees its citizens political and civil rights. A second, Turkey, teeters precariously between democratic and military rule, while a third, Lebanon, despite some democratic traditions, barely has a functioning government and is largely under the control of Syria, its powerful neighbor to the east. The rest of the countries of the Middle East are either dictatorships, sometimes dressed up with powerless parliamentary institutions, or despotic monarchies. Four of them—Iraq, Libya, Saudi Arabia, and Syria—were listed as being among the world's most repressive countries in the 1999–2000 report by Freedom House, a highly respected independent foundation. Iran, Iraq, and Saudi Arabia were listed in 1999 by the U.S. State Department as being among the world's most repressive countries in denying religious freedom. Finally, of the seven countries in the world listed by the U.S. State Department as promoting international terrorism, four—Iran, Iraq, Libya, and Syria—are in the Middle East.

THE GEOGRAPHIC SETTING: THE DRY WORLD

The Middle East has an area of about 3.4 million square miles (8.8 million square kilometers) and a population of approximately 230 million people. These figures are only slightly less than those for the United States, which has an area of 3.6 million square miles (9.3 million square kilometers) and a population of 278 million people. The natural boundaries of the Middle East are the Black, Aegean, Mediterranean, Arabian, and Caspian seas, and the Caucasus Mountains. The Persian Gulf, sandwiched between the Arabian Peninsula and Iran and under whose shores and waters lie more than 60 percent of the world's oil resources, lies entirely within the region. The Gulf of Aden on the southern shore of the Arabian Peninsula and the Gulf of Oman to its northeast are extensions of the Arabian Sea.

The Middle East has several distinct regions, a large variety of topographical features, and environmental contrasts even within individual countries. There are extremes of cold and heat, flat plains and jagged mountain ranges, mighty life-giving rivers, and the salty and lifeless Dead Sea. At the same time, one overriding characteristic—an arid climate—unites the entire region. The Middle East has aptly been called "the dry world." For thousands of years water has been the key to survival in the Middle East. Even today, despite the overwhelming importance of oil, nothing is of greater concern to its population than water. Only about 3 percent of the region's land receives enough rain—more than 12 inches (300 millimeters) per year—to be agriculturally useful. Some of the Middle East's desert regions are among the driest places on Earth. Years can pass without rainfall in parts of Egypt, southeastern Saudi Arabia, and western Oman. Iran's Great Salt Desert reportedly is the largest area in the world with no vegetation at all.

A few areas along the fringes of the Middle East do get adequate rainfall, mainly parts of northern Iran and Iraq, the upland areas of northern Turkey, the Mediterranean coastal areas of Turkey, Syria, Lebanon, and Israel, and the mountainous areas of Yemen. Yet even in these areas rainfall is a problem: It is concentrated in the winter months, while summers are hot and dry. Summer winds blowing in from the desert parch what in winter were well-watered landscapes. And there is always the danger in any given year or period of years that the rains will be too light and there will be drought.

The Middle East's largest and most reliable sources of water year-round are its two great river systems, the Nile and the Tigris-Euphrates. The Nile carries water into Egypt from the interior of Africa via two main branches, the Blue Nile and the White Nile, that join into a single river several hundred miles south of Egypt in the Sudan. The Nile's waters make its river valley one of the most fertile and agriculturally productive places in the world. The Tigris and Euphrates both rise in Turkey and flow generally southeast until they meet just short of the Persian Gulf. The fertile land between them, where a series of ancient civilizations beginning with the Sumerian developed, is called Mesopotamia, Greek for "between the rivers." The third major river in the Middle East is the Jordan, the river that plays such a prominent role in the Bible. Compared to the Nile, Tigris, and Euphrates, the Jordan River is little more than a large stream, much of whose length forms the border between Israel and Jordan.

Another source of year-round water in the Middle East is groundwater, which in the form of springs has fed the region's oases for millennia. Today newly discovered groundwater, buried in rock formations deep beneath baking desert sands, is being tapped in both Saudi Arabia and Libya. However, unlike the water from rivers or permanent springs, this groundwater is not a renewable resource. It has been there for thousands, and in some cases tens of thousands, of years. Some of it consists of deposits left over from the last Ice Age, when rainfall in the region was much greater, and is literally 30,000 years old. The rest, about 6,000 years old, dates from more recent, but still prehistoric, periods of heavier rainfall. This so-called fossil water is not being replaced as it is used, which means its consumption must be managed carefully. Even then, this "new" source of ancient groundwater eventually will be used up.

Not surprisingly, deserts are the single most common land formation in the "dry world" of the Middle East. Most of Egypt and Libya is taken up with North Africa's Sahara, the largest desert in the world. The vast Arabian Desert covers a huge plateau that dominates the Arabian Peninsula. Jordan, on the edge of that peninsula, is mainly desert, as is the southern part of Israel, which is known as the Negev. Yet another desert covers part of the plateau that makes up most of Iran.

Deserts have their own form of beauty, be it sand dunes shaped by the wind or monoliths like these formations in Libya's Sahara.

The Middle East is divided into four major geographic regions. A huge mountainous plateau that runs from Iran through Turkey forms the region's northern tier. The western section of that region, which constitutes most of modern Turkey, is a peninsula known as Anatolia or Asia Minor, which separates the Mediterranean and Black seas. Anatolia in turn is separated from Europe by two narrow and strategic straits, the Bosporus in the northeast and the Dardanelles in the southwest, and by the Sea of Mamora, which lies between the two straits. South of that rocky highland is the Fertile Crescent. Its name comes both from its curved shape and, for the Middle East, its relative abundance of water. The Fertile Crescent runs from the Mediterranean coast of Israel and Lebanon northeastward into Syria and Iraq, where it turns southeastward, following the courses of the Tigris and Euphrates to the Persian Gulf. Its moisture comes from rainfall of approximately 24 inches (600 millimeters) per year in northern Israel, Lebanon, and southern Syria, and the waters of the Tigris and Euphrates. South of the Fertile Crescent is the barren Arabian Peninsula, one of the hottest and driest places on Earth. Its most important features are underground: saucerlike rock formations, with their low point near the Persian Gulf. Eons ago these structures trapped the oil deposits that today are the largest in the world. The peninsula has mountainous areas in its southwestern and eastern corners. Finally, the North African section of the Middle East is part of the Sahara Desert. Its parched landscape is broken only by the long and slender green strip of the Nile River valley and the huge triangular delta where the Nile flows into the Mediterranean Sea.

THE PEOPLES OF THE MIDDLE EAST

When we think of the Middle East we usually think of Arabs, often in their traditional dress: men wearing a headcloth held on by a cord called a *kaffiyeh*, and women in modest loose-fitting clothing, their hair covered by a scarf, their faces often hidden by a veil. This picture no longer fits many

Arabs, who at least in urban areas frequently have adopted Western styles of dress. Nor are the Arabs the only people in the Middle East. They are the largest single group in the region and the vast majority in thirteen of its sixteen countries. But in the Middle East as a whole Arabs constitute about 60 percent of the total population.

Originally the term Arab referred to the inhabitants of the Arabian Peninsula, an ancient Middle Eastern people mentioned both in the Bible and in other contemporary records. Their conquests beginning in the seventh century A.D. spread both Islam and the use of the Arabic language across the Middle East and North Africa and in the process assimilated non-Arab peoples such as the Egyptians into the Arab fold. Today the term Arab refers both to the original Arabs and the descendants of those conquered people who continue to speak Arabic as their native language, approximately 150 million people. Arabic itself belongs to the Semitic family of languages. It is related to languages formerly spoken in the Middle East, such as Aramaic, as well as to Hebrew.

The Turks are most the populous non-Arabic-speaking people in the Middle East. By Middle Eastern standards they are recent arrivals: The first Turkic groups settled in the region approximately a thousand years ago. The Ottoman Turks, founders of the empire that for five hundred years dominated much of the Middle East, arrived in what today is Turkey only seven hundred years ago. They speak a language that originated in Central Asia and did not adopt Islam as their religion until after migrating to Middle East.

The Iranians, the second largest non-Arab group in the Middle East, are the direct descendants of the ancient Persians. They have lived in what today is called Iran since ancient times, probably arriving in the region in the third millennium B.C. The Persians are mentioned as great conquerors in the Bible. In later centuries they battled the ancient Greeks and Romans, as well as the Byzantines, for control of large parts of the Middle East. The Iranian language belongs to the Indo-European family of languages that includes English and most other European languages, as well as Sanskrit, the ancient language of India. Iranian is the third most widely spoken language in the Middle

East, after Arabic and Turkish. Most Iranians follow the Muslim faith.

About 25 million Kurds live in the Middle East in a region called Kurdistan, which is divided between Turkey, Iran, and Iraq. They continue to be persecuted in all three countries, often with great brutality, because of their desire for an independent Kurdish state. They are, by far, the largest single Middle Eastern ethnic group without an independent country of their own. The Kurds, who trace their Middle Eastern roots to ancient times, are Muslims and speak a language related to Iranian.

Jews have lived in the Middle East as an identifiable people for close to four thousand years. Over the course of their long history they lived in virtually every part of the region. However, since 1948 Jews have fled persecution in Arab countries and settled in Israel. Sizable Jewish communities still survive in Iran, where all non-Muslims share a precarious existence, and in Turkey, where Jews are full-fledged citizens. Most Middle Eastern Jews live in Israel, where they constitute slightly less than half of the country's Jewish population.

All of the groups just mentioned, with the exception of the Jews, are predominantly Muslim. The Muslims themselves are divided into two main sects, the Sunnis and the Shiites. The split between the two groups dates from the mid-seventh century. Between 85 and 90 percent of all Muslims are Sunni; most of the rest, who are concentrated in Iran and, to a lesser degree in Iraq, are Shiite. Sunnis and Shiites in turn are divided into many smaller sects. Christians make up a small and declining proportion of the Middle East population. The largest Christian group in the Middle East is the Coptic community of Egypt, which accounts for about 6 percent of the country's population of 61 million. About 30 percent of Lebanon's 3.6 million people belong to several different Christian churches. Approximately 1 million people in Lebanon, Syria, Israel, and Jordan follow the Druze faith, a secretive offshoot of Islam dating from the eleventh century. There are, of course, many small ethnic and religious groups scattered throughout the vast Middle East. Prominent among them are the Christian Armenian communities in Turkey, Syria, and Iran, and the Berbers in Libya.

A BRIEF HISTORICAL OVERVIEW

The long history of the Middle East can be divided into seven periods. The first, and by far the longest, dates from the origins of the ancient Sumerian and Egyptian civilizations shortly before 3000 B.C. to the conquests of the Greek king Alexander the Great between 334 and 323 B.C. That period saw the rise and fall of numerous great states and empires, beginning with Egypt and the empire of Sargon of Akkad in Mesopotamia, and followed, among others, by empires dominated by the Hittites, Babylonians, Assyrians, and Persians. The development of monotheism by the Israelites began in the Fertile Crescent sometime after 1800 B.C., with the Israelite exodus from Egypt and settlement in what today is Israel probably occurring in the thirteenth century B.C. The first period of Middle Eastern history ended with the first conquest of the region by an outside power, Alexander the Great.

The second period, the era of Greek and subsequently Roman domination, lasted until the end of the fourth century A.D. Although Alexander's empire broke up after his death, large parts of the Middle East from Anatolia southward along the Mediterranean coast into Egypt were absorbed into the Greek, or Hellenistic, world. Egypt especially became the center of a thriving Greek culture, although there and elsewhere in the Middle East that culture was limited to the ruling elite. During the second and first centuries B.C., Rome conquered the Hellenistic part of the Middle East. In the first century A.D., a time of extensive religious ferment, Christ preached in Roman-dominated territory that today lies mostly within Israel, and Christianity was born. Christianity eventually became the official religion of the Roman Empire and thereby the dominant religion in much of the Middle East, a status it lost after the Arab conquests of the seventh century.

The Roman Empire was divided into western and eastern portions in A.D. 395 and ceased to exist in the west just fifteen years later. Rome's decline and fall marked the beginning of the Middle East's third historical period. During this period, which lasted until the seventh century, two empires, the Byzantine (or Eastern Roman Empire) and the Persian, fought for dominance in the region. Having exhausted each other, neither could prevent the Arab armies that burst out of the Arabian Peninsula from overrunning much of the region. The Byzantine Empire lost much of its territory, but still survived the storm, beating back several Arab assaults on its capital of Constantinople between 673 and 677. The Persian Empire was conquered between 637 and 650, after which the Persians gradually abandoned their native Zoroastrian faith for the religion of their conquerors.

The Arab conquest began the fourth period in the history of the Middle East. The Arabs brought a new religion, Islam, to the Middle East. Islam had originated on the Arabian Peninsula and was based on the teachings of Mohammad, who in about the year 610 began preaching what he claimed was the word of God as revealed to him. Mohammad's revelations were collected and written down in the Koran. By the time of his death in 632, most of the Arabian Peninsula had been won over to Islam, either as a result of Mohammad's preaching or by force. The Arabs then began a campaign of conquest to spread their new religion. The Arab armies had important advantages over their opponents. They were inspired by the idea of *jihad*, or holy war, which was to be waged, either militarily or by other means such as proselytism, until the entire world either converted to Islam or accepted Muslim rule. Arab warriors, fired by Islamic religious teaching that promised they would instantly be transported to paradise if they died fighting for their faith, often fought seemingly without fear, thereby terrorizing opposing soldiers. However, while the Arabs were ruthless and destructive conquerors, they usually did not force Christians and Jews to convert to Islam, and Jews in particular often lived more securely and suffered from less persecution under Muslim rule than under Christian rule. But the Arabs did compel Christians and Jews to live as inferiors to Muslims. As inferiors, or *dhimmi*, they had to pay a special tax and were subject to many humiliating restrictions, such as not being allowed to testify in Muslim courts or ride horses. In part because of these restrictions and other discrimination, Christianity declined in the Middle East and Islam became the region's dominant religion, a status it retains to this day.

By the eleventh century Arab military and political power had waned, and large parts of the Middle East passed to non-Arab control. Islam, however, remained the dominant religion. The main exception to Islamic rule was the existence of several Christian states established in the late eleventh century by the Crusaders from Europe along the eastern coast of the Mediterranean Sea. But the Crusader states lasted less than two hundred years. Muslim forces were able to regroup, and the last Christian stronghold fell to them in the late thirteenth century.

The rise of the Ottoman Turks in the fourteenth century marked the beginning of the fifth era, which lasted into the nineteenth century. The Ottomans, who were Sunni Muslims, succeeded an earlier group of Turkish conquerors known as the Seljuks. At its peak, the Ottoman Empire controlled most of the Middle East, with the exception of Persia and parts of the Arabian Peninsula. It also controlled the Balkan Peninsula in Europe and all of North Africa.

Although the Ottoman Empire survived until 1918, by the mid-nineteenth century it was in a state of decay. That decline opened the door for European powers to increase their influence in the region and began the sixth era of Middle Eastern history. It was during this period that the Suez Canal was built. Completed in 1869, the canal fulfilled an age-old dream of linking the Mediterranean and Red seas and opening a direct water route between Europe and eastern Asia. It immediately became one of the world's most strategically important waterways. European influence in the Middle East reached its peak after World War I, when the Ottoman Empire was dismantled. The empire's former territories that encompassed the Fertile Crescent were placed under the control of Great Britain and France by the newly founded League of Nations. These territories, however, were not held as colonies, but rather as what were called mandates, which meant that Britain and France were to prepare the local populations for eventual independence. France received the mandate for Syria (which included what today are Syria and Lebanon), while Britain received the mandate for Iraq and the mandate for was then called Palestine (the area that today includes Israel, Jordan, and the territories administered by the Palestinian Authority).

Meanwhile, in the 1920s, oil was discovered in the Middle East near the Persian Gulf. The discovery of the world's richest oil deposits made the Middle East a region of vital concern to the world's industrial powers. Control of the Middle East and its oil resources was critically important during World War II. In the battle of El Alamein in northern Egypt in 1942, one of the key battles of the war, the British stopped the Nazi German drive toward the Suez Canal and the invaluable oil wells of the Persian Gulf that lay beyond. The era of peak European influence lasted until after World War II, when the weakened European powers saw their empires in Asia and Africa dissolve.

The seventh and current era is one of independence from foreign control. The Middle East now has sixteen independent states: thirteen Arab states and individual Turkish, Iranian, and Jewish states. The current era, however, has not been a peaceful one. Since World War II Israel and Arab states that refuse to recognize Israel's right to exist have fought four wars. These wars are part of what is known as the Arab-Israeli conflict. The Middle East has also been the

The U.S.S. *Enterprise* in the Suez Canal on its way to join U.S. forces in the Gulf in 1996.

scene of an eight-year war between Arab Iraq and non-Arab Iran, as well as wars and civil wars among Arabs themselves. Traditional monarchies have been overthrown in several Arab states and in Iran and replaced, depending on the case, by secular or religious dictatorships. Vast oil resources have made several states bordering the Persian Gulf wealthy, in some cases fabulously so. But riches from oil, and the economic development and social change that accompanied it, have also created problems. They have contributed to rivalries between countries and social unrest within countries where oil wealth is concentrated in very few hands.

In addition, from the end of World War II until the early 1990s, largely because of the region's oil resources, the Middle East was an important arena in the Cold War struggle between the United States and the Soviet Union. Both the Americans and the Soviets provided their allies and clients in the region with powerful ultramodern weapons that took their toll in lives during wartime and burdened countries with enormous military budgets in times of peace. Today the countries of the Middle East devote a greater percentage of their annual gross national product to military spending than countries in any other region in the world. Since the end of the Cold War, several of the region's most dictatorial and aggressive states including Iraq and Iran have redoubled their efforts to acquire nuclear, chemical, or biological weapons, which are known as weapons of mass destruction because they can kill huge numbers of people. This has increased the danger that a disastrous war could break out in the region. At the turn of the millennium, the future of the Middle East, notwithstanding its long and creative past, is anything but secure.

CHAPTER 2

North Africa: Egypt and Libya

EGYPT

Egypt has the longest continuous history—more than 5,000 years—of any country in the world. While it is true that today's Egyptians no longer speak their ancient language, worship their old gods, or live according to their original culture, there remains a sense of continuity and national identity that runs back to when Egypt first was unified around 3100 B.C. The linkage goes beyond historical memory or sentiment: Most experts agree that the modern Egyptians by and large are genetically similar to the people who lived there in ancient times. The name "Egypt" itself is a Greek adaptation from an original ancient Egyptian word, *Kemet*, meaning "black land," a reference to the fertile black soil along the Nile River.

Today Egypt is no longer a world power or technological pacesetter, as it was in ancient times. It is, however, the political and cultural leader of the Arab world, a position it has held, with only one brief interruption, for generations. That role is the result of several factors. With more than 61 million people, Egypt by far has the largest population of any Arab nation. It is centrally located in the Arab world, midway between the North African states that stretch to the

Atlantic Ocean in the west and the Fertile Crescent and Arabian Peninsula in the east. Egypt has a long tradition as a center of Islamic scholarship that dates from the founding of the Al-Azhar Mosque in Cairo during the tenth century. Today the nation has 150 institutions of higher learning, including 13 universities.

Most important, however, Egypt's leadership in the modern Arab world evolved from its central role in the Arab revival after centuries of decline and foreign domination. That revival began in the early part of the nineteenth century and accelerated during the era of British control of Egypt that began in 1882 and lasted into the twentieth century. The era saw the birth of modern Egyptian nationalism. When Egyptian army officers overthrew the country's monarchy in 1952 and set up a military dictatorship, they firmly established Egypt as the leader of Arab nationalism throughout the Middle East and North Africa. The new regime, under President Gamal Abdel Nasser, also made Egypt the Arab world's leading military power, a position it holds to this day. Egypt also is the Arab world's center of literature, art, book publishing, music recording, theater, and film. The Arab world's most prominent fiction writer, Nobel Prize–winner Naguib Mahfouz, is a native and lifelong resident of Cairo. Egypt's broadcasting stations are the most powerful in the Middle East and their transmissions are heard in many foreign languages as well as in Arabic. Egyptian Arabic is considered the common language, or "lingua franca," of the Arab world. The country has played a central role in most major issues that have absorbed the Arab world, from the struggle against the Ottoman Empire and resistance to European colonialism to the Arab-Israeli conflict and the 1991 Gulf War against Iraq.

To be sure, Egypt remains terribly poor and is dependent on aid from the United States, Europe, and the wealthy Arab oil powers such as Saudi Arabia. It is burdened by a huge and growing overpopulation problem that consistently overwhelms all development programs. Furthermore, as in several other Arab countries, Egypt's secular leadership faces serious, and increasingly violent, threats from Islamic fundamentalists who want to overthrow the current regime and establish an Islamic state based on Muslim religious law, the *Sharia*. Yet so far no other Arab country has seriously challenged Egypt's place of primacy in Arab and Middle Eastern affairs.

Geography and People

Egypt is a large, almost-square quadrilateral, slightly wider in the south than in the north, that occupies the northeast corner of Africa and a small triangular chunk of western Asia called the Sinai Peninsula. Egypt is about 640 miles (1,030 kilometers) from north to south, 600 miles (965 kilometers) east to west in the north, and 770 miles (1,240 kilometers) east to west in the south. Almost all of its total area of 385,229 square miles (999,739 square kilometers), about the size of Texas and New Mexico combined, is desert. The only exception, aside from a few scattered oases, is the region watered by the Nile River: a long, narrow valley, never more than 9 miles (14 kilometers) wide, that extends southward into inner Africa; and a broad 11,000-square-mile (28,500-square-kilometer) delta along the Mediterranean Sea. The Nile Valley and delta together account for about 4 percent of Egypt's land area, but are home to 99 percent of its population. This region is one of the most densely populated places on Earth.

Egypt's northern boundary is the Mediterranean Sea. To the northeast, bordering on the Sinai Peninsula, is Israel. The rest of Egypt's eastern border is formed by the Red Sea. Egypt's western neighbor is Libya, its southern neighbor Sudan. Its largest city is Cairo (population 6.6 million). Several miles west of Cairo, in the desert, is the Giza plateau, home to Egypt's famous great pyramids, collectively the only remaining member of the ancient Seven Wonders of the World. A few hundred yards from the two largest pyramids—the Great Pyramid of Khufu and the Pyramid of Khafre—is the Great Sphinx. Half man and half lion, 240 feet (73 meters) long and 66 feet (20 meters) high, the Sphinx was carved at least 4,500 years ago from a single huge block of stone. It is known in Arabic as *Abu al-Hol*, the "Father of Terror." Along with the pyramids it seems to guard, the Great

The pyramids at Giza, built about 4,500 years ago

Sphinx is the most recognizable symbol of Egypt. Nearby these massive ancient monuments is Giza, officially Egypt's third-largest city (population 2.4 million), but really a part of greater Cairo. Alexandria (population 3.3 million), Egypt's second-largest city, is on the Mediterranean coast just west of the Nile delta.

With virtually all of Egypt desert, the country averages only 1 or 2 inches (25 to 50 millimeters) of rain per year. The main exception is a strip of Mediterranean coastline by the city of Alexandria, where winter rains average about 7 inches (178 millimeters) per year. Winters are warm and comfortable; summers are scorchingly hot, especially in the south. Whereas summer temperatures average around 85°F (30°C) along the Mediterranean coast, they soar to 122°F (50°C) at Aswan in the far south.

Two-thirds of Egypt consists of the Western—or Libyan—Desert, which covers all of Egypt from the Nile Valley to the Libyan border. The Western Desert, a part of the gigantic Sahara that covers North Africa, is a barren low plateau pockmarked by basins and depressions. They include the huge Qattara Depression, a 7,000-square-mile (18,130-square-kilometer) expanse of salt marsh and quicksand lying below sea level that contains the lowest point (436 feet, or 133 meters, below sea level) in Africa. Along the Libyan border in the Western Desert is an expanse of dunes called the Sand Sea. The Western Desert was virtually impassable until invading Persians introduced camels to Egypt and North Africa in the sixth century B.C. But it often was more than a match even for camels. The Persians found this out to their sorrow in 525 B.C. when, according to the Greek historian Herodotus, one of their armies totaling 50,000 men attempting to cross the desert was lost and buried in a sandstorm.

The Western Desert is not entirely devoid of life. Jackals, hyenas, gazelles, and a variety of rodents and insects survive there. Humans also can live, and even thrive, in a few places. Deep beneath the desert's sands opposite the Nile Valley is an arch-shaped underground aquifer that supports five oases, pinpoints of green on the vast brown Western Desert canvas. The largest, Al-Daklah, has 30,000 acres (12,150 hectares) of farmland and a population of 60,000. A sixth oasis, Siwah, is far to the west near the Libyan border. Siwah is unique in Egypt. Its isolation over the millennia has given it a distinct culture and language that persists to this day against the ever-growing inroads of the modern world. The Siwah oasis is crowded with 250,000 date palms that make it Egypt's main producer of highly prized dates. Just west of the Nile on the edge of the desert, about 60 miles (100 kilometers) southwest of Cairo, is Al Fayyum, an oasis fed by an ancient canal leading from the Nile. Originally largely a swamp fed by the overflow from the Nile, this 1,620-square-mile (4,200-square-kilometer) so-called "Garden of Egypt" was reclaimed by Pharaoh Amenemhet I almost 4,000 years ago. His efforts created a lake, Birket Qarun, and a productive agricultural area in the desert. Today, however, under pressure of increasing population and over exploitation, the lake has shrunk to about 85 square miles (220 square kilometers), half its former size, and become as salty as the Mediterranean.

East of the Nile, the Eastern, or Arabian, Desert, extends to the Gulf of Suez and Red Sea. East of the Gulf of Suez is Asia and the Sinai Peninsula, yet another desert. It contains

Mount Sinai, where the Bible records Moses and the Israelites received the Ten Commandments from God after fleeing Egypt. (The actual Mount Sinai is unknown; the peak currently called Mount Sinai is only one of several candidates for the site where the Bible says this episode took place.) Another peak in the Sinai desert is Mount Catherine, at 8,652 feet (2,640 meters) the highest point in Egypt.

More than 2,000 years ago the Greek historian Herodotus called Egypt the "gift of the Nile." It still is. Without the Nile River, the "long river between the deserts," Egypt simply would not exist. In fact, it seems fair to say that the Nile Valley and the Nile's delta are Egypt. The ancient Egyptians evidently thought so when they named their country *Kemet* after the "black land" along the river, in contrast to *Deshret*, the "red land," of the surrounding desert. The main function of the deserts on either side of the Nile for thousands of years was to protect its valley and delta and their inhabitants from invasion. If nothing else, peering down from the air at Egypt's Nile Valley—that slender 550-mile-long (885-kilometer) green ribbon of life, squeezed precariously between huge seemingly lifeless brown blocks of desert—is a lesson on the fragility of human existence. As if to emphasize that point, ancient Egyptians likened their country to a delicate lotus: The Nile and its valley were the stem, the Al Fayyum oasis its bud, and the Nile delta the flower.

Egypt traditionally was viewed as divided into Upper Egypt and Lower Egypt, names that reflect the course of the Nile rather than the directions north and south. Upper Egypt ran from Aswan in southern Egypt near the Sudanese border—that is, *up*stream along the Nile—to where Cairo stands today, just south of the Nile delta. Lower Egypt began where the Nile fans out to form its delta—that is, *down*stream along the river—about 125 miles (200 kilometers) from the Mediterranean. Traditionally, Aswan was the frontier where Egypt ended, the site of a natural barrier of rapids on the Nile called the First Cataract. (The Second Cataract is just north of the current Egyptian-Sudanese border.) Today both cataracts are gone, vanished hundreds of feet beneath the warm shimmering waters of Lake Nasser, the artificial lake that rises behind the huge Aswan High Dam, completed in 1971.

Today the increasingly crowded Nile Valley still is a garden of water plants, including dozens of types of grasses, growing along the river bank. It also remains a refuge for more than four hundred species of birds that feed on the river's fish. Some wild mongooses and ibis still roam the delta region. But these are the remnants of a biologically much richer and diverse past. The elephant, Nile crocodile, lion, monkey, and baboon are gone. The lotus, the ancient symbol of Egypt, still grows in the delta. But papyrus, which at the dawn of history was made into a durable material on which to write, thereby playing a crucial roll in the development of Egyptian literacy, has almost vanished. All are victims of the unstoppable spread of agriculture and urbanization fueled by Egypt's growing population.

The Nile Valley is also a huge outdoor museum. In the northern part of the valley is Tel al-Amarna, the city built by the Pharaoh Akhenaton as the home for his short-lived monotheistic religion dedicated to the worship of the sun god Aton. In the center of the valley, where the Nile completes its semicircular detour eastward before returning to its southward course, stand the ruins of the ancient city of Thebes, Egypt's capital for almost five hundred years (1550–1070 B.C.). Here, less than 2 miles (3 kilometers) apart, are two enormous temple complexes: Luxor and Karnak. At Luxor, successive pharaohs for several hundred years tried to outdo each other in their building projects. Pharaohs built at Karnak for more than 1,300 years. Both Luxor and Karnak are on the east bank of the Nile; across the river a few miles away in the desert is the Valley of the Kings. Here are buried some of Egypt's most famous rulers including Ramses II, considered by some historians to be the pharaoh of the biblical Exodus; Hatshepsut, the only woman to rule as a pharaoh; and the boy-king Tutankhamen, whose small tomb, discovered in 1922, was the only one in the valley not looted by robbers and therefore contained thousands of objects providing priceless information about life in ancient Egypt.

For eons the Nile flowed unobstructed from the interior of Africa to the Mediterranean Sea. The ancient Egyptians tried to dam the Nile about 2600 B.C., but that dam collapsed during construction. Although the British successfully built a dam on the Nile at Aswan in southern Egypt between 1898 and 1902, it was too small to control the mighty river. The great change for the Nile and the people living along its banks occurred between 1960 and 1971, when Egypt, with the help of the Soviet Union, built the Aswan High Dam. Located about 4 miles (6 kilometers) south of the older and much smaller dam, the Aswan High Dam is a colossus, 364 feet (111 meters) high and about 2 miles (3 kilometers) long, dwarfing even the pyramids. Thirty thousand workers took eleven years to build it. Behind the dam, stretching for 500 miles (800 kilometers) into Sudan, is Lake Nasser. The dam was a significant engineering accomplishment and has provided many benefits for Egypt. The country finally has a regular year-round water supply, allowing farmers to grow three crops annually. The dam increased Egypt's cultivable land by 2 million acres (810,000 hectares), or 30 percent, while its hydroelectric energy doubled Egypt's power supply. But these benefits came at a price, much of it unanticipated by the dam's builders. Because the Nile no longer floods annually downstream from Aswan, the farmland south of the dam no longer benefits from its yearly dose of soil-enriching silt. This means that farmers must resort to chemical fertilizers, which they often cannot afford. Meanwhile, the silt, now building up behind the dam, will someday fill the lake.

Nor is enough silt or water reaching the Nile delta, which contains more than half of Egypt's cultivatable land. The delta therefore increasingly is threatened by the encroaching salt water of the Mediterranean and by erosion. It is, in fact, sinking, some parts by as much as a quarter of an inch (half a centimeter) a year. The cutback in fresh water downstream from Aswan also is harming local fishing, although Lake Nasser has become a major new source of fish. Meanwhile, the slower flow of less water has allowed parasites to flourish in the river that spread serious diseases to humans.

Despite many problems, Egyptian agriculture—which consists mostly of small labor-intensive farms—is highly productive. The most important cash crop is cotton; Egypt is the world's sixth-largest producer and one of its leading exporters. Other crops include rice, wheat, millet, corn, citrus fruits, and dates. Egypt's main domestic animals are dairy cattle, goats, sheep, and water buffalo.

In recent decades the percentage of Egyptians engaged in agriculture has fallen rapidly to about a third of the workforce. About a fifth of the workforce is engaged in manufacturing; the major industries are petroleum refining, chemicals, fertilizers, cement, and textiles. About 40 percent of the workforce is in services, much of that in the huge government bureaucracy. Egypt has a serious problem with child labor. Children under twelve make up a tenth of the workforce and they are terribly exploited. For example, children who plant and harvest rice earn only eighty cents for working a twelve-hour day under the sweltering Egyptian sun.

Egypt's most important natural resource is oil, which is found in the Western Desert and the Sinai Peninsula. Although Egypt's oil deposits are tiny compared with the major Arab oil producers, it produces enough to supply its local needs and also be an exporter. Tourism, a major source of foreign currency, is very important to the Egyptian economy, one reason attacks on tourists by Islamic fundamentalist in the 1990s met with such a vigorous government response. Egypt's single-largest supply of foreign currency comes from tolls collected from ships passing through the Suez Canal. Another important source is money sent home by more than 3.5 million Egyptians living and working abroad, especially in the major oil-producing Arab countries.

The People of Egypt

Egypt has a population of more than 61 million people, 99.8 percent of whom are Arabs. Approximately 94 percent of all Egyptians are Muslims, and Islam is the official state religion. Most non-Muslim Egyptians are Coptic Christians, the descendants of the Egyptians who did not abandon Christianity for Islam fourteen centuries ago. The Copts often have been subject to discrimination in Islamic Egypt, and the violence against them has increased dramatically in recent decades with the rise of Muslim fundamentalism. Other minorities—small ethnic European communities, Nubians in the south, and a few other groups—account for less than 0.2 percent of the population.

With so many citizens squeezed into a limited area, Egypt's most serious problem is overpopulation. Despite government efforts to encourage birth control, the population in the mid-1990s was growing at a rate of 2.3 percent per year, or 1 million every ten months. That has made it impossible to keep pace in terms of food, social services, jobs, and a host of other necessities. Egypt's rate of population growth, in the face of limited resources, is crippling. The country's population has risen from 10 million in 1900 to 30 million in the 1960s, to 60 million in the mid-1990s. In the mid-1800s Egypt had 5 million acres (2 million hectares) to feed 5 million citizens; today it has 7 million acres (2.8 million hectares) to feed twelve times that number. A country that was once the granary of the Roman Empire, and which could feed itself until relatively recently, now imports half its food. Among the world's nations only Russia and Japan import more food.

EGYPTIAN HISTORY

From Ancient Times to the Islamic Conquest

The ancient Egyptians were a Mediterranean ethnic group whose language belonged to the Hamito-Semitic language family spoken elsewhere in northern Africa and in southwest Asia. They viewed themselves as ethnically and culturally distinct from their neighbors to the south in Africa and to the east in Asia. The Egyptians were ruled by pharaohs, their ancient god-kings, for almost three thousand years. This long epoch is divided into three main parts: the Old Kingdom (3100–2258 B.C.), the Middle Kingdom (2000–1786 B.C.), and the New Kingdom (1750–332 B.C.) The Old Kingdom, whose pharaohs built great pyramids and the Sphinx, was the era of Egypt's most significant cultural achievements. The Middle Kingdom was an age of empire, when Egypt's power extended southward into lands then called Nubia and Kush, westward into Libya, and eastward into Asia as far as the Euphrates River. It also was an age of monument building. The New Kingdom brought another age of empire. Its famous pharaohs included religious reformer Akhenaton and conquerors and builders like Ramses II. However, after 1000 B.C., Egypt was ruled intermittently by foreign powers, including the Assyrians and Persians.

The New Kingdom, and the era of the pharaohs, came to an end when the Greek king Alexander the Great conquered

Egypt in 332 B.C. Alexander built a new city on the Mediterranean that he named Alexandria in his own honor. After his death, Egypt was ruled by a dynasty founded by the Greek general Ptolemy. The Greeks ruled as a tiny minority over a native Egyptian population. They made Alexandria the country's capital and the leading center of Greek learning in the Hellenistic world. The city was home to accomplished mathematicians, astronomers, historians, philosophers, and poets, and it contained the greatest library in the ancient world. The Ptolemaic dynasty ruled Egypt until it was overwhelmed by Rome in 30 B.C. During that troubled time a fire swept through Alexandria's magnificent library, destroying almost 500,000 papyrus rolls and with them much irreplaceable knowledge of the ancient world. By the second century A.D., Christianity had taken hold in Egypt. In the mid-fifth century disputes over religious doctrine gave birth to the country's Coptic Church. By then the western part of the Roman Empire had collapsed. Except for a twelve-year interlude of Persian control, Egypt would be ruled by the Byzantine Empire from its capital of Constantinople until the Arab conquest of the mid-seventh century.

From the Islamic Conquest to 1952

The Arab conquest and the triumph of Islam was an important turning point in Egyptian history. At the time of the Arab conquest in the mid-seventh century, the Egyptians were speaking Coptic, a variant of their ancient native language. Over the next several centuries most Egyptians converted to Islam and Arabic replaced Coptic as the national language. This severed an important link with the past and gave Egypt a new identity, an Islamic one. The Arabs, however, could not bring political stability to Egypt. After being ruled by Arab dynasties based respectively in Damascus and Baghdad, Egypt in the tenth century fell to the Fatamids, Arab invaders from the west. The Fatamids founded Cairo in 969 as Egypt's new capital. They also established the Mosque of Al-Azhar as a Muslim university, thereby making Egypt a center of Islamic learning. The Fatamids then weakened, in part under pressure from the European Crusaders. They were succeeded in the twelfth century by the short-lived Ayyubid dynasty founded by Saladin, best known for conquering Jerusalem from the Crusaders. From 1250 until 1517 Egypt was ruled by the Mamlukes, Turkish slave soldiers who had overthrown their Ayyubid masters. The Mamlukes were both great builders and warriors. In 1260 they defeated the Mongols in Syria, dealing the first serious defeat to invaders who conquered and terrorized much of Eurasia.

In 1517 Egypt fell to the Ottoman Empire. The country endured both economic and cultural decline under Ottoman rule. This was especially true beginning in the seventeenth century, when the Ottoman Empire began its own long decline that lasted into the twentieth century. The result in Egypt, as elsewhere in the empire, was misrule, corruption, and further decline. By the late eighteenth century Ottoman control of Egypt was more official than real. A short period of French occupation (1798–1801) further weakened Ottoman control. The French occupation, however brief, was significant. In 1799 French soldiers found a basalt slab with identical texts written in three scripts: hieroglyphic (the ancient Egyptian script), demotic (a simplified form of ancient Egyptian writing), and Greek. The Rosetta Stone, as it was called, dated from the Ptolemaic era and enabled scholars, after years of effort, to decipher ancient Egyptian hieroglyphics. This enormously expanded our knowledge of ancient Egyptian history, culture, and life.

After the British drove the French from Egypt, the Turkish sultan appointed a new governor, or *pasha*, for Egypt named Mohammad Ali. Within a few years of taking office in 1805 he was operating as a virtually independent ruler. Mohammad Ali began the job of modernizing Egypt. He improved the government bureaucracy, expanded education, promoted new agricultural methods, and encouraged industrial development. Ali's successors continued his policies, promoting the cotton industry and, in the 1860s, the building of the Suez Canal by a French company. However, mismanagement and corruption left Egypt deeply in debt to the British and French, and in 1882 the British occupied Egypt, even though in theory it remained part of the decaying Ottoman Empire.

Official independence came in 1922, but it was less than what it seemed. Egypt had a king, Ahmed Fuad, and a parliament, but the parliament had little power and the British controlled the government from behind the scenes. When Ahmed Fuad died in 1936, he was succeeded by his son Farouk, but the British kept their influence in Egypt until after World War II.

In 1948 Egypt attacked the newly founded state of Israel, joining with four other Arab countries in an attempt to wipe the Jewish state from the map. The Egyptian army's poor performance and eventual defeat in the Arab-Israeli war of 1948–49 infuriated many nationalists, and in 1952 a military group calling themselves the Free Officers overthrew Farouk. They declared Egypt a republic, undertook a series of wide-ranging reforms, and began a new era in the country's history.

Under Nasser and Sadat: 1952 to 1981

Although General Mohammad Nagib was the apparent leader of the coup that overthrew the Egyptian monarchy, the strongman behind the scenes was Colonel Gamal Abdel Nasser. The new military government quickly arrested many prominent politicians, abolished all political parties, and declared Egypt a republic. In fact, it was a military dictatorship and a one-party state. By 1954 Nasser was Egypt's undisputed leader. He officially became president in 1956 in an "election" in which he ran unopposed. The voters also approved a new constitution that proclaimed Islam as Egypt's state religion, but also granted women, for the first time in Egypt's history, the right to vote.

The Nasser regime had an ambitious agenda, one that matched its charismatic leader's grand vision of remaking not only Egypt but the entire Arab world. A primary goal was to modernize and industrialize Egypt's economy. Another objective was to reduce the great differences in wealth between a tiny minority that was very rich and the vast majority who were very poor. Nasser was equally intent on promoting Arab unity under his leadership. As part of that effort Nasser was determined to avenge the defeat of 1948–49 and destroy the state of Israel. He also wanted Egypt to be a leader of the countries of Asia and Africa (called the "Third World") that were neutral in the Cold War between the Soviet bloc and the West.

The new regime was not without opposition at home. Nasser's government was primarily secular in orientation. This soon brought it into conflict with Egypt's leading Islamic organization, the Muslim Brotherhood, which in 1954 tried to assassinate Nasser. The government responded by suppressing the Muslim Brotherhood, hanging several of its leaders, and driving it underground. Meanwhile, it promoted industrialization by expanding the role of the state in the economy, a policy Nasser called "Arab socialism." The government seized foreign assets, including those of thousands of Jews who had been forced to flee Egypt in the years after 1948. It took over banks, newspapers, and most industrial and mining enterprises; by the 1960s it controlled 85 percent of all manufacturing and a third of the total economy. Arab socialism also meant breaking up large estates and turning farm land over to Egypt's millions of poor peasants, a program that won the government wide popular support. Laws establishing minimum wages and reducing working hours brought Nasser and the new regime further support from Egypt's poverty-stricken millions.

It was, however, in foreign affairs that Nasser made his reputation. By 1955 he was recognized as one of the Third World's most influential leaders. In 1956 Nasser seized control of the Suez Canal from its British owners. He intended to use its revenues to finance his dream development project: the Aswan High Dam. Earlier, the United States had refused to finance the project because of Egypt's growing friendship with the Soviet Union. Great Britain and France responded to Nasser's bold step by attacking Egypt. They were joined by Israel, whose purpose was to end years of Egyptian-sponsored terrorist attacks on its territory launched from the Sinai Peninsula and the Gaza Strip. The British/French/Israeli assault was successful militarily, but it failed politically. The attack won Nasser and Egypt international sympathy, including strong backing from the Soviet Union. Despite Egypt's military defeat, Nasser himself emerged as the Arab world's leading hero for standing up to the British and French colonial powers. International pressure forced the British and the French to withdraw from the Canal Zone and Israel from the Sinai Peninsula. A United Nations force was placed in the Sinai to prevent further military conflict between Egypt and Israel. Egypt subsequently received large amounts of aid from the Soviet Union, including funding for the Aswan High Dam and Soviet experts to help build it.

Nasser was not successful in promoting Arab unity under Egyptian leadership. A union with Syria called the United Arab Republic lasted only from 1958 to 1961 before Syria withdrew, leaving bitterness on both sides. A second union forged in 1958, this one with Yemen, also collapsed after three years. Within a year Nasser was again involved in Yemen. In 1962, military officers who supported Nasser overthrew Yemen's conservative monarch and declared Yemen a republic. Royalists rallied to oppose the new regime, and a civil war broke out. Nasser intervened on the republican side, while Saudi Arabia backed the royalists. Egypt ended up mired in a bloody and expensive struggle that involved 50,000 of its troops. During the fighting Egyptian troops committed numerous atrocities against pro-royalist villages, including, on Nasser's orders, attacking them with chemical weapons. These actions embarrassed both Egypt and Nasser in the Arab world before Nasser finally withdrew his troops from Yemen in 1967.

Still, Nasser overwhelmingly remained the most popular and respected leader in the Arab world. One issue that served his ambitions was the Arab-Israeli conflict. His rallying cry for unifying the Arab world centered on hatred of Israel and a determination to destroy the Jewish state. In 1967 Nasser's obsession with Israel again led Egypt to war, and to a military disaster worse than the debacle of 1948–49. In the spring of 1967 he demanded that the United Nations peacekeeping force leave Sinai. When the UN complied, he massed thousands of troops along the Israeli border and forged military alliances with Jordan and Syria. Nasser also blockaded Israel's port of Elat by closing the Strait of Tiran at the southern end of the Gulf of Aqaba to Israeli shipping.

Meanwhile, Nasser and other Egyptian officials proclaimed that the time had come to crush Israel once and for all. After weeks of waiting for international diplomatic action to restrain the Egyptians, a response that never came, in early June the Israelis attacked Egypt and Syria. Jordan then joined the fighting on the Arab side. The Arab-Israeli war of 1967, which became known as the Six-Day War, ended with an overwhelming Israeli victory. Egypt's defeat, which again put Israel in control of the Sinai Peninsula, left Nasser a broken man. He remained Egypt's president, but died in 1970 of a heart attack.

Nasser's successor was his little-known vice president, Anwar Sadat. Sadat turned out to be a man of many surprises. First, he was not pushed aside as expected, but established himself firmly in power. Sadat relaxed Nasser's police-state measures, releasing some political prisoners and allowing political parties, banned since 1953, limited freedom to operate. To promote economic development, he reduced state interference in the economy in order to attract foreign investment. In foreign policy, he began to turn Egypt away from the Soviet Union and toward the United States, hoping to win U.S. support to force Israel to return the Sinai Peninsula to Egypt. In October 1973, frustrated by his lack of progress, Sadat got together with Syria and launched a surprise attack on Israel on the Jewish holy day of Yom Kippur. The initial battles of what is known as the Yom Kippur War gave the Arabs their first military victories over the Israelis. However, after bloody fighting and heavy losses on both sides, Israel again triumphed. Yet even in defeat Sadat won enormous prestige in the Arab world.

Sadat's last, and greatest, surprise was his role as peacemaker. In early November 1977 he stunned the world, and especially his fellow Arabs, by announcing in a speech to the Egyptian parliament his willingness to negotiate with the Israelis to establish peace; he thus became the first Arab leader to do so. Said Sadat:

> I am willing to go to the ends of the earth for peace.
> Israel will be astonished to hear me say now, before
> you, that I am prepared to go to their own house, to
> the Knesset [Israel's parliament] itself, to talk to them.[1]

Sadat meant what he said: In mid-November he went to Jerusalem and spoke to the Israeli parliament. Long and difficult negotiations followed. Finally, in September 1978, with

A historic moment at Camp David that surprised the world—a spontaneous hug between Menachem Begin and, with his back to the camera, Anwar Sadat. Former U.S. president Jimmy Carter stands to the right.

American president Jimmy Carter playing a central role, Sadat and Israeli prime minister Menachem Begin signed a preliminary agreement, the Camp David Accords. Additional negotiations were needed to settle difficult issues. A conference of Arab nations met in November 1978 to plan measures against Egypt if it signed a peace with Israel; the conference even offered Egypt $5 billion in aid to scrap the peace process, an offer Sadat rejected. In March 1979, on the White House lawn, Sadat and Begin signed an Israeli-Egyptian peace treaty, ending more than three decades of war between the two nations.

While the peace treaty won enormous respect for Sadat in the United States and Europe, the Arab world reacted with fury. Sadat was accused of betraying his fellow Arabs. Almost every Arab country broke diplomatic relations with Egypt and it was suspended from the Arab League. The league moved its headquarters from Cairo to Tunis, the capital of Tunisia. The Arab states also imposed economic sanctions on Egypt, making it increasingly dependent on American aid. Syria, Iraq, and Libya even tried, but failed, to have Egypt expelled from several organizations related to the United Nations. The peace with Israel also was denounced in Egypt by critics who ranged from extreme Islamic fundamentalists to supporters of Nasser's policies.

These reactions did not deter Sadat, who continued to improve relations with Israel. In 1980 the two countries exchanged ambassadors. But Sadat's peace with Israel had made him too many enemies among the Arabs. On October 6, 1981, while watching a parade in Cairo commemorating Egypt's successful October 1973 attack across the Suez Canal on Israeli troops, he was assassinated. The killers belonged to a small Islamic fundamentalist group called al-Jihad ("Holy War"). While Anwar Sadat was deeply mourned in the West, and especially in Israel, there was little genuine mourning for him in Egypt. Three former American presidents—Richard Nixon, Gerald Ford, and Jimmy Carter—attended his funeral, but not a single Arab head of state.

The Mubarak Era: Egypt Since 1981

Sadat was succeeded as Egypt's president by his vice president, Hosni Mubarak. In contrast to his two charismatic predecessors, Mubarak was a cautious and practical technocrat. His tendency was to seek a safe middle course whenever possible. The problems Mubarak faced fell into three broad categories. First, he had to promote economic development to relieve Egypt's massive poverty. Second, he had to cope with an increasingly violent Muslim fundamentalist challenge to secular rule. By the 1990s this issue dominated Egypt's domestic agenda. Third, Mubarak wanted to restore Egypt to its leadership position in the Arab world while maintaining peace with Israel. Any one of these problems was daunting; having to deal with all three simultaneously was nothing less than overwhelming.

Mubarak made a little progress on the economic front. During the late 1990s Egypt's economy grew at a strong rate of 5 percent per year. Furthermore, in appreciation, or perhaps more accurately, in payment for Mubarak's central role in mobilizing Arab support for the 1991 Gulf War against Iraq, the United States and the wealthy Arab states of the Persian Gulf region each wrote off $7 billion (for a total of $14 billion) of Egypt's $50 billion foreign dept.

But these were little more than bright spots, surrounded on all sides by darkness. Mubarak continued Sadat's attempt of slowly moving Egypt from a state-controlled to a market economy, while at the same time trying to curb the corruption that pervaded the country's economic life. Progress was painfully slow. By the late 1990s, after three five-year plans, most industrial plants were still owned by the government. Although the private sector's share of the economy increased, about half of Egypt's total gross domestic product, or GDP, still was produced by the state. Loans secured in the early 1980s, when oil prices were high and foreigners were willing to lend, added their heavy weight to Egypt's crushing foreign debt. Egypt, an oil exporter, suffered badly when oil prices fell in the mid-1980s. There were serious food riots in 1984, as there had been under Sadat in 1977. By the 1990s unemployment, fueled by unrelenting population growth, was growing at an alarming rate. After 1992, murderous attacks on foreign visitors by Islamic fundamentalists badly hurt the tourist industry, an important source of jobs and foreign earnings for Egypt. Egypt became increasingly dependent on foreign aid; American aid alone totaled $35 billion in the twenty years after the Camp David Accords. In the mid-1990s four million people staffed the government's bloated, inefficient, and expensive bureaucracy, yet another anchor on the economy. Another burden was Egypt's military forces, which were being equipped with modern high-tech weapons at the cost of billions of dollars. In fact, Egypt spent 70 percent of its American aid on armaments.

Mubarak also fought an uphill battle against Islamic fundamentalism. During 1980 and 1981 Sadat had been using harsh measures against Islamic extremists, including a series of arrests in September 1981, just before his assassination. Sadat's murderers were tried and executed in 1984. Meanwhile, the number of fundamentalist groups was growing rapidly, as were the number of clashes between them and government security forces. Fundamentalists assassinated the speaker of parliament in 1990 and the head of Egypt's State Security Investigative Section in 1994. In 1995 they attempted to assassinate Mubarak himself while he was visiting Ethiopia.

In their battle to change Egyptian society, the Islamic fundamentalists targeted more than government officials. In 1992 the well-known writer and political figure Dr. Faraj Fuda was murdered because he had said that Egypt should be a secular society. Two years later an Islamic extremist tried to kill Nobel Prize–winner Naguib Mahfouz, who was eighty-two at the time. Meanwhile, militant Muslims sued a highly respected professor of Arabic literature at Cairo University, Nasr Abiu Zeid, to force him to divorce his wife. The militants argued that Zeid's writings showed that he had rejected Islam, which made him unfit to be married to a Muslim woman. Zeid had written that the Koran should be viewed as a seventh-century document rather than as the basis for Egyptian society in the twentieth century. In 1995 Egypt's highest court accepted the argument of the Islamic militants and decreed that Zeid must indeed divorce his wife. Under threat of death from the militant Islamic group "Holy War," Zeid and his wife left Egypt to live abroad.

Egypt's Coptic Christian minority, the largest Christian community in the Middle East, repeatedly fell victim to Islamic extremists. Hundreds of Copts were killed in numerous acts of violence that began with bloody assaults in villages in southern Egypt in 1991.

During the 1990s Copts were victims of assaults and murders both in southern Egypt, where most of them live, and in other parts of the country as far north as the Nile delta region. The impact of these attacks was magnified by the government's failure to prosecute Muslims who committed them and by official anti-Christian discrimination, such as long-standing restrictions against building or repairing churches. The government made matters even worse by permitting Islamic clerics to denounce the Coptic faith in fiery sermons broadcast on government-run television. Probably the worst incident erupted in the southern village of al-Kosheh on December 31, 1999, the eve of the millennium, and culminated in riots by Muslim mobs on January 2, 2000, that left more than twenty Copts dead. Although the government arrested several people, the investigation and the trials that followed amounted largely to a cover-up, and all of the murder suspects were acquitted in February 2001.

Foreign tourists also became fundamentalist targets during the 1990s, and some were killed. An attack on a Cairo hotel in April 1996 left eighteen Greek visitors dead; the attackers claimed they were trying to kill Israelis. In September 1997 nine German tourists died in an attack on their bus. The worst incident was the gruesome murder of more than seventy people, among them fifty-eight foreigners, at Luxor in 1997. This act caused such public revulsion that the organization which carried it out announced it would no longer target tourists in its struggle with the government.

The Mubarak government cracked down hard. It arrested an estimated 10,000 Islamic fundamentalists in 1989 alone. In 1993 the government hanged convicted Islamic terrorists for the first time since the execution of Sadat's assassins. In 1997, it extended the state of emergency in Egypt, in effect since 1981, until the year 2000.

Of the many Islamic groups confronting the government, two stood out. The most active and dangerous organization was Gama'a al-Islamiya ("Islamic Group"), whose "spiritual leader" was Sheikh Omar Abdel Rahman. During the early 1990s, Islamic Group launched a terrorist campaign in an attempt to overthrow the Mubarak government and replace it with a strict Islamic regime. It attacked thousands of people and was responsible for the carnage in 1996 in Cairo and 1997 in Luxor. The insurgency lasted eight years and cost more than one thousand lives before the government finally crushed it. Meanwhile, Islamic Group's reach extended far beyond Egypt. In 1993 the Islamic Group tried to blow up the World Trade Center in New York City, an act that, had it succeeded, would have killed tens of thousands of people. Rahman, who was living in the United States at the time, was sentenced by an American court to life in prison without parole for his role in that bombing, in which six people died. The Islamic organization with the broadest support in Egypt was and continues to be the Muslim Brotherhood, which was founded back in 1928. It agrees with Gama'a al-Islamiya about the goal of establishing an Islamic Egypt, but opposes violence to achieve that goal.

A small sign that the violence might decline came in March 1999 when Islamic Group announced that it would lay down its arms. The Egyptian government responded by freeing hundreds of its members, but pointedly kept thousands more securely in jail. These actions, however, had little impact on Holy War, the assassins of Anwar Sadat. Holy War pledged to continue its fight. It condemned what it called Islamic Group's "cease-fire with the United States and Israel," saying it was "a step back in the face of a new Christian crusade which aims to uproot Islam and give Israel the upper hand."[2]

Like Nasser and Sadat, Mubarak enjoyed his greatest successes in foreign affairs. One goal he achieved was to restore Egypt to its leadership position in the Arab world. This required a delicate balancing act, as Mubarak also was committed to Egypt's peace treaty with Israel. He maintained formal relations with Israel, but in such a distant and limited way that disappointed Israelis called their relationship with Egypt a "Cold Peace," as opposed to a normal peace in which countries interact on many levels. In fact, the only time Mubarak visited Israel was to attend the funeral of assassinated Israeli prime minister Yitzhak Rabin. At the same time, Mubarak was a diligent and effective peacemaker in intra-Arab disputes, such as that between Jordan and the Palestine Liberation Organization (PLO). He also encouraged other Arab states and the PLO to join Egypt in making peace with Israel.

Mubarak's efforts to restore Egypt's leadership position in the Arab world were helped by the fears of the oil-rich nations of the Persian Gulf. Those wealthy but militarily weak nations were increasingly concerned for their safety during the Iran-Iraq war of 1980 to 1988. The war was one reason the Persian Gulf states resumed financial aid to Egypt in 1987. By then Jordan, in 1984, had resumed diplomatic relations with Egypt. Most Arab states followed suit over the next five years. In 1989 Egypt was readmitted to the Arab League, and the organization returned its headquarters to Cairo.

In 1990, following the Iraqi invasion of Kuwait, Mubarak was instrumental in lining up Arab support for the international effort, led by the United States, to drive the Iraqis from their oil-rich neighbor. Egypt contributed 35,000 troops to the multinational force that did the job in 1991. Egypt's growing international stature was reflected in the election of its foreign minister, Boutros Boutros-Ghali, to the post of United Nations secretary-general. Boutros-Ghali took office on January 1, 1992. To Egypt's great disappointment, in 1996 the United States blocked Boutros-Ghali's attempt to win a second term.

At the same time, Mubarak worked hard to facilitate Israeli-Palestinian peace negotiations. He played an important role in bringing together a peace conference that met in Madrid, Spain, in the fall of 1991. Egyptians also reportedly were involved as advisers in the secret talks that produced the Israeli-Palestinian Oslo Accords in 1993. Of course, even as he pushed his fellow Arabs to follow Egypt's example and sit down with Israel, Mubarak was anything but a neutral in this process. Egyptian diplomats worked continuously behind the scenes to coordinate Arab strategy. Mubarak also tried to persuade the United States and Western Europe to increase their pressure on Israel to make concessions.

Beginning in 1995, Egypt faced growing tensions on several fronts. Mubarak accused the fundamentalist Islamic regime in Sudan of aiding an attempt to assassinate him in Ethiopia and openly began supporting exiled opponents of the Sudanese regime. Tensions with Israel increased over Israel's possession of nuclear weapons, and for a time Egypt threatened not to sign the renewal of the Nuclear Non-Proliferation Treaty (NPT) of 1968 unless Israel abandoned its nuclear program. American pressure, especially a threat to discontinue aid to Egypt, ultimately persuaded Egypt to sign the NPT. Egyptian-Israeli relations worsened further after the 1996 election of Benjamin Netanyahu as Israeli prime minister. Netanyahu, a critic of the Oslo Accords, took a harder line in negotiations with the Palestinians than either of his two immediate predecessors, Yitzhak Rabin and Shimon Peres.

During 1997 Mubarak criticized the United States for not applying sufficient pressure on Israel and Netanyahu to make more concessions to the Palestinians. The strain in relations with the United States was evident in 1998 when Egypt objected to American plans to bomb Iraq for violating its agreement to allow United Nations arms inspectors to search for Iraqi weapons of mass destruction.

Egyptian Politics, the Press, and the Law

Egypt has an authoritarian form of government. It is, however, not nearly as brutal as the dictatorships of Iran or Syria, or as absolutist and oppressive as the monarchies of Saudi Arabia and the Persian Gulf states. Prior to 1952 Egyptian political life was freer and more open than it is today, but that interlude ended with the Free Officers revolution. Egypt became a one-party state, whose leader ruled with dictatorial power. In 1962 Nasser named the Arab Socialist Union as Egypt's ruling party. Anwar Sadat loosened Nasser's system a little. Amendments to the constitution in 1980 permitted a limited multiparty system. But Egypt's political system still operated under tight controls. The country's leading party, which inevitably won every election, was Sadat's National Democratic Party. In presidential elections, the candidate was "nominated" by the parliament and ran in an election where he was the only candidate. Thus in 1994 Mubarak won his third six-year term as president in a typical "election" in which he took 94.9 percent of the vote. In 1999, the process and results were the same: With the National Democratic Party controlling 95 percent of parliament's seats, Mubarak was nominated to a fourth term and "reelected" with just under 94 percent of the popular vote.

At the same time, under Sadat and Mubarak opposition parties have held a few seats in parliament, called the People's Assembly. It contains 454 members, 444 elected for a five-year term and 10 members appointed by the president. The president also appoints the country's prime minister and council of ministers, who are in charge of day-to-day governing.

Egypt's leading opposition party is the New Wafd Party (*wafd* means "delegation" in Arabic). It is a descendant of the most popular party that existed before 1952 and represents Egypt's middle class and business interests. The New Wafd Party has chafed under the restrictions of Egyptian political life. In 1995 it called the parliamentary elections the "worst in history," and it boycotted the 1997 elections. Several other parties also exist, although they are insignificant. Far more important than the legal opposition parties are the illegal Islamic groups. They include the Muslim Brotherhood, which has elected representatives to parliament running under New Wafd Party auspices, and Islamic Group and Holy War. Another illegal group is Thawrat Misr ("Egypt's Revolution"), whose leading figure is Khaled Abdel Nasser, son of the former president.

Egypt's press reflects the country's form of government. As with political parties, the press was freer before the 1952 revolution than after it. The government owns 51 percent of all major newspapers and is careful to control much of what they print. After a period of relative freedom in the 1980s, the government imposed harsher censorship. A new law in 1995 provided for long prison sentences and harsh fines for various crimes, including "insulting" public officials. The law was modified and made less severe in 1996, after international criticism.

Egyptian law for the most part does little to support individual rights. Before 1980 the constitution identified the Islamic legal code (Sharia) drawn from the Koran as *a* source of Egyptian law. In 1980, that *a* was changed to *the*. Egypt also continues to have strict censorship laws. In May 1999, the parliament passed a law severely restricting human rights groups. Another 1999 law put all nongovernmental organizations more firmly under state control. Still, Egyptian law, even while imposing limitations unacceptable by Western standards, allows citizens considerably more freedom than in most Arab countries. For example, in January 2000 parliament changed the country's divorce laws to make it easier for women to get a divorce. Previously it was almost impossible for a woman to get a divorce without her husband's consent, while a husband could divorce his wife simply by saying "I divorce thee" three times or by filing a paper with the government stating that he was divorcing his wife. The new law, while still leaving wives at some disadvantage relative to their husbands, allows a woman to demand a divorce if she and her husband cannot get along with each other and requires that he help support her if he is able to do so. Only Tunisia among the world's Arab nations grants women similar rights when it comes to divorce.

MODERN EGYPTIAN CULTURE

Egyptian cultural life is a colorful and cosmopolitan pastiche of traditional and modern that reflects the impact of outside influences. The movie industry is a prime example. The first Egyptian movie was made in 1927, the same year Hollywood produced the world's first "talkie." More than three hundred films were produced in the 1960s, the heyday of Egyptian filmmaking. Egyptian directors borrowed many of the plots they used from Hollywood. Today it is not easy to make a good film in Egypt. Egyptian filmmakers must walk a thin line in dealing with political and sexual themes to avoid getting into trouble with religious authorities and government censors.

Egyptian's greatest film star of the twentieth century was Umm Kalthoum, the "Star of the East," who also was Egypt's most popular singer and a superstar throughout the Arab world. In 1956 the director Salah Abou Seif won the critics' prize at the Cannes Film Festival, one of the international film industry's most prestigious awards. The Egyptian actor who probably achieved the most international recognition is Omar Sharif; his most notable role was as the Russian physician Dr. Zhivago in the British-made classic of that name. The country's most distinguished director is Youssef Chanine, who has excelled at his trade for half a century. He won a lifetime achievement award at the 1997 Cannes Film Festival.

Theater also remains popular in Egypt. Adel Imam, currently the most popular local movie actor, is a leading actor in the theater as well. The belly dancer Fifi Abdou is one of Egypt's leading theater actresses. Belly dancing, whose roots run deep into Egyptian history, remains popular, although in the 1990s it has been under attack by Islamic extremists.

One of the more interesting aspects of twentieth-century Egyptian culture has been the development of painting and sculpture. These art forms flourished in ancient Egypt, as the tombs and monuments amply demonstrate. However, Islam, which forbids painting or sculpting living creatures, severely limited these traditions for centuries. Stimulated by Egypt's growing contact with Europe, art and sculpture revived in the twentieth century, growing along with Egyptian nationalism. Influenced by nationalist thinking, Egyptian artists tried to create a distinctly Egyptian style. Their influence can be seen today in the work of artists such as Adel al-Siwi and Chant Avedissian.

No discussion of Egyptian cultural life would be complete without a reference to the coffeehouse. Coffeehouses are popular gathering places throughout the Middle East, where along with conversation, patrons enjoy drinking strong coffee and smoking tobacco. Sipping and puffing—the latter often through a *sheesha*, or water pipe—are interspersed with games of dominoes, dice, and cards. Interestingly, both coffee and tobacco are foreign imports into the Middle East. Coffee probably was introduced in Egypt, Turkey, and Syria from Ethiopia via the Arabian Peninsula in the sixteenth century. English merchants probably brought tobacco to the region a century later. There are about 30,000 coffeehouses in Cairo alone, many catering to specialized groups of customers of every conceivable variety, from physicians, musicians, and retired generals to political radicals, Muslim extremists, and homosexuals. Many coffeehouses also serve a variety of concoctions that are supposed to cure ailments from stomach problems to coughs.

Coffeehouses remain, as they have been for centuries, largely a male bastion. A common complaint today in Egypt, as elsewhere in the world, is that television and other electronic media have had a negative impact on local traditions and culture, such as coffeehouse life.

LIBYA

If Egypt is the country with the world's oldest continuous history, Libya, its North African neighbor directly to the west, is at the opposite end of the spectrum. Libya had no history as a nation prior to becoming independent in 1951. The term "Libya" is an ancient one that traditionally referred to most of North Africa. It was revived in 1934 when Italy cobbled together three areas it controlled in North Africa—Tripolitania, Cyrenaica, and Fezzan—and called its new creation Libya. After gaining independence, whatever its troubles, Libya functioned more or less normally as a country for eighteen years. That ended in 1969 when military officers led by Muammar Qaddafi overthrew the monarchy of King Idris I. Since then, rather than functioning as a country in the normal sense of the word, Libya has been dominated and even defined by one man: Qaddafi. The only comparable situation in the second half of the twentieth century is in Cuba, where Fidel Castro has been in power since 1959, ten years longer than Qaddafi. But not even Castro, it seems fair to say, has cast a personal shadow over his country as completely as has Qaddafi. And if Castro has his detractors and bitter enemies, there are few who would go so far as to call him insane, something that cannot be said for Qaddafi.

Libya's official name, changed several times by Qaddafi, currently is the Great People's Socialist Libyan Arab Jamahiriya. Jamahiriya means "state of the masses." Islam is Libya's official religion and Arabic its official language.

GEOGRAPHY AND PEOPLE

Libya is a huge country of 679,358 square miles (1,759,540 square kilometers), slightly larger than Alaska. It is the fourth-largest country in Africa, and the second largest, after Saudi Arabia, in the Middle East. Libya's northern border is the Mediterranean Sea. To the east are Egypt and Sudan, to the west Tunisia and Algeria, and to the south Chad and Niger. Almost all of the country is desert and barren rock; it has no rivers that flow year-round. More than 90 percent of Libya's people live within 10 miles (16 kilometers) of its 1,100-mile-long (1,770-kilometer) Mediterranean coastline. The climate is cooler along the coast than in the searing desert, where temperatures as high as 135°F (57°C) have been recorded. Western coastal areas receive a enough rainfall to make agriculture possible. Libya's main crops are wheat, citrus fruits, and olives. A few oases dot the bone-dry southern part of the country, deep in the Sahara desert.

Libya consists of three regions that have few historic ties. Tripolitania, the western coastal area, makes up about 16 percent of the country. Tripoli (population 980,000), Libya's largest city and capital, is in that region. Tripolitania is most closely linked with the western part of North Africa called the Maghreb, which consists of Algeria, Tunisia, and Morocco. South of Tripolitania is the desert region of Fezzan. Libya's eastern half is called Cyrenaica. Historically linked most closely to Egypt and the east, Cyrenaica is where most of Libya's oil and gas deposits are located. Part of Cyrenaica's coastline cradles the Gulf of Sidra, the scene in 1981 of an air battle between American and Libyan jets. Benghazi (population 650,000), Libya's second-largest city, lies on the northeastern coast of the Gulf of Sidra.

Libya has a population of about five million people, a number that is increasing rapidly (4 percent per year, one of the highest rates in the world), in part because of government encouragement. Almost half the population is less than fifteen years old. Virtually all Libyans are Sunni Muslims and most are Arabs. There is a significant community of Berbers, the indigenous people of North Africa. The Berbers probably migrated to North Africa from southwestern Asia at least 5,000 years ago. They have been partially, but not entirely, assimilated into Arab culture, and many still speak the ancient Berber languages, which are related to ancient Egyptian.

Libya has natural resources such as iron, potash, and gypsum. Oil, however, discovered in the late 1950s, is by far Libya's most important resource. While the oil industry employs less than 2 percent of Libya's workforce, it accounts for a third of the country's domestic product and virtually all (along with natural gas) of its export earnings. Libya is the world's thirteenth-largest oil producer, but consumes less than 10 percent of what it pumps from the ground. The rest is exported, mainly to Europe. Libyan oil is in demand because it contains very little sulfur and therefore burns cleanly. Oil wealth has enabled the regime to provide a vast range of social services, including free education until age fifteen and medical care, that has helped it keep the population economically satisfied and under control.

LIBYAN HISTORY

Since ancient times, a variety of groups including Phoenicians, Greeks, Romans, Byzantines, Arabs, Spaniards, and Ottomans have ruled Libya. Between 1711 and 1835, when Ottoman control weakened, the city of Tripoli and its environs was ruled by a local dynasty. Tripoli earned its income, as did the other so-called Barbary states of North Africa, from piracy or from collecting tribute from countries in return for *not* attacking their ships. In effect, what was going on was state-sponsored terrorism. To protect its ships and citizens after enduring more than a decade of attacks, a young and vulnerable United States under President Thomas Jefferson sent a naval squadron to attack Tripoli. The successful capture of the city in 1805 by a small force of Marines secured the safety of American ships. The achievement was memorialized in the U.S. Marine Corps hymn by the line "To the shores of Tripoli."

After 1835 Tripoli returned to Ottoman control until Italy seized what today is Libya in 1911. Libya remained an Italian colony until occupied by British and French forces during World War II. In 1951, in accordance with a 1949 United Nations resolution, Libya became independent under King Idris I. A period of conservative rule and stability followed. Libya under Idris had good relations with the conservative Arab monarchies of the region and with Britain, the United States, and other Western powers. Both the United States and Britain were permitted to have military bases in Libya and Western oil companies developed the country's newly discovered oil deposits.

Libya Under Qaddafi

After military officers led by twenty-eight-year-old Muammar Qaddafi seized power in 1969, Libya was transformed from one of the most conservative states in the Arab world to arguably the most radical. Qaddafi's idol was Nasser, but the Libyan leader quickly went far beyond Nasser in his radicalism. Qaddafi rejected Western capitalism and democracy as well as communism. His ideology is a unique and volatile mixture of Islamic theology, revolutionary socialism (but *not*

A young Muammar Qaddafi views a battlefield with President Nasser, in sunglasses.

Marxism), Arab nationalism, populism, anti-Semitism, and an absolute faith in his fate as a man of destiny. Qaddafi's revolutionary vision for the Arab world, or "Third Universal Theory," was outlined in his *Green Book*. Part one was published in 1976, followed by parts two and three respectively in 1978 and 1979.

The Qaddafi regime moved swiftly. It closed down British and American military bases (the day the last U.S. forces left became a national holiday), nationalized all banks, took over all heavy industry and mining, and negotiated far more favorable terms for Libya with foreign oil companies. It also seized the property of Italians and Jews and forced them to leave the country. Eventually the regime seized all foreign oil assets. A new organization, the Arab Socialist Union (ASU), became the country's only political party. In 1973, declaring that the Libyan people were not sufficiently revolutionary, Qaddafi announced a "cultural revolution" that rejected all "non-Islamic thinking." In the mid-1970s, after spending most of 1974 in seclusion, Qaddafi introduced what he called direct "people's power." Libya's government was now called the "General People's Committee." Private economic activity was severely restricted, and traditional Koranic law—including punishing thieves by cutting off their hands—became the country's basic legal code.

By the late 1970s Libya supposedly was being run by "people's" or "revolutionary" committees. In fact, even though Qaddafi resigned his position as head of the government in 1979—announcing he was leaving his post to devote full time to "preserving the revolution"—Libya has remained a strict military regime under his personal dictatorship. There have been at least five serious attempts to overthrow Qaddafi—in 1975, 1984, 1993, 1996, and 1999—and dozens more may have gone unreported. Unrest has been a constant factor since Qaddafi seized power, but none of his opponents have been able to topple him.

Life for ordinary Libyans ranges from unpredictable to dangerous. Among the things most feared are the "purification committees" of army officers and students the government often uses to enforce its laws and decrees. For example, in October 1998 Qaddafi decided the prices in private shops were too high. He warned shopkeepers that "prices must be cut by whatever means, and if they are not, there will be violence."[3] Shopkeepers took Qaddafi seriously, terrified that purification committees would find them in violation of the new decree. While Qaddafi's enforced price slashing was popular with the poor—salaries in Libya have been frozen since 1981—many shopkeepers simply shut their businesses, unable to make a living under the new rules. The wife of one spoke for many when she complained, "This is not fair, but what is fair in this country anyway?"[4]

Libya from the start was much too small a stage for the historical role Qaddafi envisioned for himself. Only the international arena, including not only the Arab world but well beyond it, could provide a venue large enough to match his grandiose ambitions. Libyan foreign policy under Qaddafi therefore has been militant, unconventional, and aggressive. Qaddafi is bitterly anti-Western in general and anti-American in particular. He has supported extremist Islamic movements and what he considers "liberation movements" worldwide, from the Middle East to Latin America, Western Europe, and east Asia. Many of the movements receiving Libyan money, training, and arms are terrorist groups. The Libyan government also has been directly involved in terrorist acts. All this has made it one of the world's leading sponsors of international terrorism.

In the Middle East, Qaddafi has uncompromisingly opposed all attempts to solve the Arab-Israeli conflict peacefully. Instead, he supported the most extreme Palestinian groups that share his vision of seeing Israel completely destroyed. This posture at times has brought Libya into conflict with Egypt. Libyan attempts to undermine the Sadat regime in the 1970s led to armed clashes along their mutual border. Libya also played a leading role in ostracizing Egypt from the rest of the Arab world after Sadat made peace with Israel. Interestingly, Libya supported the militantly Islamic and anti-Western, but non-Arab, Iran in its eight-year war with Saddam Hussein's Iraq, an Arab state, during the 1980s.

Qaddafi's confrontations with the United States also have led to clashes. In 1981 American and Libyan jets fought in the Gulf of Sidra when Qaddafi claimed the gulf lay within Libyan territorial waters, an assertion belied by the geography of the region. In 1986 American aircraft bombed Libya after Libyan agents were linked to the bombing of a nightclub in Europe in which several American soldiers were killed. Another American-Libyan air battle took place over Mediterranean waters in 1989.

In addition, two Libyan intelligence agents were linked to the bomb explosion that destroyed an American passenger airplane (Pan American Flight 103) in midair over Lockerbei, Scotland, in 1988. This terrorist act cost 270 lives (259 on board, 11 on the ground). When Qaddafi refused to turn the agents over for trial, undoubtedly fearing the trial would point the finger of guilt directly at him, the United Nations Security Council imposed economic sanctions on Libya. Those sanctions—which, significantly, did not include a boycott of Libyan oil exports—remained in place until Libya, fearing the sanctions were about to be tightened, finally turned the agents over to international authorities in May 1999. In July, Libya in effect admitted involvement in a 1986 bombing of a French airliner over Africa when it paid the families of 170 victims in that incident $31 million. A year and a half later, in February 2001, a Scottish court convicted one of the two Libyan agents tied to the Pan American bombing of murder. The second agent was acquitted. U.S. president George W. Bush reacted by stating that the verdict was not reason enough to lift UN sanctions against Libya and that the Libyan government should be required to pay compensation to the families of the bombing victims.

Libya's international adventures also extended into Africa. For fifteen years Libya intervened in Chad, Libya's poor African neighbor to the south. Qaddafi's goal was to annex Chad's northern region, called the Aouzou strip, which reportedly has rich uranium deposits. Supported by French and American aid, Chad finally expelled Libya from the Aouzou strip in 1987. Qaddafi's ambitions in Africa ranged further than Chad. As one American analyst commented in 1999, "there has been a consistent effort in the past to destabilize West Africa."[5] At the same time, over the years Qaddafi sponsored a series of Libyan "unions" with other Arab states, none of which amounted to anything concrete.

The key question concerning Libya in the twenty-first century is what will happen to Qaddafi? Islamic extremists reportedly tried to assassinate him in 1996. Another better-documented attempt on his life in June 1999 left him wounded. A few weeks after that incident, the governor of Benghazi, who was linked to the plot, was killed. According to state-run Libyan newspapers, he died when kicked in the forehead by a horse. Meanwhile, there have been growing signs of opposition to the regime. In particular, Islamic militants are increasingly difficult to control despite brutal repression. One thing seems certain: With or without Qaddafi in charge, Libya's future is likely to be unpredictable and unstable.

CHAPTER 3

Israel, the Palestine Authority, and Jordan

ISRAEL

During their long history the Jewish people have settled on every continent and in some of the most remote areas in the world. Their roots, however, are in a tiny part of the Middle East, where in the twentieth century, after a lapse of 1,900 years, they re-created the state of Israel. The goal of the founders of the modern state of Israel was to build a country in their ancient homeland where Jews could live securely and freely. An independent Israel would enable Jews to escape the insecurity and persecution they had known as a scattered minority and become a nation able to defend itself and develop its national culture.

The ancient Israelites, the ancestors of today's Jews, emerged as an identifiable people almost four thousand years ago along the eastern shore of the Mediterranean Sea, approximately where Israel is today. Unlike other ancient peoples that appear in our history books, the Israelites' main distinguishing feature was not their cultural sophistication or military conquests, or their impressive monuments or expertise in science and technology. Rather they were remarkable for their unusual religion, one that assumed the existence of a single God who demanded his followers live according to a strict moral code. That religion—Judaism—was the world's first monotheistic faith. It later provided inspiration for two other monotheistic religions, Christianity and Islam, which are the two most widely followed religions in the world today.

After several centuries of being organized into twelve separate tribes, the Israelites established a unified but short-lived kingdom in the eleventh and tenth centuries B.C. After that kingdom split in two in the late ninth century B.C., the Israelites often were ruled by a succession of powerful empires. Still, for the next one thousand years they were able to develop their religious life and moral principles while occasionally reasserting their political independence.

Two unsuccessful revolts, respectively in the first and second centuries A.D., against the mighty Roman Empire brought catastrophe. The Romans drove most of the Jews, as they were called by then, from the land at the time known as Judea. The Romans then changed its name to *Syria Palestina,* or Palestine, which means "Land of the Philistines" (the Philistines had lived in the region centuries earlier) in order to sever its ties with the Jewish people. That name, although it referred to a people long since vanished, would remain in use until 1948.

For about 1,800 years the Jews lived in the region as a minority of the overall population. But beginning in the late nineteenth century Jews from distant countries returned in growing numbers to what they called *Eretz Yisrael*, the land of Israel, to reestablish their national life. Unlike the Egyptians, who never left the Nile Valley but who have lost direct touch with their ancient religion and language, modern Israelis follow the religion and speak the language—an updated Hebrew—of their ancient ancestors. They also share with their ancestors the burden of living in a region that remains, as it was long ago, one of the most tumultuous and dangerous in the world.

GEOGRAPHY, ECONOMY, AND PEOPLE

Israel is a narrow sliver of land with great topographical variety along the eastern coast of the Mediterranean Sea. Its boundaries and area still are not permanently settled; in

A sign warning travelers that the border between Israel and Lebanon lies ahead

many places they remain jagged armistice lines left over from a series of wars between Israel and its Arab neighbors. According to the armistice lines that existed between 1949 and 1967, Israel has an area of 7,992 square miles (20,700 square kilometers). If one includes the eastern part of the city of Jerusalem, which Israel annexed in 1967, and the Golan Heights, to which Israel applied its laws in 1981, Israel's area is 8,473 square miles (21,946 square kilometers). In either case, Israel is about the size of New Jersey.

Israel also exercises external military control (but not direct day-to-day administrative control) over most of an area known as the West Bank, 2,260 square miles (5,860 square kilometers), and part of the Gaza Strip, 140 square miles (360 square kilometers). Altogether, the total area under Israeli control in one form or another currently amounts to about 10,800 square miles (28,000 square kilometers).

Israel's 170-mile-long (273-kilometer) Mediterranean coastline is its western border. Egypt lies to the southwest. Due south from its southernmost point is the Gulf of Aqaba, which

Israelis call the Gulf of Elat. Jordan borders Israel to the east, Syria to the northeast. Due north of Israel is Lebanon.

Despite its small size, Israel has four distinct geographic zones. The heart of the country is the fertile and densely populated coastal plain. At its center on the Mediterranean coast is Tel Aviv, Israel's second largest city (population 375,000). Approximately 2 million people, one in three Israelis, live in the Tel Aviv metropolitan area. Farther north on the coastal plain is Haifa, Israel's third-largest city (population 264,000), its most important port, and its high-tech industrial center. Haifa begins at the seashore and then climbs the steep, wooded slopes of 1,792-foot-high (546-meter) Mount Carmel, a dramatic and scenic 13-mile-long (20-kilometer) mountain ridge that towers over the coastal plain.

Not far inland is Israel's second geographic zone, a region of hills bisected by the fertile Jezreel Valley (Valley of Israel), the largest valley in Israel. The area north of the Jezreel Valley is the Galilee. Its shimmering liquid jewel is the 64-square-mile (165-square-kilometer) Sea of Galilee (Lake Tiberias), Israel's only freshwater lake and its most important water resource. Its Hebrew name, the *Kinneret*, probably comes from Hebrew word for "harp" (*kinor*), referring to the lake's shape. Looming above the lake and the Galilee is a dark block of gray volcanic rock called the Golan Heights, a 444-square-mile (1,150-square-kilometer) plateau. The Golan's highest point, and the loftiest in Israel, is Mount Hermon, 7,300 feet (2,224 meters). South of the Jezreel Valley are the Judean Hills. Perched on a peak in those hills is Jerusalem, Israel's capital and largest city (population 575,000) and possibly the most fought-over piece of real estate in human history.

Israel's third zone is the Jordan Valley, where the Jordan River flows from the Sea of Galilee to the Dead Sea. The Jordan Valley is a small section of the Great Rift Valley, a huge gash in the earth, the largest of its kind, that runs 3,000 miles (4,830 kilometers) from northern Syria in southwest Asia to Mozambique in east Africa. The Jordan, Israel's longest and most important river, also marks a large part of its border with the Kingdom of Jordan to the east. The Dead Sea, eight times as salty as the ocean, is actually a salt lake with no outlet. At 1,292 feet (394 meters) below sea level, it is the lowest point on the surface of the Earth. Summer temperatures in the hot and arid Dead Sea basin reach 122°F (50°C). The main relief from the baking heat is the oasis of Ein Gedi, a series of springs and cliffs covered with lush vegetation that also is a nature reserve. Gazelles, ibex, oryx, foxes, jackals, leopards, and many other animals and birds flourish there.

Israel's fourth geographic zone, and by far its largest, is the Negev Desert. The Negev—its name comes from a Hebrew word meaning "to dry"—is a large arid triangle that occupies about 60 percent of the country. Its main city is Beersheba, a sprawling vibrant town of about 150,000 people on its northern fringe. At the Negev's southern tip stands Elat, a port and resort city that is Israel's main outlet to the Far East. The Negev is not all desert. Its northern and western section around Beersheba is a dusty plain that really is a transition zone that supports agriculture. Winter rains here often produce flash floods. Farther south is the rocky and desolate, but also dramatic, landscape of the real desert. The eastern fringe of the Negev is the Arava Valley, another section of the Great Rift Valley and a stretch of desert between the Dead and Red seas.

Israel lies at the southeastern edge of the Fertile Crescent. This is reflected in the country's rainfall statistics, which vary considerably despite its small size. Northern Israel has a Mediterranean climate, with warm, reasonably wet winters and hot dry summers. Rainfall reaches about 28 inches (710 millimeters) in the far north, and 19 to 21 inches (480 to 530 millimeters) in the central part of the country. Farther south, the Fertile Crescent ends and the desert begins. The northern fringe of the Negev, the transition zone, gets about 12 inches (300 millimeters) of rain per year, enough to support agriculture with the aid of highly efficient Israeli irrigation techniques. Rainfall declines to virtually zero near the city of Elat. The Arava gets less than an inch (25 millimeters) of rain per year.

Israel's rainfall, although marginal, enables its farmers to feed the country and produce many crops for export. Israel is the world leader in making maximum use of limited quantities of water in agriculture. In the 1960s it built the National

Water Carrier, a huge network of pipelines, pumping stations, tunnels, aqueducts, canals, artificial reservoirs, and dams. It carries water from the Sea of Galilee, the upper Jordan River and its tributaries, and other water sources in the north to the drier parts of the country. Israeli farmers make extensive use of a technique invented in the country called drip irrigation, in which water is delivered on a timed basis directly to individual plants through pipes or hoses with tiny holes in them, rather than being sprayed wastefully over an entire field. Recent improvements in drip irrigation include computer controls and the addition of fertilizer to the irrigation water. Effective irrigation has enabled Israel to increase its farmland by 250 percent since 1948. Local farmers also make extensive use of greenhouses and plastic sheeting to cover plants, which allows them to grow crops out of season for the export market.

The Economy
Although Israel must import certain items, such as cereals and feed grains, on balance it is self-sufficient in food. Major export crops include citrus fruits, a variety of noncitrus fruits and vegetables (eggplants, tomatoes, avocados, melons, bananas, and peaches), and flowers; most of them find customers in Western Europe. Other important crops include cotton, olives, and grapes. Israeli agriculture has a feature that is unique in the world: The majority of its farmers live and work on democratically run cooperatives. There are two main types of cooperatives: the *kibbutz* and the *moshav*.

The kibbutz is essentially based on communist principles. All property is collectively owned, work is done cooperatively, and earnings are distributed equally among the members. Earnings are not even distributed in the form of wages, but as necessities and services such as housing, medical care, education, and vacations. Many kibbutzim also engage in manufacturing, so that along with a third of the country's agricultural products they produce more than 6 percent of its manufactured goods. A moshav is a village in which each family farms an individual plot and profits accordingly, but the village buys its supplies and sells its product cooperatively. About 125,000 people live on 269 kibbutzim, while

160,000 people live in 411 moshavim. All Israel's cooperatives lease the land they farm from an agency called the Jewish National Fund. A few Israelis operate private farms.

Israel focused on developing agriculture during its early years. Today agriculture produces just 4 percent of the country's total output, employs only about 2.5 percent of its population, and accounts for 7 percent of its exports. This is because Israel has become a modern industrial society. While the single-largest category of industries is engaged in food processing, the country has a competitive and rapidly growing high-tech sector. That sector has been boosted by investment by American and European companies seeking to make use of the country's highly skilled workforce. Israeli-made software, computer chips, and other electronic equipment including sophisticated medical and printing equipment— have excellent international reputations. So does the high-tech military equipment that Israel has learned to produce in its own defense. The United States military is a leading buyer of Israeli equipment. Israel's leading exporter, Israel Aircraft Industries, manufactures both military equipment such as unmanned reconnaissance aircraft and, increasingly, civilian products such as executive jets. Israeli industries also produce modern plastics, petrochemicals, and metal products. In addition, the country is a world leader in the production of polished diamonds and other precious stones.

Israel has almost no natural resources. Golda Meir, Israel's third prime minister, used to joke that Moses led the ancient Israelites through the wilderness for forty years and then took them to the only place in the Middle East where there is no oil. (Actually, Israel has a tiny amount of oil and is exploring for more.) Its only valuable mineral resources are bromides, potash, magnesium, and other materials extracted from the Dead Sea. Israel is the world's largest exporter of bromides, which are used to make photographic chemicals, antiknock mixtures for gasoline, and a number of other products. About 40 percent of Israeli exports go to Western Europe, 30 percent to North America, and 20 percent to the Far East. Israel also benefits from traffic flowing the other way in the form of tourists, most of whom come to see its many sites connected with the Bible.

Like every industrial country, Israel suffers from pollution and environmental problems. Industrial pollution and urban sprawl threaten both Israel's limited farmland and its precious natural open space. At the same time, Israelis have dramatically improved the environment of their country. Since 1948, they have planted more than 200 million trees in what was once an almost totally deforested countryside. These ongoing efforts have expanded the tree cover from almost nothing to 770 square miles (2,000 square kilometers), about 10 percent of Israel's total area. The trees have helped regenerate Israel's soil and enabled the land to absorb rainwater, thereby restoring dried-up wells to productivity. The Israeli government also has established more than 250 nature reserves; they cover a fifth of the country's total land area and provide a refuge for wild flowers and animals. Some native animal species, such as the white oryx and Mesopotamian fallow deer, that had disappeared from the region, have been reintroduced, while others, among them the magnificent golden eagles, have returned on their own.

People

In 1998 Israel's population topped 6 million, an increase of 2.3 percent over the previous year. Just over 79 percent of the population are Jews. Muslim Arabs account for just under 15 percent of the population; Christians—most, but not all, of whom are Arab—about 2 percent; and Druze about 2 percent.

Statistics do not convey the complexity of Israel's population profile. Israel is a very young country that since its founding has attracted Jewish immigrants from all over the world. Although they shared a common religion, they came from radically different cultural backgrounds. Some came from modern industrial countries, others from traditional agricultural societies. Blending them together into a single nation has been an ongoing and sometimes difficult task that remains unfinished after more than fifty years.

What virtually all the immigrants had in common is that they were escaping from persecution, or, as in the case of more than 270,000 Holocaust survivors in the years immediately after World War II, far worse. The Holocaust survivors were joined by hundreds of thousands of Jews fleeing persecution in Arab countries, from Morocco in the west to Iraq in the east to Yemen in the south. Some of those communities were 2,500 years old. The 700,000 refuges who reached Israel by 1951 helped swell its Jewish population of 650,000 in 1948 to 1.4 million. In the 1970s a new wave of immigrants escaping persecution came from the Soviet Union. That wave swelled after the Soviet Union collapsed in 1991 and by 1999 totaled over 1 million people. Tens of thousands of immigrants came in the 1980s and 1990s from the African country of Ethiopia. Smaller numbers of immigrants who were not fleeing persecution but who wanted to live in the Jewish state also arrived from the United States and Western Europe.

Israel's Jewish population is divided into two main groups: *Ashkenazic* and *Sephardic* Jews. Ashkenazic Jews, who make up slightly more than half the Jewish population, trace their roots to the medieval Jewish centers of Central and Eastern Europe. Sephardic Jews are the descendants of Jewish communities from the Iberian Peninsula, Greece, Turkey, North Africa, and the Middle East. The two communities have somewhat different religious rituals, but the most important differences between them are economic and social. Israel was founded by Ashkenazic Jews, who have comprised most of the country's political and economic elite ever since. Sephardic Jews, by contrast, began arriving in Israel in large numbers after the founding of the state. The great majority came from Arab countries and were poorly educated, with few skills suitable for a modern economy. In addition, they arrived virtually penniless, most of their property having been confiscated by Arab governments when they departed for Israel. Most of these Sephardic Jews therefore found themselves near the bottom of Israeli society in economic terms.

Over time this situation began to change as Sephardic Jews gradually improved their social, economic, and political positions. In the government formed after the 1996 elections, three of the most senior positions—defense minister, foreign minister, and deputy prime minister—were held by men born respectively in Iraq, Morocco, and Iran. In 2000, for the first time, a Sephardic Jew became Israel's president. Intermarriage between Ashkenazic and Sephardic Jews also is common. Still, significant economic, educational, and social gaps remain; most poor Israeli Jews are Sephardic. This continues to create intergroup tensions. At the same time, because of the high rates of immigration throughout Israel's history, half of its Jewish citizens—whether Ashkenazic or Sephardic—were born abroad.

A third, smaller group, numbering about 50,000, are black Jews from Ethiopia. Their origins are uncertain; they probably are an amalgam of Jews who arrived in Ethiopia in ancient times and native converts. In any event, Ethiopian Jews were cut off from the rest of world Jewry for two thousand years. They lacked any knowledge of Jewish learning and traditions that had developed since ancient times. Yet in exceedingly difficult circumstances they preserved their Jewish identity until rescued by Israeli authorities from the turmoil and starvation in Ethiopia and brought to Israel, initially by sea in 1981 and then in two dramatic airlifts: Operation Moses in 1984–85 and Operation Solomon in 1991. In a young country, they are a young community: Half of all Ethiopian Jews are under eighteen years of age.

Jews in Israel are divided in another way that transcends ethnic origins: the division between secular and religious (often called Orthodox). It is difficult to say precisely where this dividing line is. Orthodox and ultra-Orthodox Jews, who strictly observe traditional Jewish religious law, are themselves divided into many groups. Ultra-Orthodox Jews wear distinctive traditional clothing and live in their own neighborhoods, such as the famous Mea Shearim section of Jerusalem. The state of Israel is a secular state. However, from the beginning the Orthodox community was given control over certain areas of life that seemed to be most closely connected to religion, such as marriage and burial. Other accommodations were made as well; for example, automobile traffic was banned in Orthodox neighborhoods during the Jewish Sabbath. Orthodox and ultra-Orthodox Jews, who account for perhaps 20 percent of Israeli Jews, also traditionally have voted for their own political parties. They usually have held the balance of power in the Knesset (Israel's parliament) and used that position to win concessions for causes they support. The result has been a degree of tension between secular and Orthodox, especially ultra-Orthodox, communities.

That tension, however, should not be exaggerated, or seen simply as a secular-Orthodox divide. There are significant differences between Orthodox groups, who usually get along well with the secular majority, and the ultra-Orthodox sects, who themselves have major areas of disagreement. There are, to be sure, also divisions in the secular community, which means that the shifting tides of political life cause bewildering alignments and realignments that defy a simple secular-Orthodox distinction.

Most of Israel's non-Jews are Muslim Arabs. Israel's 900,000 Muslim Arabs occupy an awkward and difficult position in Israeli society. They live on a tightrope, suspended between their relatively new identity as Israeli citizens and their much older identity as Arabs in a world where Arab states (and Muslim Iran) remain the greatest threat to Israel's security. Israel's Arab citizens enjoy full legal rights.

Teenagers enjoy a sunny day on Tel Aviv Beach

But they live apart from the country's Jewish majority, mainly in all-Arab villages or in Arab sections of towns and cities. Most Israeli Arab parents send their children to Arabic-language schools, which also teach them Hebrew. The main legal difference between Arabs and Jews in Israel—and it is a big one—is that Arabs are not subject to being drafted into the army. (They may, however, volunteer.) Because army service is so important for social acceptance in Israel, not serving creates a stigma. Yet the current policy is understandable since Israel's main enemies are Arab states and the Israeli army inevitably must fight and kill Arabs when it goes to war. Israeli Arabs ordered to defend Israel would have to choose between loyalty to their country and to their fellow Arabs in opposing armies.

Israeli Arabs maintain that the government has taken land that legally belongs to them and that their communities do not receive services equal to those given to Jews. While they have legitimate complaints, the fact remains that they have done well in Israel. The Arab literacy rate has climbed since 1948 from 5 to 95 percent. (It is 57 percent in Arab nations.) Arabs have prospered economically, and have the same access as Jewish citizens to the best medical treatment in the Middle East. Israeli Arabs enjoy a free press and the political rights of a democratic society, neither of which exist in the Arab states. Arab women, who make up most of the illiterate population in the Arab world, in particular benefit from living in a modern democratic society. In Israel they enjoy legal equality with men and legal protection unmatched by women in Arab countries. In the 1999 elections, 13 of the 120 representatives elected to the Israeli parliament were Arabs, who belonged to six different political parties. In the government formed after those elections, the post of deputy foreign minister was filled by an Arab. Meanwhile, two Arab members of parliament served on the Knesset's important foreign affairs committee, and one Arab jurist was a member of Israel's 9-person supreme court. Yet while Israeli Arabs have increased their participation in Israeli political life, there also is a disturbing trend in the opposite direction. In recent years many Israeli Arabs, including college students, increasingly have been identifying less with Israel and more with Arabs living under the Palestinian Authority. This trend worries both Jewish and Arab Israelis who are working to encourage Jewish-Arab coexistence in Israel.

The Druze religion is an eleventh-century offshoot of Islam. About 100,000 Druze live in Israel. Since 1957 they have been recognized as a separate religious community. Still, the Druze speak Arabic and most of them seem to view themselves as Arabs. Nonetheless, in 1948, many Druze sided with Israel against the invading Arab armies, and since 1957, by their own request, they have been subject to conscription in the Israeli army. Their long tradition of self-defense makes the Druze excellent soldiers, and many serve in elite Israeli army units such as the paratroopers.

The great majority of Israeli Christians are Arabs. Most belong to three Christian groups: Greek Orthodox, Greek Catholic, and Catholic. Although they are not Muslims, the Arab Christians of Israel usually side with the Muslim Arab community in its disputes with the Jewish community and Israeli government. But not always. In 1998 a dispute broke out in the city of Nazareth, the largest Arab city in Israel, whose population of about 60,000 is about two-thirds Muslim and one-third Christian. The trouble began with Christian plans to build a plaza on a half acre of land in front of the city's church in preparation for the millennium. The church itself stands on the site where tradition says the angel Gabriel told Mary she was pregnant with the child of God. Muslims protested and responded with plans for their own project, a huge mosque financed by Persian Gulf nations, on that same half acre, which they claim is a Muslim holy site.

Nazareth's Muslims were in a position to carry out their project because in the most recent elections they had taken over the city council for the first time in decades. Among those who tried unsuccessfully to dissuade local Muslims from going ahead with their project was Yasir Arafat, who feared the dispute would hurt tourism in Bethlehem, which the Palestinian Authority governs. Tension built until it boiled over into fights and rock throwing between Muslim and Christian youths on Easter Sunday of 1999. In the end, the Israeli government, which actually owns the land in question and found itself caught in the middle of the dispute, imposed a compromise. The Muslims could build their mosque, but it would have to be smaller than planned so as to leave some room for the Christian plaza. Not surprisingly, the compromise satisfied neither side.

At the same time, the Christian presence in Israel is not limited to Arabs. Christian groups of all sizes from all over the world maintain a presence in Israel, where their faith was born two thousand years ago. One of their major concerns are the many Christian holy sites in Israel, a shared interest that not infrequently leads to competing claims and disputes.

Political System

Israel is a democracy, the only one in the Middle East. Its parliament, the Knesset, has 120 members who are elected by proportional representation. Every political party that receives more than 1.5 percent of the vote receives seats according to its percentage of the vote. Proportional representation, while very democratic in theory, can be divisive. It allows small political parties to proliferate and makes it very difficult for one party to win a majority of the vote. In fact, no single party has ever won a majority in an Israeli election; every government, including the current one, has been a coalition of several parties. In recent years, the number of parties has increased, complicating the task of governing the country. The person ultimately responsible for that job is the prime minister, who heads the cabinet. From 1948 until 1996, the prime minister was the leader of the largest party in parliament. However, in 1996 the system was changed so that the country's voters as a whole chose the prime minister in an election similar to the presidential election in the United States. The hope was to increase the authority of the prime minister and overcome some of the division and weakness in parliament caused by the proportional representation system. That hope was disappointed. In the elections of 1996 and 1999, voters split their ballots. In the election for prime minister, they voted for a candidate from one party, while in the parliamentary election they voted for another party. The result was a weakening of Israel's two largest parties, increased division in parliament, and two unstable governments in a row, neither of which lasted very long. By 2001, most Israelis understood the reform had failed, and after the prime ministerial election in February of that year, parliament restored the old system by which it chooses the person for that office.

THE HISTORY OF MODERN ISRAEL

The Zionist Movement and the Establishment of Israel
The history of modern Israel begins in the late nineteenth century with the founding of the Zionist movement. Zionism is the belief that Jews should return from the countries where they live as a minority and build their own nation in Israel, the land of their ancestors. Zionism is properly considered the modern Jewish nationalist movement, basically similar to many other nationalist movements that also began in the nineteenth century. At the same time, it is more than 2,500 years old, dating back to the time when the ancient Israelites first were exiled from their homeland by the Babylonians in the sixth century B.C. Psalm 137, written during that exile, contains the famous admonition:

> If I forget thee, O Jerusalem, let my right
> hand forget her cunning.
> If I do not remember thee, let my tongue
> cleave to the roof of my mouth...[1]

The founder of the modern Zionist movement was Theodor Herzl, a Jewish journalist born in Austria. He organized the first Zionist Congress in 1897. Between his death in 1904 and 1914, about 30,000 Jews from Eastern Europe settled in the ancient homeland of their people, which was at the time was called Palestine and was part of the Ottoman Empire. In November 1917, during World War I, the British government responded to Zionist appeals and issued the Balfour Declaration, which called for the "establishment in Palestine of a national home for the Jewish people." After World War I, the British took control of Palestine under the League of Nations mandate when the Ottoman Empire was dismantled. The League mandate repeated the Balfour Declaration's endorsement of a Jewish national home in Palestine. However, as early as 1920, the same year they officially received the League mandate, the British imposed restrictions on Jewish immigration into Palestine. Those restrictions were tightened in the 1930s, just when Jews in Europe attempting to escape from Nazi persecution desperately needed a place to go.

The British imposed these restrictions because the Arabs of Palestine, at the time the overwhelming majority of the population, strongly objected to Jewish immigration. During the 1920s and 1930s their anger erupted into protests and acts of violence directed at the Jews, whose population nonetheless rose from 50,000 in 1917 to 350,000 in 1939. Yet Jews were far from the only immigrants into Palestine. In fact, during the years the British restricted Jewish immigration, they did nothing to restrict extensive Arab immigration from neighboring countries that had been going on for decades. By the 1930s most of the Jewish immigrants were refugees from Nazi persecution in Germany. They had help in adjusting to their new situation from the well-organized Jewish community in Palestine. Among its most effective leaders was David Ben-Gurion, later Israel's first prime minister.

During World War II, more Jewish refugees entered Palestine. This occurred despite strict restrictions put in place by the British, who during the war were worried about growing Arab support for Nazi Germany and did not want to antagonize the Arabs by allowing too many Jews into Palestine. After the war, the British found it increasingly difficult to keep peace in Palestine in the face of intensifying Arab-Jewish conflict. At the same time, there was widespread international sympathy for the Jewish people because of the murder of 6 million Jews by Nazi Germany during the Holocaust. There also were hundreds of thousands of Jewish refugees—the survivors of the Holocaust—in European displaced persons camps with no place to go. The Jews of Palestine tried to smuggle refugees into the country, usually on old ships that were barely seaworthy, but the British navy caught most of those ships and interned the Jews in detention camps.

In 1947, the British, burdened by their own domestic problems, announced they would withdraw from Palestine. The United Nations General Assembly then voted in November of 1947 to partition the country into two states, one Arab and one Jewish. The proposed borders were based largely on population patterns, that is, where each group was the majority. The Jewish community of Palestine accepted the partition, but the Arabs rejected it, demanding complete control of the country. They warned they would fight any attempt to establish an independent Jewish state, and that if one was created they would drive the Jews into the sea. On May 14, 1948, the British withdrew from Palestine and the Jews, led by Ben-Gurion, declared the independence of the state they called Israel. Five Arab armies from neighboring countries immediately invaded the new country, which found itself fighting for its very existence. The head of the Arab League was very clear about what his side intended to do:

> This will be a war of extermination and a momentous massacre which will be spoken of like the Mongol massacres and the Crusades.[2]

From War to War: Israel, 1948–1982

There would be no "momentous massacre." In fighting that lasted from May of 1948 to the spring of 1949, Israel defeated the armies of Egypt, Syria, Iraq, Jordan, and Lebanon in what Israelis call their War of Independence. But victory came at a very high price in terms of lives, destroyed property, and money. Nor did the end of the fighting bring peace: The Arab states refused to sign peace treaties with Israel and agreed only to an armistice. The armistice also left Egypt in control of a small but strategic coastal area called the Gaza Strip and the Kingdom of Jordan in control of a large kidney-shaped area called the West Bank, which it soon officially annexed. Jerusalem ended up divided. Jordan controlled the eastern part of the city, which included the Old City and its Jewish Quarter—from which the Jordanians expelled all the Jewish inhabitants—and the Western Wall, Judaism's holiest site. Israel controlled the new, western part of Jerusalem. The war also produced about 500,000 Arab refugees. The Arab flight began immediately after the UN voted to partition the country, when thousands of wealthy business leaders moved their families and assets to the safety of Egypt and Lebanon. By the spring, before the British left but after fighting had begun between local Arab and Jewish forces, many Arab political and community leaders joined a second wave leaving the country. By the time Israel declared its independence in May of 1948, about 175,000 Arabs had left to escape the fighting. Then, as the tide of battle turned in favor of the Israelis, large numbers of ordinary Arab town dwellers and peasants, having seen their leaders flee, left their homes to seek safety behind Arab lines. Often these refugees had been frightened by rumors and false claims of atrocities spread by Arab leaders themselves in an attempt to demonize the Jewish enemy and thereby mobilize the Arab side. In a few cases, Israeli troops expelled Arab civilians from villages with strategic military importance, including along the vital highway connecting Tel Aviv and Jerusalem. In any event, the Arab refugees were unable to return to homes that ended up on the Jewish side of the 1949 armistice lines. No Jews were allowed to remain in Arab-controlled territory; all were expelled, most of them from areas seized by the Jordanians. The jagged armistice lines of 1949 gave Israel about 21 percent more territory than provided by the original UN partition plan.

Over the next decade Israel took in hundreds of thousands of Jewish refugees, mainly from Arab countries where growing hostility had made life for Jews impossible. The newcomers changed the face of Israel. In 1948 it had been largely European and Ashkenazic, but by the 1960s it was about 50 percent Middle Eastern and Sephardic. Under the Law of Return, passed in 1950, Jews from anywhere in the world were given the right to come to Israel and immediately become citizens.

In 1956 Israel again went to war, this time with Egypt. Israel attacked Egypt hoping to end Egyptian-sponsored terrorist raids from the Sinai desert and Gaza Strip that had claimed hundreds of civilian lives. These raids had increased dramatically during 1955, when the death toll approached

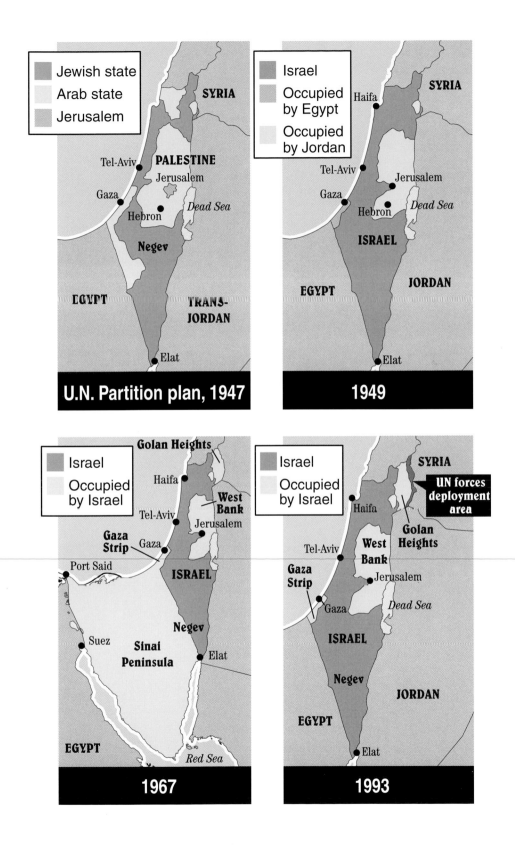

U.N. Partition plan, 1947

Jewish state
Arab state
Jerusalem

SYRIA
PALESTINE
Tel-Aviv
Jerusalem
Gaza
Hebron
Dead Sea
Negev
EGYPT
TRANS-JORDAN
Elat

1949

Israel
Occupied by Egypt
Occupied by Jordan

SYRIA
Haifa
Tel-Aviv
Jerusalem
Gaza
Hebron
Dead Sea
ISRAEL
EGYPT
JORDAN
Elat

1967

Israel
Occupied by Israel

Golan Heights
Haifa
West Bank
Tel-Aviv
Jerusalem
Gaza Strip
Gaza
Port Said
ISRAEL
Negev
Suez
Sinai Peninsula
Elat
EGYPT
Red Sea

1993

Israel
Occupied by Israel

SYRIA
UN forces deployment area
Haifa
Golan Heights
West Bank
Tel-Aviv
Jerusalem
Gaza Strip
Gaza
Dead Sea
ISRAEL
Negev
JORDAN
EGYPT
Elat

250. A second goal, shared by Britain and France, countries that also attacked Egypt in 1956, was to bring down the Nasser regime. Israel defeated the Egyptian army in the Sinai Peninsula and occupied the region, but bowed to international pressure and withdrew in 1957.

Israel's prime minister from 1948 until 1963, with the exception of 1953 to 1955, was David Ben-Gurion. His political party, a socialist group called Mapai (now the Labor Party), controlled the government in coalition with smaller partners even longer, until 1977. The 1950s and 1960s were tense for Israel. All its Arab neighbors officially maintained a state of war with the Jewish state. Furthermore, the Arab League enforced an economic boycott against Israel. Arab states not only refused to trade with Israel, but pressured European, American, and Asian companies not to do business with Israel, on pain of losing Arab business. Still, Israel enjoyed a period of rapid development and growth. Hundreds of thousands of refugees, most of them penniless and uneducated when they arrived in Israel, became productive citizens. Israel built a powerful army and air force, the best in the Middle East. It constructed its National Water Carrier, drained swamps, planted forests on barren hillsides, and established new industries in the cities. These included armaments factories that made Israel less dependent on foreign suppliers.

In 1967 Israel faced its most serious crisis since its War of Independence in 1948–1949. It began when Egypt's President Nasser demanded that the UN peacekeeping troops in the Sinai Peninsula, in place since 1957, withdraw. Nasser then quickly moved tens of thousands of Egyptian troops up to the Israeli border. He signed military alliances with Syria and Jordan, and blockaded Israel's port of Eilat by closing the Strait of Tiran at the southern end of the Red Sea to Israeli shipping. On May 27 he announced, "Our basic objective will be the destruction of Israel." Three days later Cairo radio proclaimed that Israel either "will be strangled by the Arab boycott, or it will perish by the fire of Arab forces. . . ."[3] By early June, the Egyptian force along Israel's southern border included nearly 120,000 well-trained troops and almost 2,000 tanks.

The Israelis were convinced that they could not afford to let the Arabs strike first. Israel was too small and vulnerable, only 9 miles (14 kilometers) wide at its narrowest point. Therefore, on June 5 they launched a preemptive attack against Egypt, the enemy they feared most. Six days later, after hard fighting on three fronts, Israel had won a total victory over all three of its Arab opponents, Egypt as well as Jordan and Syria. Israel now controlled the Gaza Strip and West Bank, the Sinai Peninsula, and the Golan Heights. It also controlled all of Jerusalem, including the holy sites in the eastern half of the city from which all Jews had been barred since 1948. The Israelis were shocked to find that between 1949 and 1967 the Jordanians had destroyed every Jewish synagogue in Jerusalem's Old City and used tombstones from Jewish graves in the ancient Mount of Olives cemetery to pave army latrines. Upon entering Jerusalem's Old City, Defense Minister Moshe Dayan spoke for the country when he said:

> We have returned to all that is holy in our land. We have returned never to be parted from it again.[4]

Israel's victory in what is known as the Six-Day War was a great boost to morale and left the country, at least temporarily, much more militarily secure than ever before. But it also left many urgent problems unsolved. The Arab world remained united in its opposition to Israel's right to exist. Israel now ruled over more than one million Arabs living on the West Bank and in the Gaza Strip who were not Israeli citizens and who were bitterly hostile to Israeli control. In addition, Israeli Arabs were increasingly restive. Until 1966 they had lived under special military rules that limited their freedom of movement. After 1967 they were influenced by their increased contacts with the West Bank and Gaza Arabs. This heightened their sense of Arab identity at the expense of whatever ties they felt with the state of Israel.

There also was a new and destabilizing element in the already volatile political Middle East political mix. In 1964, at a time when Israel did not yet control the West Bank, Gaza Strip, or eastern Jerusalem and the Old City, the Arab League decided to set up the Palestine Liberation Organization (PLO). The PLO's goal was the destruction of the Jewish state and its replacement by an Arab-dominated state from which most Jews living in Israel would be expelled. After the defeat of Arab armies in 1967 the PLO's importance grew. It received effective leadership for the first time in 1969 when Yasir Arafat became its chairman. In the years that followed, Israel increasingly found itself under attack by terrorists sent by the PLO or other Palestinian terrorist organizations. Their civilian victims included airline passengers, Israeli athletes at the 1972 Olympic Games, and schoolchildren.

Israel's prime minister at the time of the Six-Day War had been Levi Eshkol. When he died in 1969 he was succeeded by Golda Meir, the first woman head of state in the Middle East. In 1973 it became Meir's fate, like that of her predecessors, to lead Israel as it fought another costly war. The war began with a coordinated Egyptian-Syrian attack against Israeli forces in both the Sinai Peninsula and Golan Heights that caught the Israelis unprepared. The attack came on October 6, the night of Yom Kippur, the Day of Atonement, the holiest day of the Jewish year; hence the name the Yom Kippur War. Outnumbered twelve to one at the front, initially the Israelis were thrown back, but they then regrouped. With the help of a massive airlift of supplies from the United States, they defeated the Egyptian and Syrian forces, but at a price in lives that stunned the nation. Israel lost nearly 2,600 soldiers in the war. Only the War of Independence had cost more lives. For Israel, whose population was about 3 million at the time, 2,600 dead was the equivalent of 250,000 dead in a country the size of the United States. Almost 9,000 soldiers were wounded. Three weeks of intense warfare had cost $9 billion, more than Israel's gross national product for an entire year.

The Yom Kippur War was a catalyst for political change. In April 1974 Golda Meir resigned following criticism that her government had not been prepared for the 1973 attack. Her replacement as prime minister was Yitzhak Rabin, the general who had led Israel's forces during the Six-Day War. Rabin, who after retiring from the army had served as ambassador to the United States, was the first native-born Israeli to lead his country. The high point of his term in office was the spectacular rescue of almost 100 people—most of them Israelis but also some non-Israeli Jews—taken hostage by Palestinian and German terrorists. The terrorists had hijacked a passenger airliner in Europe and diverted it to Entebbe, Uganda, 2,600 miles (4,100 km) from Tel Aviv. On July 3, 1976, Israeli soldiers, having secretly flown seven hours from Israel and landed at Entebbe in the dead of the night, freed the hostages in a daring raid. A minor financial scandal—Rabin's wife had illegally kept a foreign bank account—forced Rabin's resignation in 1977. His successor was Shimon Peres, a former close aide to Ben-Gurion, and a longtime rival of Rabin in the Labor Party. Peres had played a key role in building Israel's defense industries and its nuclear program. His problem, as his party faced parliamentary elections in May, was that after almost thirty years in power the Labor Party had lost touch with many Israelis, especially the Sephardic community. The election ended Labor's long era in power. The winner was the Likud Party, led by Polish-born Menachem Begin.

Begin's Likud Party differed from Labor in two main policy areas. During Labor's years in power Israel had a mixed economy: Most of it was in private hands, but there also was a large government-run sector. Likud strongly favored free-market reforms to reduce the role of the government in the economy. The more important difference concerned the territories Israel had won in the Six-Day War. From the start, Labor had favored territorial compromise in exchange for peace. Labor did not even want to retain areas with a large Palestinian Arab population, fearing that such control would undermine Israeli democracy. Labor did insist on keeping Jerusalem as the united capital of Israel, a position that had almost universal support among Israelis. When it came to other territories—the Sinai Peninsula, the thinly populated Golan Heights and Jordan Valley, and selected parts of the West Bank and the Gaza Strip—the decisive issue was security. Areas deemed not essential to security could be given up in return for peace; those deemed vital would remain under Israeli control.

Begin and Likud had a different view from Labor. They were prepared to yield territory that was not part of biblical ancient Israel, such as the Sinai Peninsula, but not land that was part of what they considered Israel's biblical heritage. For that reason, while Labor restricted Jewish settlements to thinly populated and strategically critical areas, Likud promoted Jewish settlement throughout the West Bank and the Gaza Strip, even in areas with large Arab populations.

In the end, however, it was Begin, the hard-liner, who made Israel's first peace with an Arab country. In 1977 he reacted positively to Egyptian president Anwar Sadat's offer to "come to Jerusalem." Begin then negotiated the Camp David Accords, a framework for peace, with Sadat and U.S. president Jimmy Carter in September 1978 and a peace treaty in March 1979. In that treaty, in exchange for peace Israel returned the Sinai Peninsula and its oil wells, which the Israelis had developed, to Egypt. The treaty also called for further negotiations to establish autonomy for the Arabs of the West Bank and Gaza Strip. Begin then moved to shore up Israel's legal position over areas he considered crucial. In 1980, the Knesset passed a law declaring Jerusalem Israel's permanent and undivided capital, and in 1981 Israeli law was extended to the Golan Heights, in effect annexing that territory. However, neither act received international recognition. That same year, in another daring raid that rivaled the Entebbe operation, Begin sent Israeli warplanes to bomb the nuclear reactor being built in Iraq. Begin feared, correctly as it turned out, that Iraq, a country still officially at war with Israel, was planning to build nuclear weapons. The Israeli raid, criticized at the time in Europe and America, almost certainly spared the United States and its allies from facing a nuclear-armed Iraq in the Gulf War ten years later.

In June 1982 Begin sent the Israeli army into civil-war torn Lebanon to destroy bases the PLO had been using to attack Israel. The war in Lebanon, despite achieving its military goal, turned into a long and bloody occupation that deeply divided Israeli society. The first major disaster of the war occurred in September when Christian Lebanese forces, who were allied with Israel, murdered hundreds of Palestinian refugees in two refugee camps near Beirut. Although it was Lebanese and *not* Israelis who committed that crime, many Israelis began to turn against the war. The second disaster developed over time when Israel kept its troops in southern Lebanon and ended up fighting Lebanese and Palestinian guerrillas there.

In 1983 Begin resigned as prime minister, in part because of his despair over the growing Israeli casualties in Lebanon. His successor was Yitzhak Shamir, a veteran Likud politician. When the 1984 elections produced a virtual Labor-Likud standoff, the two parties formed a "national unity" government. They agreed that Shimon Peres would be prime minister from 1984 to 1986, and that Shamir would take over from 1986 to 1988. In 1985, the midpoint of Peres's short term, Israel finally left most of southern Lebanon. It withdrew to a narrow "security zone" just north of the Israeli border, which its army patrolled along with local Lebanese Christian allies.

Meanwhile, there was trouble closer to home. In December 1987, a Palestinian uprising, known as the *intifada* (the term means "shaking off" in Arabic), began in the Gaza Strip and spread to the West Bank. The intifada reflected the deep frustrations of the Palestinian Arabs, especially the youth, with the ongoing Israeli occupation. While the intifada began spontaneously, within a month the PLO controlled many of its activities. Two radical Islamic fundamentalist groups, Hamas and Islamic Jihad, also were deeply involved in the intifada. When Israel tried to crack down on the demonstrators, who often were teenagers, but whose rocks and gasoline bombs could kill, its public image abroad suffered. At home, many Israelis, who understood when their soldiers had to go to war against Arab armies, were troubled watching them use tear gas and clubs against rioting Palestinian teenagers. But the continued political stalemate—there was another indecisive election in 1988—prevented new initiatives that might lead to useful negotiations between Israel and the Palestinians.

In 1991 Israel became involved in the Gulf War, but not as a direct participant. The war was fought between Iraq, which had invaded Kuwait in 1990, and a U.S. led coalition formed to force the Iraqis to withdraw. During the war Iraq attacked Israel with dozens of guided missiles. The United

States urgently requested Israel not to retaliate, fearing an Israeli response would cause the Arab states allied with the U.S. to quit the coalition. The Israelis honored the request, despite the damage and terror the missiles caused. The next year Israel finally held an election that produced relatively decisive results. The Labor Party, led by Yitzhak Rabin, won a solid plurality and formed a new government with Rabin as prime minister. For the first time in almost a decade, Israel had a government capable of taking decisive action on urgent issues facing the country.

Israel in the 1990s

When Yitzhak Rabin took office in July 1992 he told his fellow Israelis, "We are going to change the national order of priorities." His main goal would be to "promote the making of peace and take vigorous steps that will lead to the end of the Arab-Israeli conflict." He also directed some of his remarks to the Palestinians, urging them, "Don't lose this opportunity that may never return. Take our proposals seriously...."[5] During 1993, while public talks that had begun back in 1991 were getting nowhere, Israeli and PLO officials met secretly for months in Oslo, Norway. In August they surprised the world by announcing an agreement, or Declaration of Principles, popularly known as the Oslo Accords. The agreement provided for a transition to Palestinian self-rule in the Gaza Strip and West Bank over a five-year period. Israel would turn over territory to a newly created Palestine Authority in stages, beginning with most of the Gaza Strip and the West Bank city of Jericho. Exactly how much territory Israel eventually would retain and how close "autonomy" would come to actual independence were two of the many difficult issues left unsettled. A third critical issue left unsettled was the final status of Jerusalem.

On September 9, Israel and the PLO exchanged letters in which Israel recognized the PLO as the representative of the Palestinian people and the PLO recognized Israel's right to exist and promised to abandon the use of terror against the Jewish state. The two sides formally signed the Oslo agreement in Washington on September 13, 1993. Additional essential details took further negotiations; they were worked out in an agreement signed in Cairo on May 4, 1994. The peace process and establishment of Palestinian self-rule was supposed to be completed in five years.

The Oslo Accords, despite deeply felt skepticism and mistrust of the PLO and Arafat, initially won widespread support in Israel. Rabin admitted to his people that it was not easy to make peace with people he called "murderers," but added that Israel had to consider what he called the "comprehensive" picture. Significantly, the former general, known for his careful and meticulous planning, bluntly and simply said, "We have to take risks."[6] The benefits of the peace process for Israel became more evident to many when Israel and Jordan signed a peace treaty in October 1994, finally ending a forty-six-year state of war between the two nations. Low-level diplomatic relations and economic ties also were established with several other Arab states.

But Israeli faith in the process was shaken by a series of terrorist attacks by Islamic fundamentalist groups that killed a total of seventy-seven people in the sixteen months following the accords. Nonetheless, in September 1995 Israel and the PLO reached an agreement often called "Oslo II." It provided for Israel's withdrawal from six more West Bank towns, a legislature called the Palestinian Council, and the election of a president of that council. Oslo II also divided the West Bank and Gaza Strip into three unequal areas: territory under full Palestinian control (the smallest at 3 percent, but including the major urban areas), territory under Palestinian administration and Israeli military control (24 percent), and territory under full Israeli control (73 percent).

Oslo II was controversial in Israel, and barely won Knesset approval in October. Then the peace process and virtually everything else in Israel was disrupted on November 4, 1995, when an extremist Jewish law student assassinated Rabin just after his appearance at a peace rally in downtown Tel Aviv. The assassination united Israelis of virtually all political camps in shock and mourning. Although the assassin belonged to a tiny fringe group opposed to territorial concessions to the Palestinians, his deed grimly highlighted the deep and bitter divisions in Israel over the peace process and how to guarantee the country's security. At the same time, the assassination was so shocking precisely because it was such an exception to the rules and practices of Israeli society and because Israelis were accustomed to closing ranks, whatever their differences, in times of crisis.

Shimon Peres succeeded Rabin as prime minister and prepared for elections in May 1996. For the first time, voters would not only cast ballots in a parliamentary election, but also would vote directly for Israel's prime minister. Although Labor and Peres were favored, a new series of deadly terrorist attacks by Palestinian groups opposed to the peace process cost Peres and his party support. The voters narrowly chose Likud leader Benjamin Netanyahu as prime minister. Netanyahu was a critic of what he said were excessive Labor concessions to the Palestinians under the Oslo agreement; his campaign stressed that Israel must negotiate a "secure peace." Once elected, Netanyahu had to cobble together a coalition of eight parties to form a majority in the Knesset. This was further testimony to the growing fractionalization of Israeli political life.

Netanyahu's domestic program called for reducing the government role in the economy, cutting the budget deficit, and encouraging foreign investment in Israel. In foreign affairs, Netanyahu focused on the peace process, but with a tougher and more cautious stance toward the PLO than that of Labor. Netanyahu and Likud, also in contrast to the former government, encouraged additional Israeli settlement on the West Bank. In addition, the new Israeli government demanded stricter Palestinian compliance with agreements already signed. Its demands included carrying out Arafat's long-standing but unfulfilled pledge to eliminate numerous articles in the PLO Charter that called for Israel's destruction and for real efforts to combat terrorism.

Notwithstanding Netanyahu's skepticism about the Oslo agreement, in January 1997 his government and the Palestinian Authority negotiated the Hebron Protocol, under which Israeli troops withdrew from most of the West Bank city of Hebron. After the Hebron agreement, the peace process again ground to a halt for the rest of the year. Netanyahu's government was weakened when one of its coalition partners withdrew, leaving it with a razor-thin

61–59 majority in the Knesset. An entire year without meetings between Israeli and Palestinian leaders finally ended with an American-sponsored meeting in New York in September 1998. In October, Netanyahu and Arafat began a summit meeting with American president Bill Clinton at the Wye River Conference Center in Maryland. Later they were joined by King Hussein of Jordan, already seriously ill with cancer. It took nine days of intense negotiations to reach an agreement, the Wye River Memorandum. Israel agreed to withdraw its troops from an additional 13 percent of the West Bank in three stages. In return the Palestinians again agreed to step up antiterrorist efforts and eliminate the clauses from the PLO Covenant calling for Israel's destruction. This pledge, made five times since 1993, finally was carried out by a vote of the PLO's governing body, the Palestinian National Council (PNC), in December 1998. The PNC voted to approve a January 1998 letter from President Arafat to President Clinton that stated fifteen articles (out of thirty-three) had been "nullified" and parts of nine others "modified."[7] The vote itself did not reflect any enthusiasm, or even serious involvement, on the part of the general PNC membership. It was conducted, without discussion, by PNC members standing with their hands raised.

In the months after the Wye River Memorandum defections from the Likud coalition cost the government its parliamentary majority. This forced new elections for parliament and prime minister in May 1999. Although both Labor (now calling itself "One Israel") and Likud lost seats—Labor fell from 34 to 27 and Likud from 32 to 19—smaller parties sympathetic to Labor did better than those favoring Likud. More importantly, Labor's candidate, former general Ehud Barak, the most highly decorated soldier in Israel's history, decisively defeated Netanyahu in the prime minister's race. Barak was considered tough and security minded, but also more flexible than Netanyahu in terms of negotiating with the Palestinians. His reputation as being strong on security was important. Between the signing of the Oslo Accords in 1993 and the end of 1998, 279 Israelis were killed in terrorist attacks, more than in any comparable period in recent years. Most died in suicide attacks by bombers who blew themselves up along with their victims. Barak appeared to many as the man who could wear the mantle of Yitzhak Rabin and negotiate a secure peace for Israel.

It took Barak six long weeks to cobble together a coalition of seven political parties. Aside from One Israel, the coalition ranged across Israel's divided spectrum and included both leftist secular and ultra-Orthodox parties. When he took office on July 6, Barak told Israelis his main priority would be a "true lasting peace." He directed remarks to Israeli mothers "who don't sleep at night," but also told Palestinians he recognized their "suffering."[8] Less than two months later, on September 3, after tough negotiations in which the United States again played an important role, Barak and PA president Arafat signed an agreement in Sharm al-Sheikh, Egypt. The agreement simply modified the Wye River Memorandum: Its main significance was that it restarted the peace process. Israel agreed to complete the withdrawals agreed to at Wye in three stages, which would leave the Palestinian Authority in full or partial control of 40 percent of the West Bank. As at Wye, the Palestinians agreed to carry out security measures that included arresting terrorists wanted by Israel, collecting weapons from Palestinian civilians, and reducing the size of its police force to the limits specified by the Oslo Accords. The two sides also agreed to begin negotiations within months for a final settlement, and to achieve that goal by September 10, 2000. The first Israeli withdrawal, fixed for September 10, 1999, took place a day earlier than scheduled.

Israel Since the Millennium

The hopes for peace raised by the election of Ehud Barak and the Sharm al-Sheikh agreement did not survive the year 2000. The year began well enough when Israel completed the withdrawals agreed to in the Wye River Memorandum in March. Late in May, Israel withdrew its soldiers from its security zone in southern Lebanon, where they had been for almost two decades. The occupation, while bringing some security to Israel's northern villages and towns, had been extremely costly. More than nine hundred Israeli soldiers had been killed in battles with various Lebanese and Palestinian guerrilla groups, in particular the Lebanese Shiite group Hezbollah, which drew much of its inspiration and financing from Iran. It was against this background that U.S. president Bill Clinton called for a summit between Prime Minister Barak and President Arafat at Camp David, Maryland, the same presidential retreat where more than two decades earlier President Jimmy Carter had negotiated the agreement with Israeli and Egyptian leaders that had led to the peace treaty between the two countries. Clinton set an ambitious goal: to resolve the most difficult issues remaining in the Israeli-Palestinian peace effort dating from the 1993 Oslo Accords.

The negotiations at Camp David lasted two weeks, from July 11 to July 25. Barak offered the Palestinians unprecedented concessions. He was prepared to turn over about 95 percent of the West Bank and Gaza to an independent Palestinian state. That state would have sovereignty over part of eastern Jerusalem and over the surface of the Temple Mount, where two Muslim mosques stand. Barak even offered to allow 100,000 Palestinian refugees to return to Israel under a onetime "family reunification" program, to uproot more than 40,000 Israeli settlers living on territory that would become part of the Palestinian state, and to cede to that state some land inside Israel's 1949 borders adjoining the Gaza Strip. In return Israel would annex about 5 percent of the West Bank where three major blocs of Jewish settlements housing about 130,000 settlers stood.

These concessions went far beyond anything Israel had offered before and shocked and dismayed many of Barak's countrymen, who believed he was doing irreparable harm to Israel's security. President Clinton, both in private during the negotiations and in public comments to the press later on, made it clear that he believed that these were terms that Arafat and the Palestinians should accept. But Arafat wanted more, including full sovereignty over all of eastern Jerusalem. The negotiations dragged on. Finally, with time running out, Clinton gave Arafat a series of yes-or-no options that could have led to an agreement and an independent Palestinian state. Arafat said no. The Camp David negotiations were over, the best opportunity for the Palestinians to have a state of their own since 1947 had been lost, and the Israeli-Palestinian peace process had broken down.

Although the Camp David negotiations collapsed over the specific issue of Jerusalem, the Israeli public was perhaps even more disturbed and deeply shaken by another Palestinian demand, one that directly challenged the assumption that the Palestinians finally were prepared to accept Israel's existence. The Palestinians insisted on the right of all refugees from the 1948–49 war and their descendants to return and live in Israel. That eventuality, which by 2001 would have involved three million people, literally would have meant the end of Israel's existence as a Jewish state.

It was not long before large-scale violence resumed in the form of an explosion of Palestinian demonstrations and attacks against Israelis throughout the West Bank and Gaza Strip. Israeli soldiers, generally badly outnumbered, responded with nonlethal means when possible such as tear gas and rubber bullets, but often found those means were not enough to contain the situations they faced and therefore turned to more powerful weapons. Initial reports erroneously depicted the violence by Palestinians as a spontaneous reaction to a visit by Israeli hard-line politician Ariel Sharon to the Temple Mount—a visit approved by the PA. In fact, it soon became clear that the campaign of violence, soon known as the "second" intifada, had been planned by PA authorities well in advance, after Yasir Arafat's return from the failed Camp David negotiations.

The second intifada escalated the violence that had taken place during the original intifada of the late 1980s and early 1990s. It involved the direct participation of militias controlled and armed by al-Fatah ("Conquest" in Arabic), the group headed by Arafat since the 1950s. They used an arsenal of weapons that included automatic rifles, machine guns, mortars, hand grenades, explosives, and antitank missiles to attack Israeli soldiers. Israeli civilians living in settlements on the West Bank also came under attack, often by rifle fire. In October, a Palestinian mob destroyed a Jewish shrine, Joseph's Tomb, in the West Bank city of Nablus; a week later another mob in the city of Ramallah lynched two Israeli soldiers, a gruesome incident captured by journalists on videotape. The Palestinian Authority meanwhile released hundreds of jailed Hamas and Islamic Jihad terrorists, a practice it had followed on and off since 1994 in violation of the Oslo accords and subsequent agreements. In April 2001, the United States State Department reported that the members of the PA security services and groups associated with al-Fatah had "instigated and participated in anti-Israeli violence."[9] By then, more than 400 people were dead, about 350 Palestinians and almost 70 Israelis. Thousands of people had been injured, mainly Palestinians but also hundreds of Israelis.

In only six months, events seemingly had come full turn, and for the worse. Far from sensing that peace was at hand, as many had hoped in mid-2000, Israelis once again worried about the danger of a full-fledged war. Many Israelis who had considered themselves part of the peace camp were deeply disillusioned. With Israel facing the worst violence in years, the government of Ehud Barak fell apart and Israelis again went to the polls, for the third time in less than five years, to elect a new prime minister. This time, more than 62 percent of the voters turned to Ariel Sharon, the leader of the Likud Party.

Sharon was one of Israel's most charismatic and controversial politicians. He was a war hero, the man who in the 1973 Yom Kippur War had led Israeli troops across the Suez Canal to trap the Egyptian army on the other side. He also had been defense minister during the 1982 invasion of Lebanon, which many Israelis believed had been a costly mistake. He was known for his daring and toughness, and for his hard-line views when it came to dealing with the Palestinians. Within Israel, he had both fervent admirers and bitter enemies. By 2001, he also was the man most Israelis believed could at least provide them with some measure of security.

Sharon began his term after successfully weaving together a "unity" government that included both the Labor and Likud parties and six other smaller parties. His foreign minister was prime minister Shimon Peres, the architect of the Oslo peace process whose approach to dealing with the Palestinians differed markedly from Sharon's. The new cabinet also included Labor Party member Saleh Tarif, the first member of the Druze community ever to hold a cabinet post in Israel. It said something about the fractured state of Israeli politics that Sharon's ability to form a government was seen as a significant accomplishment.

Meanwhile, the intifada continued without a pause, with PA president Arafat making increasingly inflammatory statements to Arab audiences, until an especially horrifying bombing attack on June 1 in which a Hamas suicide bomber blew himself up outside a crowded Tel Aviv discotheque. What was so shocking, especially to Western Europeans and Americans, was that this time the target was not only civilians, but children. The discotheque was a teenage hangout, and most of the twenty-one Israelis killed in the attack were between the ages of fourteen and eighteen. But notwithstanding Prime Minister Sharon's reputation for toughness and readiness to use force, the expected Israeli retaliation did not come. Instead, Sharon held back as international pressure quickly built on Yasir Arafat, who, fearing what Israel might do and concerned about international criticism, called for an immediate cease-fire. After mediation efforts by the United States, what officials called a cease-fire went into effect on June 13. In reality it was a lower level of violence: Palestinians still attacked Israeli civilians and soldiers, while the Israeli military targeted and assassinated Palestinian militants who had carried out terrorist attacks or were planning to do so. The situation remained as dangerous and potentially explosive as ever.

Despite the tensions and disappointments of 2000 and 2001, Israel began the new millennium as a modern and relatively prosperous society. It had integrated Jewish immigrants from all over the world and built a modern industrial economy. Israeli schools trained world-class scientists and engineers. Its high-tech products were found in 60 percent of its exports (excluding diamonds). The Israeli military was among the world's most respected. It was working with the U.S. army to produce the Arrow antimissile system, the world's first, and a powerful laser to destroy short-range rockets often used by guerrillas. The country had a vibrant cultural life. Writers like Amos Oz and A. B. Yehoshua were known internationally, and Israeli-trained classical musicians like Itzhak Perlman and Pinchas Zuckerman were among the world's most renowned in their fields. Its problems, from secular-religious tensions to the environment, were serious and daunting, but all took second place to the search for a secure peace. Nothing could change the reality that Israel faced great dangers in the future.

PALESTINIAN AUTHORITY

Palestinian Authority (PA) is an autonomous political entity located on parts of the West Bank and Gaza Strip, areas under Israeli control from the 1967 war to 1994. The PA controls most of the Gaza Strip, a small and densely populated stretch of land along the Mediterranean coast 28 miles (45 kilometers) long and only 5 miles (8 kilometers) wide, squeezed between Israel and Egypt. It also fully or partially controls 40 percent of the West Bank, the hilly eastern region of the former Palestine Mandate. Both areas were occupied by invading Arab powers in the 1948–49 Arab-Israeli war, the Gaza Strip by Egypt and the West Bank by Jordan. They were taken by Israeli forces in the 1967 war. The West Bank and Gaza Strip make up most of the area that would have formed an Arab state had the Arabs accepted the 1947 UN partition of Mandatory Palestine and not chosen instead to go to war with Israel.

Children at play in a refugee camp in Gaza

About 1.75 million people live on the West Bank. More than 90 percent are Arabs. Christians make up perhaps a tenth of the Arab population, but their numbers are declining because of emigration. About 160,000 Israelis live in scattered settlements in the region established in the years after the 1967 Six-Day War. They and many other Israelis refer to the West Bank by its biblical names: Judea (the southern part) and Samaria (the northern part). The population of the Gaza Strip is about 1.1 million, virtually all of whom are Sunni Muslim Arabs. A quarter of the population lives in Gaza City, the region's largest urban area. One-third of the population are refugees from the 1948–49 war and their descendants. They live in eight large camps that over the years have taken on the look of permanent towns. Approximately 6,000 Israelis live in settlements in the Gaza Strip.

The "autonomy" of the PA refers to its uneasy and unresolved relationship with Israel. After exercising direct control of the area between 1967 and 1993, Israel yielded some of that control to the PA in a series of agreements. Israel, however, maintains that the ultimate fate of the region must take into account its security concerns. The West Bank in particular is a wedge that practically divides Israel in two. It also contains high ground overlooking Israel's coastal plain that provides strategic advantage in any military conflict. The West Bank could become, as it was in 1948 and 1967, a staging ground for an Arab attack on the Jewish state. Israelis therefore are deeply concerned about exactly what territory the PA controls and the degree of its control.

The Palestinians argue for complete independence of the West Bank and the Gaza Strip. They want all Israeli settlements established since 1967 to be dismantled. In addition, they want control of all of eastern Jerusalem, which Israel annexed in 1967 and considers part of its united capital city.

The PA came into being as a result of the Declaration of Principles signed by Israel and the Palestine Liberation Organization in September 1993. In May 1994, after further negotiations, the PA took control of the city of Jericho on the West Bank near the Jordan River and the majority of the Gaza Strip. At the end of 1995, after the Oslo II agreement, Israel withdrew from six of the remaining seven major West Bank cities: Nablus, Ramallah, Jenin, Tulkarm, Qalqalya, and Bethlehem. Hebron, important to both Muslims and Jews because they consider it the burial place of the patriarch Abraham, was not included in the 1995 agreement. However, 450 Palestinian villages and towns were turned over to PA administration, with Israel maintaining control over security. The bulk of West Bank territory remained under Israeli control.

In 1997 Israel withdrew from 80 percent of Hebron, but kept control over the rest of the city to protect the small group of Jewish settlers there. The agreements of 1993, 1995, and 1997 left the PA with full control of 3 percent of the West Bank land, civilian administrative control of an additional 24 percent, and full control of 60 percent of the Gaza Strip. The Wye River Memorandum of 1998 and the Sharm al-Sheikh agreement that superseded it expanded the PA's total or partial control to 40 percent of the West Bank. These agreements also left well over 90 percent of all Palestinians living in the West Bank and Gaza at least under PA civilian rule. Just under a quarter of the territory transferred to PA control under the Wye and Sharm al-Sheikh agreements was set aside as a nature reserve where building is prohibited.

In January 1996 Palestinian voters elected a legislature called the Palestinian Council. Yasir Arafat's Fatah organization, the core of the PLO, won 49 out of the 88 seats. The voters also elected a president of the council; in that election Arafat won more than 87 percent of the votes over a rival who opposed the Oslo peace agreements. In May of that year Arafat appointed what in effect was a cabinet.

Since its establishment, the PA has had a rocky history. Almost entirely dependent on foreign contributions for its budget, in 1998 it was accused by officials who audited its budget of mismanaging $300 million dollars. The PA is widely viewed as extremely corrupt, even by local Palestinians. It has been criticized both at home and abroad for operating undemocratically and for committing human rights abuses.

The PA also has had serious economic problems. It remains heavily dependent on Israel for imported goods, as a market for its exports, and as a place where many Palestinians find jobs. The economy therefore was hurt each time Israel closed its borders with the PA, which it did on several occasions after terrorist suicide bombing attacks killed Jews in Israel. Unemployment, fueled by one of the world's highest birthrates and a resulting population explosion, remained at staggering levels (34 percent in 1996). In fact, although the international community provided the PA with about $2.5 billion in aid between 1994 and 1998, almost every relevant statistic during the late 1990s indicated economic decline.

Along with their internal problems, Arafat and the PA consistently have locked horns with Israel. They were angered and disappointed by the pace and the extent of Israeli withdrawals from West Bank territory. What emerged in the course of those withdrawals was a fundamental difference in what each side expected. The Palestinians expected Israel to withdraw from virtually all of the West Bank, including all of eastern Jerusalem, which the Palestinians wanted as their capital. Israel intended to withdraw from perhaps 50 percent of the region and retain complete control of Jerusalem.

Israel had its own list of complaints about the PA. With considerable justification, it accused the PA of violating written commitments not to foment hatred against Israel. These violations included speeches by PA president Arafat, who when speaking to Arab audiences repeatedly called for *jihad*, or holy war, against Israel. Arafat and other PA officials also compared agreements signed with the Jewish state to a temporary truce the Prophet Mohammad had made with a Jewish tribe in the seventh century. Mohammad later broke the truce and destroyed the Jewish tribe. Israel also was disturbed about what the PA was teaching the next generation of Palestinians. Palestinian schoolchildren, rather than being prepared to accept Israel's existence and live along side it in peace, were being taught to hate both Israel and Jews and to believe that Israel some day would be destroyed. PA textbooks compared Zionism to Nazism and contained many anti-Semitic slurs, and PA–distributed maps of the region, including more than one hundred in various textbooks, failed to show Israel. In fact, as of 2001, not a single PA textbook or publication showed Israel on a map. One particularly disturbing incident was a 1998 Palestinian television program that showed footage of Palestinian children at summer camp training with automatic weapons and chanting, "I foresee my death and I rush toward it!" and "A hero's death, the death of a suicide warrior!"[10] Nor was this an exception; there were many programs with similar messages. In one, a Muslim cleric preached the following message:

> Have no mercy on the Jews no matter where they are, in any country. Fight them, wherever you are. Wherever you meet them, kill them. Wherever you are, kill those Jews and those Americans who are like them.[11]

Israel also pointed out that the PA police force, more than 40,000 strong and well armed, numbered at least 10,000 more than what was permitted by the Oslo II agreement. A PA law adopted late in 1998, which provided for the death penalty for both seller and buyer when any Palestinian sold land to an Israeli, likewise violated Israeli–PA agreements, the Israelis maintained. One step in the right direction from Israel's point of view came in December 1998, three months after the Wye River agreement, when the PLO at last amended its charter to eliminate its clauses calling for the destruction of Israel.

Aside from having to deal with Israeli demands, the PA and Arafat had to cope with Islamic fundamentalist organizations bitterly opposed to the peace process. The most important of these were Hamas and Islamic Jihad, the groups responsible for most of the suicide bombings since the 1993 Oslo accords. Yet PA efforts to restrain Hamas and Islamic Jihad from terrorist acts were interspersed with cooperation with those organizations, a pattern typified by a revolving-door policy regarding jailed terrorists, who often were released shortly after their arrests or convictions. Meanwhile, the PA had little leverage of its own in dealing with Israel, whose power far exceeded its own. Any headway Arafat made toward his goal of an independent Palestinian state depended on outside help. The most important outsider was the United States, whose close relationship with Israel at times enabled it to persuade the Israelis to make concessions and to apply pressure when persuasion did not work.

Arafat's dilemma was well illustrated as May 4, 1999, the deadline for the final self-rule settlement fixed by the Oslo agreements approached. He was under intense pressure from Palestinian militants to declare an independent Palestinian state. There was equally strong pressure from the United States not to do so, for fear of disrupting the ongoing peace process. In the end, Arafat chose caution over militancy and let May 4 pass in silence. Not surprisingly, angry youths rioted on the West Bank. Still, Arafat, as he had done many times before, managed to neutralize his opponents on all sides and ride out yet another crisis. He also could claim with considerable justification that the building blocks of a Palestinian state were being put into place. For example, in November 1998 the PA opened a new airport, built with foreign aid, in the southern Gaza Strip. In addition, under the Sharm al-Sheikh agreement, the PA could immediately start planning a new seaport.

By the year 2000, the series of agreements reached with Israel since 1993 had created optimism among Palestinians that their goal of an independent state was within reach. However, that picture changed with the failure of the Camp David peace talks in July and the new Palestinian intifada, which the Palestinians called the "al-Aksa intifada" after one of the mosques on the Temple Mount. The fighting brought death and economic hardship to both Palestinians and Israelis. Aside from the loss of life, the first half year of the Al-Aksa intifada left the Palestinian economy in ruins. Unemployment, which had dropped to 11 percent by 2000, soared to 45 percent. Per capita income dropped from $2,000 to $1,400, leaving half the population living in poverty. Loss of income, including lost wages because Palestinian workers could no longer go to their jobs in Israel and trade with Israel, approached $1 billion. The United Nations increased its aid programs to try to fill the gap, and European nations had sent $60 million to pay PA salaries. But the Arab nations, despite large promises, had sent almost to help the PA.

By the spring of 2001, the Palestinians clearly had missed their best chance since 1947 for independence. The Israelis under Ehud Barak had offered them most of what they had been demanding, and they had turned it down. The second intifada had produced nothing but more bloodshed, a public relations disaster for the PA when a Hamas suicide bomber killed twenty-one young Israelis outside a Tel Aviv discotheque, and a ceasefire that failed to end the violence. At the same time, conditions in the West Bank and Gaza Strip meant that if and when Yasir Arafat achieved his goal of an independent Palestinian state, his problems would hardly end; they would only be beginning.

JORDAN

Modern Jordan occupies an area where the ancient kingdoms of Edom and Moab stood in biblical times. Mentioned often in the Bible as enemies of the Israelites, the Edomites and Moabites nonetheless were closely related to them. Both peoples disappeared from history under the same successive waves of conquests that overwhelmed the Israelites in ancient times. The Arab conquest of the seventh century permanently made the region part of the Arab world. Other conquerors—the Crusaders, Mamlukes, Ottomans, and British—took their turns ruling the country into the twentieth century. Jordan finally became fully independent in 1946.

GEOGRAPHY AND PEOPLE

Jordan is a jagged-shaped country that looks a bit like a Muppet with its oversized nose pointing to the northeast. Mostly desert, its only outlet to the sea is 15.5 miles (26 kilometers) of coastline on the Gulf of Aqaba. Its only lake is its section of the salty and lifeless Dead Sea. Jordan has an area of 34,442 square miles (89,206 square kilometers), about the size of Indiana. Its eastern border, formed in part by the Jordan River and Dead Sea, faces Israel and the West Bank. Syria lies to the north, Iraq toward the northeast, and Saudi Arabia to the east and southeast. Amman (population 961,000) is Jordan's capital and largest city. Other major urban centers are Irbid (population 802,000), in its northwestern corner, and Zarqa, also in the northwest. Aqaba, in the far south Jordan's only port, has a population of about 85,000. Its main rivers, aside from the Jordan, are two of the Jordan's tributaries, the Yarmuk in the north and the Zerqa in the south. The Yarmuk forms part of Jordan's border with Syria and supplies water to a major irrigation project before reaching the Jordan just south of the Sea of Galilee.

Jordan has three distinct topographical areas. Its western edge is the Jordan Valley. The valley's mild winters and hot summers, combined with fertile soil and adequate water supply, make it a rich agricultural region. People have lived in the Jordan Valley for millennia. Stone tools have been found there dating back almost one million years. Evidence of farming and raising livestock is ten thousand years old. The center of the country is an upland area above and east of the Jordan Valley. Its northern section near the Syrian border contains a small forest region that makes up 1 percent of Jordan's territory. Jordan's eastern section is a parched barren plateau that belongs partly to the North Arabian desert in the south and the Syrian Desert in the north.

The 10 percent of Jordan's land that is arable produces wheat, barley, lentils, tomatoes, eggplants, citrus fruits, and grapes. Sheep and goats are raised for their milk and meat. Jordan's industries produce or process phosphates, potash, fertilizers, cement, and a tiny amount of oil. Most oil, consumer goods, and more than half Jordan's food must be imported. Jordan prospered during the oil boom of the 1970s and 1980s when about 350,000 of its citizens, including many educated and skilled professionals, took jobs in the wealthy oil-producing Persian Gulf states. The money they sent home to their families stimulated the local economy. The collapse of the oil boom at the end of the 1980s cost Jordanians their jobs and ended the flow of money. At the same time, aid from the wealthy Gulf states dried up. Jordan was hurt again in the wake of the 1991 Gulf War when Kuwait expelled 300,000 Palestinian workers. Many ended up in Jordan, where they added to the ranks of the unemployed. Overall, as the new century began, Jordan was burdened by poverty, large foreign debts, and unemployment.

People

Jordan's population is 4.4 million, about 98 percent of whom are Arabs. Approximately 96 percent of the population are Sunni Moslems, while 4 percent are Christians. Jordanians

A young Jordanian boy with his camel

are well educated. The literacy rate is more than 93 percent for men and almost 80 percent for women. Jordan has the highest number of university graduates of any Arab country. Its official language and religion are respectively Arabic and Islam.

The homogeneity of Jordan's population suggested by the percentage of Arabs and Sunni Muslims is deceiving, because there are different groups of Arabs. Jordan's ruling dynasty, the Hashemites, is a relatively recent arrival from the Arabian Peninsula. Its base of support is the Bedouin Arab community, which until recently lived the traditional Arab nomadic life. The Bedouin continue to make up a large part of the Jordanian army and the core of the officer corps upon which the Hashemites have always depended. Yet they constitute at most 10 percent of Jordan's population.

The single-largest group in Jordan's population is the Palestinians. Many of them arrived in Jordan in the last fifty years. Some simply moved from the West Bank, but hundreds of thousands came as refugees after the 1948–49 and

1967 wars with Israel. All were granted Jordanian citizenship. This movement of people is not surprising, as it is nothing new. The personal and business ties between towns on opposite sides of the Jordan River have long been very close. Many prominent Jordanian families that have been in the country for centuries, including that of a recent prime minister, trace their roots to West Bank towns. In fact, it often is impossible to distinguish who is a Palestinian and who is a Jordanian. Yet it is clear that Palestinians dominate much of Jordan's economic life, from banking, to retailing, to the import-export trade. At the other end of the economic spectrum, hundreds of thousands live in poverty in refugee camps. Whatever their status, Palestinians often are neutral or hostile toward the Hashemite dynasty. They also have opposed various Jordanian efforts since 1949 to reach a peaceful solution of the Arab conflict with Israel, since those attempts would have left the Palestinians without a state of their own.

HISTORY OF MODERN JORDAN

The Hashemite Kingdom of Jordan takes its name from the dynasty that has ruled the country throughout its brief history. The Hashemites ended up the rulers of Jordan because in the wake of World War I and the partition of the Ottoman Empire they were willing to cooperate with Great Britain, the new dominant power in the Middle East. In 1920, the area that today is Jordan was included in Britain's Palestine mandate that was supposed to be set aside for a Jewish national home. In 1922, however, the British detached the territory west of the Jordan River, about three-quarters of Palestine's total area, from the mandate. They installed Abdullah ibn Hussein as *emir* (Arabic for prince) in what from 1923 was the semi-independent Emirate of Transjordan. When the British granted full independence in 1946, Abdullah became king of the Kingdom of Transjordan.

Abdullah, uniquely among Arab leaders, did not oppose Zionism or the creation of Jewish state in Palestine. He met with Zionist leaders, including Golda Meir, later Israel's foreign minister and prime minister. In 1948 Arab pressure forced Abdullah to send his British-led and -equipped Arab Legion across the Jordan River to join the campaign to destroy the newly born state of Israel. However, he was satisfied with taking over the part of Palestine set aside for an Arab state and controlling eastern Jerusalem. Abdullah's army performed better than any of the other Arab forces, and he added valuable territory to his realm. At war's end in 1949, he controlled the West Bank and eastern Jerusalem, including the Old City and its holy sites.

Abdullah officially annexed the West Bank and eastern Jerusalem in 1950, granted the local inhabitants Jordanian citizenship (having expelled all the Jews from the territories he had seized in 1948), and changed his country's name to the Hashemite Kingdom of Jordan. The international community did not accept that annexation, which was recognized only by Britain and Pakistan. Abdullah was assassinated in 1951 while preparing to pray in the Old City's al-Aqsa Mosque. His assassin was an Islamic fanatic who considered him a traitor to the Arab cause. When Abdullah's son and successor was found to be mentally ill, the crown passed to his young grandson, Hussein ibn Talal. Hussein officially became king of Jordan on his eighteenth birthday in 1953. The new teenage king surprised almost everyone by surviving the crisis that put him on the throne and many other challenges thereafter. The worst of them, his participation in the 1967 Six-Day War, cost his country the West Bank and eastern Jerusalem. Yet Hussein was destined to rule Jordan until his death in 1999 and eventually earn a reputation as one of the Middle East's outstanding statesmen.

The Reign of King Hussein

King Hussein sat on a shaky throne from the very start. In the sharply divided world of Arab politics, he sided with the region's other conservative monarchies such as Saudi Arabia. One of the earliest threats to his reign came from Jordanian groups favoring closer cooperation with radical Arab states such as Syria and Egypt. In 1957 Hussein thwarted a military coup. The young king declared martial law and dissolved all political parties to deal with the unrest that followed. The next year Hussein survived a Syrian assassination attempt and in 1959 another military coup. That same year Jordan's prime minister, a close ally of the king, was assassinated. Hussein responded by further tightening political restrictions.

The founding of the PLO in 1964 was yet another threat to Hussein. The PLO competed with Jordan for the loyalty of its Palestinian population and constantly tried to provoke a conflict with Israel, something Hussein wanted to avoid. In 1967, however, like his grandfather in 1948, Hussein found himself unable to resist widespread Arab pressure to join the war effort against Israel. The swift Israeli victory left Jordan as the war's biggest loser, shorn of both the West Bank and eastern Jerusalem, the most valuable parts of the Hashemite kingdom.

Hussein's showdown with the PLO came in 1970. By then various guerrilla and terrorist groups that made up the PLO had created a "state within a state" in Jordan. They controlled large parts of the border area, and used them as staging grounds for raids against Israel. In September 1970 Hussein concluded the Palestinians had become a threat to his throne and sent his army against them. When Syria prepared to intervene on the PLO's behalf, Israel mobilized troops along the border, in effect forcing the Syrians to back down and thereby saving Hussein. The king's army decisively defeated the Palestinians, killing thousands, in what the latter have since called "Black September." The fighting lasted until mid-1971; some PLO fighters so feared Hussein's forces that they swam across the Jordan River and surrendered to the Israelis. The defeated PLO, along with several hundred thousand refugees, retreated into Lebanon.

The l970s and 1980s were good times for Jordan. In 1973 Hussein kept Jordan out of the Yom Kippur War until its late stages, when he sent soldiers to help Syrian troops on the Golan Heights. Meanwhile, Jordan's economy grew, fueled by money sent home by its citizens working in the oil-rich Persian Gulf region. Hussein's own popularity at home also grew and his widening base of support helped stabilize his regime. Jordan's complicated relationship with the Palestinians gradually began to sort itself out, although not always with Hussein's approval. That process in turn helped to define Jordanian identity. In 1974 the Arab League, with reluctant Jordanian support, recognized the PLO as the sole representative of the Palestinian people. Hussein held back from Egyptian president Anwar Sadat's initiative that in 1979 produced the Egyptian-Israeli peace treaty, bowing to Arab pressure to sever ties with Egypt. Meanwhile, the king continued to retreat from Jordan's claims to the West Bank. In 1984 he changed the constitution to allow Jordan to hold elections without West Bank participation, and in 1988 he renounced all Jordanian claims to the West Bank.

In 1989 Hussein felt confident enough to ease his tight grip on Jordanian political life. He permitted the country's first parliamentary elections since the 1950s. Jordanian women, to whom the king had granted the vote in 1974, voted for the first time. However, the election results were disappointing and even dangerous. Islamic fundamentalist parties whose goal was to subject Jordan to Islamic law won about 40 percent of the seats. They became the largest bloc in the parliament. This did not stop Hussein from legalizing political parties, banned since 1957, in a new law that took effect in 1992. In 1993, having changed the electoral law to minimize Islamic strength, Hussein suddenly dissolved parliament and ordered new elections. This time the largest bloc elected to parliament consisted of moderate politicians loyal to Hussein and the Hashemite regime.

Meanwhile, Hussein and Jordan endured the agony of the Gulf War. The crisis that led to the war began in August 1990 when Iraq invaded Kuwait. King Hussein was a moderate man, strongly pro-Western and pro-American, and interested in making peace with Israel. Yet many Jordanians, especially Palestinians, fervently supported Iraq in its invasion of Kuwait, largely because of Iraqi dictator Saddam Hussein's militant anti-Israel stance. (The two men were not related; Hussein is a common Arabic name.) King Hussein therefore kept Jordan neutral in the crisis, a stance that provoked Western, and especially American, anger. The war and blockade of Iraq, an important Jordanian trading partner, also hurt Jordan economically, as did its losses in foreign aid from the United States and the Persian Gulf countries.

Still, by 1992 Jordan was back in good graces with its traditional allies. In the summer of that year Hussein went to the United States for cancer treatment. He returned home, apparently cured, to huge and enthusiastic welcoming crowds. By 1994, with Israel and the PLO finally engaged in the peace process, Hussein moved quickly toward his long-standing goal of making peace with Israel. He and Israeli prime minister Yitzhak Rabin signed the treaty at an Israeli-Jordanian border village in October 1994. After the ceremony the king said, "This is my proudest accomplishment: leaving my people a legacy of peace."[12] However, not all Jordanians agreed with Hussein. The opposition to the treaty was vocal, and more extensive than expected, and the king responded with a political crackdown. Parliamentary elections in November 1997 led to new confrontations between the Hussein regime and its Islamic fundamentalist opponents. They boycotted the elections in protest of Hussein's stripping parliament of many of its powers. Not surprisingly, the election produced a pro-government majority.

In 1998 King Hussein again fell ill with cancer. This time treatment in the United States was unsuccessful. As his health declined, Hussein changed the line of succession. He removed his brother Prince Hassan as heir, a position Hassan had held since 1965. The new heir was Hussein's his eldest son, thirty-seven-year-old Abdullah. King Hussein ibn Talal, who had survived so much and led his country for forty-seven years out of its fifty-three years of independence, died on February 7, 1999. The long list of foreign dignitaries who attended his funeral was testimony to his international standing as a statesmen. His son, Abdullah II, speaking to the nation as king for the first time, pledged to continue his father's policies.

Jordan After Hussein

King Abdullah knew had enormous shoes to fill and that he had to move decisively to solidify his hold on power. He quickly named his eldest son heir to the throne and replaced several ministers who were known as supporters of his uncle and the former heir, Prince Hassan. Abdullah also announced he was ending censorship of all Arab and foreign newspapers and released about five hundred political prisoners from jail. Beginning in mid-July 1999 Abdullah moved against the radical Palestinian Islamic fundamentalist group Hamas, eventually arresting and, in November, deporting several of its leaders. Meanwhile, municipal and local elections took place through the country in July, with Islamic and independent candidates being among the groups doing well. In mid-December, the Jordanian government announced the arrest of thirteen suspected terrorists on charges of planning attacks against U.S. and tourist targets in Jordan.

In foreign affairs, Abdullah visited several Arab countries during 1999 in an attempt to strengthen and improve ties, while at the same time assuring Israel that he would continue his father's efforts to make peace between Israel and its Arab neighbors. He also made a three-week trip in May to the United States and Europe and went back to the United States to meet with President Clinton in October.

As it began a new century under a new king, Jordan had many problems. Its economy remained in poor condition. Jordan was heavily dependent on foreign aid. Unemployment, officially 15 percent, in reality was closer to 25 percent and job prospects for Jordan's young people—nearly three-quarters of the country's population was under the age of twenty-nine—were bleak. The country was deeply divided on numerous political issues. Many Jordanians, especially members of the Palestinian community, opposed Jordan's peace treaty with Israel. During 1999 those opposed to peace with Israel stepped up their efforts to ostracize any Jordanians who had friendly relations with Israelis. For example, three journalists who attended a conference at an Israeli university in September met with severe criticism and barely avoided expulsion from Jordan's press association. Islamic fundamentalists not only opposed peace with Israel, but remained determined to reverse Jordan's pro-Western policies and impose Islamic law on the country. These were only some of the divisions that for decades had induced King Hussein to keep most power in his own hands rather than allow genuine democratic reforms. King Abdullah was unlikely to find them easier to bridge than his father.

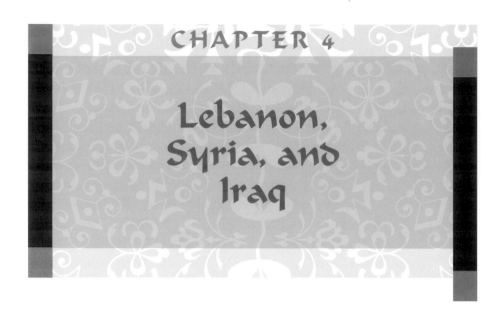

CHAPTER 4

Lebanon, Syria, and Iraq

LEBANON

There is no Middle Eastern country more divided and torn by ethnic and religious strife than Lebanon. Between 1975 and 1990, a country that once was considered the financial capital and playground of the Middle East was ripped apart by civil war. Today order seems to be restored, but only at the price of real independence. Lebanon is now a satellite of neighboring Syria, with 15,000 Syrian troops—down from the 35,000 that had occupied the country for years—in control of the northern and eastern parts of the country. Until June of 2001, about 6,000 Syrian troops were stationed in and around Beirut, Lebanon's capital. Further complicating the picture are 350,000 Palestinian refugees who came to Lebanon in several waves after 1948.

Lebanon's most fundamental problem is with Syria. Most Syrian leaders consider Lebanon to be a part of their country. Syria has never formally recognized Lebanon's independence; Syrian educational materials and official maps refer to Lebanon as a Syrian province. To this day Syria does not have an embassy in Lebanon. Syria currently does not seem interested in annexing Lebanon as its many internal ethnic problems might destabilize Syria itself. Instead, the Syrian government is content to manipulate events from Damascus, using the political figures and parties it controls and, when necessary, the Syrian military forces that occupy half the country.

GEOGRAPHY, ECONOMY, AND PEOPLE

Lebanon is a small wedge-shaped country of 3,950 square miles (10,230 square kilometers), wider in the north than in the south, about three-quarters the size of Connecticut. Its western border is its 135-mile (220-kilometer) Mediterranean coastline. To the north and west looms Syria; Israel is Lebanon's neighbor to the south. Coastal Lebanon has a Mediterranean climate of mild wet winters and hot dry summers. Its short winter lasts about three months. Altogether, about three hundred days of each year are sunny. Farther east in the mountains heavy snow falls in winter, and summers are cooler. It is perhaps symbolic of Lebanon's political divisions that its main two rivers, which rise near each other in the country's Bekáa Valley, flow in opposite directions. The Litani, the country's longest river, flows generally southwest before turning due west and emptying into the Mediterranean Sea. The Orontes River rises just north of the Litani, but flows northward into Syria. The Jordan River also rises in Lebanon and flows due south into Israel.

Four distinct geographic regions running parallel to each other along a north-south axis are squeezed into Lebanon's small area. In the extreme west a narrow coastal plain that broadens out in the north runs the length of the country. Approximately midway on the plain stands Beirut, Lebanon's capital and largest city (population 1.5 million). South of Beirut are the port cities of Sidon and Tyre; Tripoli, another port and Lebanon's second-largest city (population 160,000), is in the far north. The coastal plain is broken at several points by protrusions from a mountain range called Mount Lebanon, the country's second geographic region. It contains Lebanon's highest point, Qurnet as Sauda (10,131 feet, 3,088 meters). Gorges and rivers cut through the mountains, whose slopes are home to the small remaining stands of the

The famous cedars of Lebanon, at al-Shouf Cedar Reserve

famous cedars of Lebanon, trees that were highly valued in ancient times and are mentioned in the Bible. Today most of Lebanon's remaining trees are oak, cypress, fir, juniper, and carob. About 60 miles (96 kilometers) northeast of Beirut, Lebanon's last cedar forest clings to mountain slopes 6,500 feet (2,000 meters) above sea level. The Lebanese call these magnificent trees *ars-ar-rab*, "God's cedars." Bears and small mammals, as well as a few large predators including wildcats, still roam the forests of Mount Lebanon.

Immediately to the east of Mount Lebanon is the a fertile but narrow Bekáa Valley, only 5 to 8 miles (8 to 12 kilometers) in width. Perched at an altitude averaging about 3,280 feet (1,000 meters), the valley produces crops year-round. East of the Bekáa Valley is another range of mountains, the Anti-Lebanon range. It forms Lebanon's border with Syria. At the southern end of this range is Mount Hermon, which straddles Lebanon, Syria, and Israel. Because it is the highest point (9,232 feet, or 2,814 meters) in a region contested by Israel and Syria, Mount Hermon is of considerable strategic importance.

Economy

Lebanon was once called the "Switzerland of the Middle East" because it was the region's commercial and banking center. The country's long and destructive civil war deprived Lebanon of that status, at least for the near term. The fighting left in ruins Beirut's business section where most of the country's banks, hotels, and international businesses were located. The country's once-thriving tourist industry is a shadow of its former self. The civil war badly damaged Lebanon's economic infrastructure and cut its overall output in half.

Still, the basis for a recovery has remained. Two oil pipelines, one beginning in Iraq and ending in Tripoli and the other originating in Saudi Arabia and ending in Sidon, cross Lebanon and are potential revenue sources if they can be restored to operation. The country's main crops, grown either on the coastal plain or in the Bekáa Valley, include citrus fruits, apples, pears, grapes, olives, potatoes, tomatoes, and tobacco. Another important and profitable crop from the Bekáa Valley, grown and exported illegally, is hashish. Small- and medium-scale manufacturing industries produce processed foods, textiles, and tobacco products. The relative stability of the 1990s has attracted foreign investment and international businesses, and large parts of Beirut's business district are being rebuilt. However, the recovery has not been across the board. The gap between rich and poor widened in the 1990s, sowing the seeds for economic discontent that could add to Lebanon's formidable ethnic and religious problems.

People

Although more than 90 percent of Lebanon's estimated 3.6 million people (including Palestinian refugees) are Arabs, its population actually is a volatile mixture of religious groups that has turned it into a country of quarreling, and often warring, minorities. There are no completely reliable statistics on Lebanon's population. Early in the twentieth century the country had a Christian majority, but that has changed because of Christian emigration and higher birthrates among Muslims. Today the best guess is that Christians account for perhaps 30 percent of the population. The largest single group are Maronite Catholics, whose presence in Lebanon dates from Byzantine times, well before the Arab conquest. They number between 20 and 25 percent of Lebanon's total population and are concentrated in the Mount Lebanon region as well as in Beirut. Greek Orthodox, Greek Catholics, and Armenian Christians make up the rest of the Christian community.

On the Muslim side, the Shiites (about 32 percent of the total population) are the most numerous. Many Shiites, traditionally the poorest Lebanese, live in southern Lebanon, the Mount Lebanon region, the Bekáa Valley, and Beirut. Sunni Muslims, about 21 percent of the population, live in the major coastal cities, including Beirut, and in the Bekáa Valley. Lebanon's Druze, who make up about 7 percent of the population, have settled in the Mount Lebanon region, in the coastal towns, especially Beirut, and in the Bekáa Valley. Large numbers of Palestinians, who are Sunni Muslims, are found in refugee camps in the Beirut area and in the south.

The fundamental division in Lebanese political life, and in the struggle over control of the country, has been Christian—mainly Maronite—versus Muslim. Usually the Druze have sided with the Muslims. However, alliances often have shifted, sometimes in bewildering ways, especially with Palestinians factored into Lebanon's ethnic-religious equation. The Syrians and the Israelis have made the situation even more complicated.

LEBANESE HISTORY TO 1946

Ancient Lebanon was home to the Phoenicians, the greatest sailors of the Mediterranean world for seven hundred years from about 1250 B.C. to 550 B.C. More importantly, by about 1200 B.C. they had developed the world's first standardized phonetic alphabet. The Phoenicians and their civilization disappeared during the Roman era. Lebanon subsequently became Christianized and, significantly, remained predominantly Christian after the Arab conquest when most of the Middle East adopted Islam. Lebanese

Christians aided the Crusaders from Europe before the country again fell under Muslim rule. Ottoman rule began in the early sixteenth century.

Druze massacres of Lebanese Christians in 1860 led to French intervention on their behalf in the 1861. The French forced the Turkish sultan to create a Mount Lebanon district with a Christian governor. Its population was 80 percent Christian and more than 60 percent Maronite. After the dissolution of the Ottoman Empire after World War I, France received the League of Nations mandate for Syria and Lebanon. The French then expanded Lebanon at Syrian expense, adding territory that included Beirut and land to its south, Tripoli and surrounding territory in the north, and the Bekáa Valley. The new "Greater Lebanon" was only about 57 percent Christian and less than half Maronite. In effect, the seeds of future ethnic conflict had been sown.

Lebanon became independent officially but not in fact in 1941. In 1943 a census was taken that became the basis of the Lebanese system of government. The 1943 "National Covenant" provided that Christians would predominate over Muslims in parliament by a ratio of six to five. The presidency would be Lebanon's most powerful executive post and the president, elected by parliament, would be a Maronite Christian. The prime minister would be a Sunni Muslim and the speaker of parliament a Shiite Muslim. This system would remain in place until 1989. Lebanon was admitted to the United Nations in 1945. Genuine independence came when French troops withdrew a year later.

MODERN LEBANON

Independent Lebanon's history is divided into three periods: two decades of relative order and prosperity from 1946 to 1975, the civil war of 1975 to 1990, and the period of attempted reconciliation and reconstruction in the 1990s. At no time during its first half century of existence, even in the best of times, was Lebanon free from tensions caused by ethnic and religious strife or the volatile and unpredictable political storms of the Middle East.

Prior to the outbreak of the civil war Lebanon was a major Arab intellectual and cultural center. Beirut had some of the Arab world's outstanding academic institutions, including the French-Catholic University of St. Joseph (founded 1875), the American University of Beirut (founded 1860), and the University of Lebanon (founded 1951). After the Nasser regime in Egypt silenced the Egyptian press, Beirut had the only free press in the Arab world. While many of these institutions have survived the civil war, Lebanon's standing as an Arab intellectual center has declined along with the rest of the country's fortunes.

Politics from 1946 to 1975

Lebanon's politics during its first two decades was dominated by maneuvering among the leading families and clans of its four main ethnic-religious communities: the Maronite Christians, Shiite Muslims, Sunni Muslims, and Druze. Although Lebanon sent an army to invade Israel in 1948, it was not deeply involved in the fighting. After the 1949 truce that ended the war, Lebanon in fact coexisted with the Jewish state. The Lebanese-Israeli border was Israel's only "quiet" frontier until the mid-1960s, when Palestinians guerrillas based in Lebanon began launching terrorist raids into Israeli territory. Alone among Israel's immediate neighbors, Lebanon stayed out of both the 1967 and 1973 wars.

The most serious domestic crisis of the first two decades occurred in 1958. The precipitating issue was the Muslim community's mistrust of Lebanon's Maronite leadership and its pro-Western policies. The Muslims wanted a closer alignment with the Arab world in general and Egypt and Syria in particular. When the crisis erupted in the summer of 1958, the Lebanese government requested U.S. assistance and Washington sent 15,000 U.S. Marines to restore order. The American presence helped bring about a compromise that held into the 1970s.

The growing Palestinian presence eventually was decisive in fracturing Lebanon's fragile political structure. The PLO was firmly established in the country by the 1960s, but its activities and power increased dramatically after 1970, when thousands of Palestinians fleeing King Hussein's crackdown on the PLO took refuge there. The Palestinian influx helped upset Lebanon's Christian-Muslim numerical balance. It deepened the political fault line between conservative Christians (mainly Maronites) defending Lebanon's political system and leftist Muslims (including Palestinians) who wanted to overthrow it. The increased Palestinian presence in southern Lebanon also drew the country into conflict with Israel when Palestinian raids led to Israeli retaliation. Lebanese civilians were caught in the middle of the fighting. By 1975, the Palestinian presence had so inflamed local ethnic-religious and political conflicts that it plunged Lebanon into civil war.

The Civil War
The Lebanese civil war was a kaleidoscopic affair involving all of Lebanon's major ethnic-religious groups in shifting alliances. Christians fought Muslims, Christians fought each other, Druze fought both Muslims and Christians, Shiite and Sunni Muslims fought each other, Palestinian factions fought each other, and so on. At one point more than 40 militias and armies were active in Lebanon. Several Lebanese political leaders were assassinated, among them two presidents and one prime minister. This was compounded by direct Syrian intervention on behalf of one faction or the other, depending on Syrian interests. At one point, in 1976, the Syrians prevented a complete Christian defeat; at another, in 1981, the Syrians fought the Maronites. Eventually Syrian troop strength in Lebanon peaked at 50,000.

Further complicating matters in Lebanon were two Israeli invasions launched in attempts to put an end to PLO attacks on its territory and civilians. In both cases PLO–Israeli fighting forced hundreds of thousands of Lebanese from their homes. The first invasion in 1978 ended with the United Nations sending troops to police southern Lebanon near the Israeli border and protect northern Israel against further PLO raids. That effort failed. The second invasion in 1982 drove most PLO forces out of Lebanon, although by 1990 they had returned. It also led to a Israeli occupation of southern Lebanon until 1985 and Israel's creation of a 9-mile-wide (14-kilometer) security zone north of the Israeli-Lebanese border. The second zone was patrolled by Israeli troops and an Israeli-financed and -equipped Christian militia called the South Lebanese Army (SLA).

The international community also was dragged into the war. The UN peacekeeping force sent to southern Lebanon in 1978 failed to stop the fighting there. A multinational force of American, French, British, and Italian troops sent to Beirut in 1982 fared no better. In October 1983 Shiite suicide bombers killed 241 American Marines and 59 French soldiers; in early 1984 the multinational force withdrew from Lebanon.

In September 1989 the Arab League arranged a meeting of Lebanese leaders in Saudi Arabia. They produced the Taif Agreement, which finally set the stage for peace. The agreement, in reality dictated by Syria, balanced the parliament evenly between Muslims and Christians and increased the powers of the Sunni prime minister at the expense of the Maronite president. It also sanctioned the presence of Syrian troops in Lebanon but stipulated that Syrian troops would leave Lebanon's major cities by 1992. By then, the Lebanese civil war had cost billions of dollars and claimed 150,000 lives.

In effect, Lebanon became a Syrian satellite where the Syrians kept an occupation army of 35,000. In November 1989 Syria stage-managed the election of Lebanon's first post–civil war president. When he was assassinated eighteen days later, Syria arranged the election of Elias Harawi. A new government of "national reconciliation" was formed in 1990. The next year the government disbanded the country's ethnic militias. The only exception was the Shiite Hezbollah militia, which was allowed to keep its weapons to continue attacking the 2,500-man SLA and Israeli troops in Israel's security zone in the south. In 1992 Lebanon held its first parliamentary election in twenty-one years. By 1995 the Lebanese army was built up to a force of 45,000. In 1996, however, the south was disrupted by serious Israeli-Hezbollah fighting. Harawi served two four-year terms as president, the second term being extended for three years to 1998 by a "one-time-only" constitutional amendment. In the fall of 1998 the Syrians selected General Emile Lahoud to succeed Harawi, and the Lebanese parliament dutifully elected him.

Sunset in Beirut. The construction in the background is typical of the rebuilding that's going on all over the city. The McDonald's restaurant is not an unusual sight either.

As the 1990s drew to a close, an uneasy peace, often punctuated by violence, existed in Lebanon. Relations between the government and the Palestinians, who lived mostly in refugee camps, where they were armed, were tense. A warning shot rang out in June of 1999 when Palestinian gunmen murdered a judge and three court officials. It was the worst attack against government officials since the civil war. In October, a military court in Beirut passed a death sentence *in absentia* (the accused had not been captured) on a Palestinian militia leader. Several other leaders were arrested during the next two months. Although Israel withdrew in May of 2000 from the security zone in the south it had occupied since the 1980s, Syrian troops remained in the country. Parliamentary elections held in September 2000 served mainly to highlight the corruption in the country's political life and the deep divisions between its seventeen officially recognized religions and sects. By mid-2001, Syrian troops had left the Beirut area and their total strength in Lebanon had fallen to 15,000. Lebanon's future did not look as dark as during its violent recent past, but it was far from bright.

SYRIA

"Syria" is a Greek term that once referred to the Eastern Mediterranean region between Egypt and Asia Minor. It included what today is Syria and Lebanon, most of Israel and Jordan, and bits of northern Saudi Arabia and western Iraq. Syrian nationalists often call the area "Greater Syria." Foreign powers ruled the region for much of its history, from the ancient Hittites and Egyptians to the Persians, Greeks, Romans, and Byzantines, to the Ottoman Empire and France.

Modern Syria, a young country that has been independent barely half a century, is substantially smaller than Greater Syria. It is a chunk of the defunct Ottoman Empire that after World War I was turned over to French rule under a League of Nations mandate. Formal independence came in 1941 during World War II, but actual independence was delayed until French troops left Syria in 1946. Since then Syria has aggressively tried to assert its power in its immediate neighborhood and also play significant role in the politics of the entire Middle East and Arab world. Its official name is the Syrian Arab Republic.

GEOGRAPHY, ECONOMY, AND PEOPLE

Syria borders on the eastern shore of the Mediterranean Sea between Turkey and Lebanon and extends eastward into Asia. It looks something like a tank rumbling toward the northeast. Its area of 71,467 square miles (185,100 square kilometers) makes it slightly larger than Virginia. Syria's Mediterranean coastline is about 110 miles (180 kilometers) long. The rest of its western border is with Lebanon and Israel. Jordan lies to the south, Iraq to the southeast and

Downtown Damascus, 1989

east, and Turkey to the north. After the 1967 Six-Day War Israel occupied, and in 1981 annexed, a 500-square-mile (1,295-square-kilometer) border region called the Golan Heights. Syria still claims the region and its status remains in dispute.

Syria has four geographic zones. Its Mediterranean coastal plain is fertile and densely populated. Latakia, Syria's main port and fourth-largest city (population 315,000), as well as its most cosmopolitan and least politically and socially conservative urban area, is at the northern end of the coastal plain. The narrow plain itself extends inland only to the Jebel an-Nusariyah (*jebel* means mountain in Arabic) mountain range, which merges in the south with the Anti-Lebanon Mountains to form Syria's border with Lebanon. The Anti-Lebanon Mountains are capped by 9,232-foot-high (2,814-meter) Mount Hermon, the highest point in the region and a point of contention with Israel. East of the mountains is a fertile valley where four of Syria's five largest cities are found. The southernmost is Damascus (population 1.5 million), the capital. In the middle of the valley are Homs (population 576,000) and Hama (population 273,000). Farthest north near the Turkish border is Aleppo (population 1.6

million), Syria's largest city. The Orontes River flows north-ward toward Turkey through this lowland, which is Syria's part of the Great Rift Valley.

Syria's easternmost and largest region is an arid plateau bisected by a low range of mountains that runs diagonally northeast from the Anti-Lebanon mountains to the Euphrates River. South of the mountains is the stony Syrian Desert that stretches into Iraq. Cutting through the plateau on another diagonal, this one running southeast from the border with Turkey, is the Euphrates, by far Syria's most important river. It supplies the country with 80 percent of its water. The irrigated area northeast of the Euphrates known as al-Jizirah (Arabic for "island") is Syria's largest fertile region. It is also the area where discoveries of small but not insignificant oil deposits have given Syria its most important natural resource and main export.

Coastal Syria has a Mediterranean climate with hot dry summers and mild wet winters. Snow falls in the mountainous regions. Farther inland the climate becomes progressively dryer; about three-quarters of Syria is semiarid. Syria's southeast has a desert climate.

Economy
Although the Syria government has been promoting industrialization since the 1950s, agriculture still is the dominant sector of the economy. Major crops include wheat, barley, cotton, olives, sugar beets, potatoes, tomatoes, and grapes. Sheep, goats, and camels graze in the country's pastures. Oil is by far the country's most important natural resource and accounts for more than 60 percent of its export earnings. Major industries include refined petroleum products, cement, textiles, and processed foods. Two oil pipelines, one running from Iraq and one from Saudi Arabia, once provided Syria with valuable revenues. However, because of political disputes Syria closed the pipelines in 1982.

Syria has enjoyed several periods of impressive economic growth since the 1950s, but several factors have hurt the economy in recent years. Excessive state interference, especially over the industrial sector, limits progress. The state still directly controls about 30 percent of the economy, including the petroleum industry and most manufacturing. Foreign investment has been limited because so much of Syria's economy is subject to government planning. Enormous military expenses are another burden, made even heavier by Syria's long-term intervention in Lebanon. Those expenses are an important reason for Syria's large foreign debt, another anchor on the economy. Rapid population growth, currently higher than 3 percent per year, also makes development and raising the standard of living difficult. The largest development project in modern Syria is the Tabaqa Dam on the Euphrates. It was completed in 1978 with Soviet aid. The dam enabled Syria to expand both its irrigated farmland and production of electrical power, but it has not eliminated daily power cuts of up to four hours per day. The government will have to change its policies if Syria is to realize its economic potential.

People

Syria's population of about 16.7 million is about 90 percent Arab and 85 percent Muslim. Most, but not all, of the Muslims are Sunnis. However, about 10 to 12 percent of the total population (12 to 14 percent of all Muslims) belongs to the Alawite sect, an offshoot of the Shiite branch of Islam. While the Alawites are generally considered Muslims, most Sunnis, and even most Shiites, consider them heretics. The Alawites are concentrated along Syria's Mediterranean coast and in the mountainous northwest. Syria's Druze, another offshoot of the Shiite branch of Islam, comprise 3 percent of the population. They live mainly in mountains in the south. Christians, primarily Arabs and ethnic Armenians, account for about 10 percent of the population. The largest single denomination is the Greek Orthodox. About 6 to 7 percent of the population are ethnic Kurds, who are Sunni Muslims but not Arabs. Most Kurds live in the Jazira region of the northeast.

Syria's ethnic mix has political implications. The Alawites, and to a lesser extent the Druze, have long played a role in Syrian politics far out of proportion to their numbers. Hafez al-Assad, Syria's dictator from 1970 to 2000, was an Alawite, which means the sect has run the country for over thirty years. One of his son and successor Bashar's major problems is that Muslim fundamentalists, including the powerful Muslim Brotherhood, often have opposed the Assad regime on religious grounds. Another problem is the country's lack of deeply rooted national traditions; most Syrians generally identity first with their city or region. This tendency is intensified because different ethnic groups generally are concentrated in one or two distinct regions.

MODERN SYRIAN HISTORY

Modern Syrian history is divided into two major and sharply contrasting periods: an era of instability marked by frequent coups and intermittent military rule and the brutal but stable dictatorship of Hafez al-Assad. The first period lasted from 1946 to 1970. It began with a civilian regime that was overthrown in a military coup in 1949. The coup resulted in part from Syrian military failures in the unsuccessful 1948–49 Arab war against Israel. Military rule, punctuated by two more coups, lasted until 1954, when yet another coup restored civilian rule. The next few years saw the development of several political parties, including an active Communist Party and, most importantly, the Arab Socialist Renaissance Party (*Baath*). Baath ideology combined a commitment to socialism and an intense devotion to Arab nationalism and unity. Its secular outlook appealed to military officers, especially those belonging to the minority Alawite and Druze faiths. Syria's Baathists took Syria into its ill-fated union with Egypt of 1958 to 1961. Instability and several more coups, as well as feuds and splits in the Baath Party, followed during the 1960s. In 1967 Syria joined with Egypt and Jordan in the Six-Day War against Israel. That war cost the Syrians the Golan Heights, from which they had regularly bombarded Israeli settlements since 1949. By 1970 there had been at least a dozen successful and unsuccessful coups. That turmoil ended in November 1970 when Baath military officers led by air force general Hafez al-Assad seized power.

Syria Under Assad

Assad consolidated power quickly. In 1971 he was elected to a seven-year term as president in a plebiscite in which, as the only candidate running, he received 99.2 percent of the vote. He would be reelected in similar plebiscites in 1978, 1985, and 1991; in the 1991 "election," he received 99.98 of the vote. A new constitution in 1973 declared Syria to be a "popular-democratic and socialist state" as well as a "part of the Arab nation, struggling for the realization of its total unity."[1] The constitution also required that Islamic law be the basis of legislation and that Syria's president be a Muslim. These clauses were designed to satisfy Syria's Sunni majority and powerful Sunni fundamentalist forces headed by the Muslim Brotherhood. They did not. The clause on legislation did not go far enough for Islamic fundamentalists who wanted Syria to be an full-fledged Islamic state. In addition, many Sunnis did not consider Assad, an Alawite, to be a Muslim. By 1973, the year that Syria joined Egypt in launching the Yom Kippur War against Israel, there already were Sunni demonstrations against Assad and his largely Alawite regime. The war began with a Syrian attack and advances on the Golan Heights. It ended, after very heavy losses on both sides, with an Israeli military victory and the Israelis still in control of the strategic heights.

Assad bitterly opposed Anwar Sadat's peace initiative in 1977 that led to the Egyptian-Israeli peace treaty in 1979. After the treaty the Syrian leader led the effort that isolated Egypt from the Arab world for much of the 1980s. Syria also was on poor terms with Iraq: The two countries were led by rival wings of the Baath Party. The Syrians therefore supported non-Arab and Shiite Muslim Iran against Iraq in the Iran-Iraq war of 1980 to 1988. Meanwhile, at home the regime's conflict with the Muslim Brotherhood intensified and turned violent. Muslim Brotherhood attacks on government officials increased and were met by savage government reprisals. In 1979 Muslim Brotherhood terrorists murdered sixty-three military cadets, most of them Alawites. Further waves of government reprisals and attacks followed, reaching the state of near civil war. In early 1982 the Assad regime struck with overwhelming force against the Muslim Brotherhood's main base in the city of Hama. The government pounded the city for a week with aircraft and artillery. The city was leveled—its ruined center later became a park—and an estimated 20,000 people killed, but Assad achieved his goal by breaking the back, for many years, of the most serious threat to his regime.

Assad needed quiet at home because by 1976 Syria was deeply involved in its expensive and unending intervention in Lebanon. Although the cost was high, by the late 1990s Assad had achieved his main goals there. Lebanon was a Syrian satellite with Syria acting as the essential power broker between Lebanon's many factions. Syrian troops occupied about half the country, including the Bekáa Valley. That region served a variety of Syrian purposes. It in effect was the largest terrorist base in the world, a safe haven and training center for groups whose activities serve Syrian interests. It also was a major center for the processing and trafficking of heroin, which the Syrian government condoned and from which it profited. Much of that heroin was destined for customers in the United States. In addition, southern Lebanon remained a base for terrorist attacks on Israel, all part of Assad's strategy of forcing Israel to give up the Golan Heights. Assad meanwhile gave a cold shoulder to the Israeli-Palestinian peace process. He insisted that separate agreements undermined the overall Arab cause against Israel; a fairer assessment was that these agreements did not serve Syria's interests. Syria's on-again, off-again discussions with the Israelis yielded no serious progress.

On another front, after years of following a pro-Soviet foreign policy and sponsoring acts of terrorism in both the Middle East and Europe, Assad tried to improve relations with the West. The opportunity arose when Iraq, long a Syrian rival, invaded Kuwait in 1990. Syrian troops participated in the 1991 Gulf War in which a U.S.–led coalition of Western and Arab nations drove Iraqi troops from Kuwait. Syria's participation, however, did not secure its removal from the U.S. State Department's list of countries that support international terrorism.

As the 1990s drew to a close Syria was nearing a changing of the guard. President Assad, the unchallenged dictator for almost thirty years, was in poor health. At seventy years old, he had been suffering from heart disease and diabetes for many years and was rarely seen in public. He was elected for a fifth seven-year term as president, but few observers expected he would serve it out. Instead, Assad's most important agenda item, as one diplomat put it, could be summed up in "one word: succession. It has become the filter through which everything is filtered."[2] Assad's original choice as successor, his oldest son Basel, was killed in an automobile accident in 1994. Assad's new choice was his second son, Bashar, a British-trained physician. After his brother's death, Bashar suddenly began a belated military career. Not surprisingly, he advanced rapidly and in 1999 reached the rank of colonel. Still, Bashar was inexperienced. A Western diplomat in Damascus observed that "I don't think anyone thinks he's ready."[3]

If President Assad passed from the scene too soon, there were other ambitious sharks in Syria's political waters to challenge Bashar. The most formidable was the president's younger brother Rifaat, a hardened and ruthless political veteran unlikely to accept being pushed aside in favor of his untested young nephew. As head of an elite force of 55,000 men equipped with tanks, artillery, and helicopters, Rifaat for years was a key enforcer guarding the Assad regime. However, in 1984 the Assad brothers had a falling out, and Rifaat thereafter spent much of his time abroad, essentially living as an exile. Rifaat nonetheless made it clear that he considered Bashar al-Assad unfit to rule Syria and saw himself as Hafez al-Assad's legitimate successor. In September 1999, determined to prepare the way for his son to succeed him, an increasingly ill and frail Hafez al-Assad ordered the arrest of about one thousand of Rifaat's supporters. The next month security forces closed down a port in the city of Latakia that had been under Rifaat's control, a measure that led to violent clashes in which, according to some reports, hundreds of people died.

In June 2000, having ruled Syria with an iron fist for three decades, Hafaz al-Assad died. But he left behind a well-oiled political machine, and its wheels turned quickly to assure Bashar al-Assad's succession to the presidency. The constitution was amended to lower the minimum age for the presidency from forty to thirty-four, the age of Bashar al-Assad. Then, in rapid succession, Bashar was nominated to be commander-in-chief of the armed forces, promoted to the military rank of lieutenant-general, named head of the Baath Party, endorsed by the party leadership for the presidency, nominated for president by Syria's parliament, and then duly elected to the post with more than 97 percent of the vote. The entire process was completed by mid-July.

Once in office, Bashar al-Assad took a few small steps to ease the suffocating dictatorship Syria had lived under for thirty years. Government controls on a few areas of the economy, including banking, were eased slightly and several hundred political prisoners were released from prison. The new president also relaxed, albeit ever so slightly, controls on the press, and in March 2001 Syria saw the founding of its first independent newspaper since 1963. It sold out within hours of hitting the newsstands. At the same time, most things remained the same. The younger Assad made it clear in his inaugural address that he had no use for democracy. Syria remained under martial law, as it had been for four decades. It still was illegal for more than five people to gather for a political meeting without a permit, which could only be obtained by providing the government security services with two weeks' notice, the name of the speaker and a copy of his speech, and a complete list of everyone planning to attend.

The regime's tight web of controls extended into cyberspace. As of the spring of 2001, the Internet was not available to the general public, and only 12,000 people in a country of almost 17 million were Internet subscribers. Meanwhile, unemployment stood at 20 percent, the economy was stagnant, and a rapidly growing population meant that the need for new jobs was becoming ever more urgent. One of the most serious potential sources of trouble for the new, untested president and his supporters was the long-standing resentment in the majority Sunni community against continued Alawite control of the country and the widespread corruption that went along with Alawite power. In short, Syria was plagued with problems and uncertainty, which meant that it was possible, if not likely, that after Hafez al-Assad's passing it might face the same instability it had experienced before he came to power.

IRAQ

Iraq is Mesopotamia, the land between the Tigris and Euphrates rivers, where more than five thousand years ago the Sumerians' mastery of agriculture and invention of writing gave birth to the world's first civilization. Mesopotamia was where Sargon of Akkad forged the world's first empire, where Babylon's King Hammurabi issued the world's first systematic code of law, where the patriarch Abraham had his first inspiration about a single moral God before leaving for Canaan to found the Jewish religion, and where a succession of ancient civilizations added to the fund of human knowledge as they rose and fell. In A.D. 750 the newly founded Arab Abbasid dynasty established its capital in Baghdad, at that time a village on the banks of the Tigris not far from ancient Babylon. The Abbasids turned their new city into the Arab world's cultural and intellectual center during the eighth and ninth centuries, the period known as the Golden Age of Islam. Decline then set in, and by 1000 the Seljuk Turks held real power in Baghdad. In the thirteenth century the Mongols destroyed what was left of the Abbasid Caliphate and sacked Baghdad. Three hundred years later Mesopotamia fell to the Ottomans. Not until the twentieth century would an independent state, which would be called Iraq, exist again in the land between the rivers.

GEOGRAPHY, ECONOMY, PEOPLE

Iraq is a triangular-shaped country in southwest Asia at the northwestern edge of the Persian Gulf. It has an area of 167,924 square miles (434,923 square kilometers), slightly larger than California. Iraq is almost entirely landlocked; its only outlet to the open sea is a thirty-mile (48-kilometer) stretch of coastline squeezed between Iran and Kuwait. The geography and oil resources of the Persian Gulf have been at the core of Iraq's last two wars. The first began with Iraq's attack on Iran in 1980 and lasted until 1988. The second, the Gulf War of 1991, resulted from Iraq's invasion of Kuwait in 1990. In the first case, Iraqi dictator Saddam Hussein attacked Iran to win full control of the Shatt-al-Arab (the "river of the Arabs"), a tidal river 120 miles (193 kilometers) long formed by the confluence of the Tigris and Euphrates rivers. Basra, Iraq's main port and second-largest city (population 617,000), stands at the northern end of the Shatt-al-Arab. In the second case, the stakes were much higher, as Hussein sought to annex Kuwait and take control of its enormous oil reserves. Hussein failed to achieve his goals in either war. Between 1980 and 1988 he was stymied by ferocious Iranian resistance, while in 1990–91 the United States put together a coalition of Middle Eastern and Western nations that drove Iraq from Kuwait.

Aside from Iran, Iraq's neighbor to the east, and Kuwait, which borders Iraq on the southeast, Iraq borders on Saudi Arabia in the south, Jordan in the west, Syria in the west and northwest, and Turkey in the north.

Iraq is made up of four geographical regions. Its southeastern corner is a huge delta marshland formed as the Tigris and Euphrates approach each other near the Persian Gulf. The marshland reaches into Iran and originally covered 6,000 square miles (15,500 square kilometers). The marshes once were a world of high reeds, lakes, shallow lagoons, and narrow waterways, a natural refuge for many species of waterbirds such as pelicans, herons, and flamingos. Humans have lived there for more than six thousand years. The Marsh Arabs, as the local people are called today, were semi-nomads who herded water buffalo and hunted waterbirds. They lived in elaborate houses built on arches woven from reeds. However, the Marsh Arabs and the marshes themselves have become victims of Saddam Hussein's determination to destroy any opposition to his brutally repressive regime. In the early 1990s the Iraqi government began draining the marshes to force the Marsh Arabs out of their wetland sanctuaries. By the middle of the decade the Marsh Arab way of life and the natural environment that had sustained it for thousands of years were well on their way to being destroyed. Throughout much of the former marshland where water once stood 5 feet (1.5 meters) deep, cracking mud lay exposed to a hot sun. Only a fraction of a community that once numbered half a million survived with its traditional way of life. Tens of thousands of Marsh Arabs lived in refugee camps, mostly in Iran.

The core region of Iraq is the plain between the Tigris and Euphrates that extends from the marshland northwestward to the Syrian border. Despite problems with high soil salinity, it is a fertile region laced with irrigation canals and dotted with small lakes. This region receives very little rain and agriculture depends on irrigation. It also is subject to serious flooding. Successive Iraqi governments have built dams on both the Tigris and Euphrates to control the flooding and produce electricity. Baghdad, Iraq's capital and largest city (population 4.7 million), is in this region. Closer to the Syrian border the land rises and becomes hilly; this area receives enough rain to grow grains and vegetables without irrigation. Summers in the land between the rivers are very hot and humid. Winters are also humid, but considerably cooler.

Northeastern Iraq, the country's third geographic region, begins as a hilly upland and turns into mountains near the Turkish and Iranian borders where some snowcapped peaks reach 12,000 feet (3,660 meters). Iraq's richest oil fields are in this region, whose population is primarily Kurdish. The Kurds, Iran's largest minority group, who also live in neighboring parts of Iran and Turkey, have long sought their own independent state. Mosul, Iraq's third-largest city (population 517,000), and Kirkuk are the northeast's main urban areas. Iraq's fourth region, west of the Euphrates, is a desert that extends into Syria, Jordan, and Saudi Arabia.

Iraq's arid climate means that its survival depends on the water of the Tigris and Euphrates rivers. Both rivers rise in Turkey. The Tigris forms a very short section of the Turkish-Syrian border before entering Iraq, while the Euphrates cuts through Syria before reaching Iraq. Both Iraq and Syria are deeply concerned with Turkish damming, irrigation, and hydroelectric projects; Iraq must also worry about Syrian plans for the Euphrates River. Water is one of several issues that have contributed to tensions between Iraq and its two upstream neighbors.

Economy

Iraq has the world's second-largest reserves of oil, about 112 billion barrels, or 10 percent of the world's total. Only Saudi Arabia has greater reserves. Oil dominates the economy and for decades has provided about 95 percent of Iraq's export earnings. The country is also a leading exporter of dates. Other important crops include cotton and wheat. Iraq's small industrial sector produces a variety of products including textiles, cement, food products, fertilizers, and electronics products.

The economy suffered enormous damage as a result of the its two recent wars and their aftermath. Economic damage from the war with Iran exceeded $100 billion. The Gulf War added to Iraq's economic hardship. Allied bombing destroyed much of Iraq's infrastructure. After the war Iraq's interference with United Nations inspections of its nuclear, chemical, and biological weapons facilities—inspections designed to ensure Iraq had stopped its nonconventional weapons programs— caused the UN to impose economic sanctions. Because of those sanctions, which limited Iraqi oil exports to the value of what the country needed for vital food and medicines, Iraq was able to earn from its oil sales only about one-third of what it earned prior to the war. Between 1990 and 1997, its agricultural production dropped at an average of 2.5 percent per year. In 1999 the worst drought on record cut crop yields by 50 percent. The scarcity of goods caused severe inflation. While the elite upon whom Saddam Hussein depended continued to live well, the country's overall standard of living plunged to what it had been in the late 1950s.

People

More than three-quarters of all Iraq's 21.9 million people are Arabs. About 95.5 percent are Muslims. Iraq's small Christian minority probably accounts for between 3 and 4 percent of the population. The Muslim Arab majority is divided, often bitterly, by the gulf between Sunni and Shiite. Although Shiites account for about 60 percent of the total population, the country has long been dominated by Sunni Arabs. The Shiites are concentrated in the central and southern parts of the country, including the border region with Iran. Slightly less than 20 percent of Iraqis are Kurds, an ancient Middle Eastern people who speak an Indo-European language related to Persian. The Kurds are Sunni Muslims. Most live in the northeastern mountain region and in the cities. The Kurdish northeast also happens to contain many of Iraq's largest oil fields.

The tension between the dominant, but minority, Sunni Muslim Arabs and the majority Shiite Arabs on the one hand and the Kurds on the other has for decades been Iraq's most serious internal problem. The first Kurdish revolts against the government in Baghdad took place in the 1920s, before Iraq achieved full independence, and reoccurred periodically after independence until the present time. The Kurds came closest to success in the mid-1970s when they had Iranian help, but were defeated when Iran withdrew its support in a deal with Baghdad in 1975. The Shiites endured discrimination for centuries at the hands of the Sunni Turks and decades more after independence from the Sunni Arabs. Unlike the Kurds, who seek independence, Iraqi's Shiites want to replace the country's Sunni-dominated government

Downtown Baghdad, 1997

with one of their own. In 1980s and 1990s the Hussein regime used extremely brutal methods to repress both communities. In what was perhaps the most infamous incident, the Iraqi army in 1988 attacked the Kurdish village of Halabje with poison gas, killing five thousand people.

HISTORY OF MODERN IRAQ

Iraq is yet another state carved out of the former Ottoman Empire after World War I. The British, who governed Iraq under a League of Nations mandate, made the Hashemite prince Faisal ibn Hussein king of Iraq at the same time as they made his brother Abdullah emir (prince) of neighboring Transjordan. Iraq achieved full independence in 1932, although British influence remained strong as long as the Hashemites remained on the Iraqi throne. With British help the dynasty survived a rebellion by nationalist military officers, who also were pro-German, during World War II. The British then remained in Iraq until 1946. In 1948 Iraq joined the Arab war against Israel, sending a combat force that eventually became the largest Arab army in the war. When the fighting ended in 1949 the Iraqis withdrew, refusing to sign even an armistice with the Jewish state. In the aftermath of that war, rising anti-Semitism in Iraq caused virtually the entire Iraqi Jewish community of more than 100,000 to leave their homes and forfeit their property and flee to the safety of Israel. It was the end of a Jewish presence in Mesopotamia whose roots reached back 2,500 years, the oldest Jewish community in the Middle East outside Israel.

During the early and mid-1950s the Iraqi monarchy followed conservative policies at home and took a pro-Western approach to foreign affairs. In 1958 King Faisal II, grandson of Iraq's first king, and the Hashemite dynasty were overthrown in a bloody coup led by General Abdul Karim Kassem. The victorious plotters executed the entire royal family and many of its supporters. The Kassem regime introduced social reforms at home and followed a pro-Soviet foreign policy. However, it was opposed by other factions, including military officers who admired Egypt's President

Nasser and the Iraqi wing of the Baath Party. The regime's opponents attempted several unsuccessful coups. Then in 1963 the Baath party seized power in another bloody coup in which Kassem was murdered. Nine months later a group of pro-Nasser military officers seized power. They managed to hang on until 1968, when a new coup put the Baath Party back in control.

The Baathists, determined to crush all opposition, carried out a series of political purges and established a harsh and efficient dictatorship. Syria also was ruled by the Baath Party, but when a rival wing of the party seized power in Damascus in 1970, Syria and Iraq became bitter rivals. By the early 1970s the strongman behind the scenes of Iraqi's Baath regime was Saddam Hussein. He controlled both the secret police and the Baath Party's armed militia. In 1979 Hussein took power directly as president. A new and turbulent era in the country's history was about to begin.

IRAQ UNDER SADDAM HUSSEIN

Saddam Hussein came to power with a reputation for utter ruthlessness. He was a Baath Party executioner in his early days; one of his many victims reportedly was his pro-Communist brother-in-law. Saddam was a master of tactical alliance building and the double cross when the alliance no longer served his purposes. As he demonstrated many times in the decades to follow, he would stop at nothing to keep his iron grip on power. War, murder, mass executions, international terrorism, the use of poison gas against civilians, and the willful destruction of the environment were all part of his stock in trade.

Iraq's new dictator immediately set about making himself the center of a worshipful personality cult. Every city in the country was blanketed with his 30-foot (10-meter) portraits; stadiums, hospitals, and other public places were named for him; he was praised in songs, books, and films; statues of him sprouted up everywhere; the media praised his every move. Anyone who opposed him, or who Hussein suspected might oppose him, was arrested or executed.

The Iran-Iraq War

Hussein meanwhile turned to his goal of making Iraq into the most powerful state in the Persian Gulf region and the Middle East. His first objective was complete control of the Shatt-al-Arab. In 1975, in return for Iran ending its assistance to the Iraqi Kurd rebellion, Baghdad had agreed to divide the Shatt-al-Arab in the middle. In September 1980 Hussein repudiated the agreement and immediately launched a full-scale military assault on Iran. He calculated that the Islamic fundamentalists who had come to power less than a year earlier in Iran would be too disorganized to mount a defense. Hussein was terribly wrong. After quick early advances the Iraqi offensive bogged down. By 1982 the Iranians, often using "human wave" tactics, drove the Iraqis from their territory and crossed into Iraq. At this point, Iran rejected Hussein's attempt to end the war, demanding $150 billion in compensation from the invaders and Hussein's ouster. The war settled into a bloody stalemate. Iraq ran up huge debts to fight the war, mainly in the form of loans from Saudi Arabia, Kuwait, and other Persian Gulf states. Finally, savage Iraqi attacks on Iranian cities and poison gas attacks against Iranian troops brought the Iranians to the negotiating table. At least 500,000 soldiers on both sides were dead, and another 2 million were wounded. After eight years, the Shatt-al-Arab remained divided at its median point exactly as before the war.

Hussein suffered another defeat during the war. During the 1970s Iraq had begun a program to build nuclear weapons, and a nuclear reactor was being constructed with French help. In 1981 the reactor was about to become operational with nuclear fuel that would have enabled the Iraqis to build nine nuclear bombs. They already had aircraft and missiles that could deliver the weapons hundreds of miles away. One country that correctly considered the program a direct threat to its survival was Israel. In June 1981 Israeli bombers, in a raid that involved what a French witness called "stupefying accuracy," destroyed the reactor.[4] Because the Israeli planes destroyed the reactor *before* it was operational, no radiation was released and the only damage was to the building and equipment—and to Hussein's ambitions.

The Israeli raid meant that in his next war, in which his opponents included the United States, Saddam Hussein did not have nuclear weapons to use against them.

The Gulf War

The results of the war with Iran did not reduce Hussein's ambitions and recklessness. If anything, it increased them, for Iraq emerged from the war with enormous foreign debts of $80 billion. Hussein also had an experienced and battle-hardened military at his fingertips. He decided to use his armed forces to seize one of the biggest strategic prizes in the world: the oil reserves of Kuwait. Kuwait was a tempting target: a small country with a tiny population ruled by a reactionary royal family with oil reserves only slightly smaller than Iraq's. By annexing Kuwait, Iraq would control almost 20 percent of the world's oil supplies, giving Saddam Hussein incalculable international influence.

The Iraqis struck on August 2, 1990, and overran Kuwait in a matter of days. The United Nations Security Council reacted immediately, passing Resolution 660 on August 2, demanding Iraqi withdrawal from Kuwait and imposing a trade embargo on Iraq on August 6. Formal annexation of what Hussein called Iraq's "nineteenth province" came on August 8. There was panic in neighboring Saudi Arabia, which saw itself as Hussein's next target. By August 7, at Saudi king Fahd's request, American troops were on their way to Saudi Arabia. When Iraq did not withdraw, the Security Council responded in November with Resolution 678 authorizing "all necessary means" to force Iraqi troops out of Kuwait. A majority of Arab nations also condemned the invasion. Iraq's main support came from the PLO and the governments of Libya, Algeria, Sudan, and Jordan. Despite that narrow base, Hussein's defiance of the West and the wealthy Persian Gulf states made him the most popular Arab leader in many parts of the Arab world.

The United States brought Western nations and twelve Arab states into a military coalition to enforce the UN resolution. In January 1991 Operation Desert Storm began with air attacks on Iraq that lasted a month. In February, in a fast-moving campaign lasting only one hundred hours, Iraqi forces were routed and driven from Kuwait. Before they left, however, they sabotaged and set on fire hundreds of Kuwaiti oil wells, causing an environmental disaster in the Persian Gulf region.

Iraq Since the Gulf War

The end of the war did not bring real peace to Iraq. The most important reason for this was that UN war aims were limited to driving Iraqi forces from Kuwait and did not extend to driving Saddam Hussein from power. Still, Hussein was almost immediately faced with revolts by the Kurds in the north seeking independence and the Shiites in the south seeking to overthrow him. Both groups were encouraged by the United States and other Western powers to rebel in the hope that they could drive Hussein from power. But they received no military aid and Hussein was able to crush both rebellions by the spring of 1991. More than one million Kurds, remembering how Hussein had used poison gas against them in 1988 and fearing genocidal reprisals this time, fled to Iran and Turkey. Some of those who remained in Iraq found protection under the umbrella of two "no fly" zones—one in the Kurdish north and the other in the Shiite south—from which Iraqi aircraft were barred and which were patrolled by U.S. and British warplanes. These zones are still in existence, and continue to give Kurds and Shiites who live in the protected areas a small measure of autonomy and safety, but nothing that approaches genuine security. Those who live beyond the protection of the no-fly zones have no security at all. For example, between 1991 and 2001 the Iraqi government drove at least 200,000 Kurds living in the oil-rich region around the city of Kirkuk from their homes in an attempt to "Arabize" that Kurdish-populated area. Members of other non-Arab minorities were displaced for similar reasons.

Hussein meanwhile conducted periodic purges and mass executions to crush all opposition to his regime. Given both the secrecy under which the regime operates and the scope of its activities, it is possible to provide only a partial list of its political murders. In 1992, 80 military officers were executed for an attempted coup along with 76 demonstrators against the regime. Several civilian and military officials were executed in August 1993 for allegedly planning a coup. After an assassination attempt against Hussein's older son Udai in December 1996, Hussein executed almost 200 political prisoners in March 1997. In late 1997 several senior military officers were executed, as were an estimated 800 people suspected of belonging to opposition groups. In April 1998 the UN Human Rights Commission reported that 1,500 people had been executed in Iraq in 1997 for political reasons. Two senior Shiite religious leaders were murdered in 1998 and one more, this time the community's overall leader, in February 1999. The regime continued to execute hundreds of political prisoners every year. Nor was it necessary to be a political prisoner, or even be convicted of a crime, to be subject to the death penalty. In October 2000, dozens of women accused of prostitution, never having received any sort of trial, were executed in Baghdad and several other cities, as were some men suspected of seeking their services. The executions used swords to behead the victims, who met their fate in front of their homes.

The Hussein regime had a more difficult time imposing its will on the United Nations. During the course of the Gulf War the world was shocked to find out the extent of Iraq's programs to develop biological, chemical, and nuclear weapons. As part of the agreement with the UN that ended the fighting, Iraq accepted a UN Security Council Resolution requiring that all of its chemical and biological weapons, as well as its materials for developing nuclear weapons, be destroyed. A UN task force called the UN Special Commission on Iraq (UNSCOM) was set up to find and destroy Iraq's capacity to make these weapons. The UN also continued economic sanctions against Iraq, including a ban on oil sales, to force it to cooperate with UNSCOM. However, the UN offered to allow Iraq to sell a limited amount of oil in order to buy food and medical supplies. These oil revenues would be controlled the UN, and one-third of them would be set aside to compensate victims of Iraq's invasion of Kuwait. Hussein at first rejected that arrangement, but finally accepted the "oil for food" plan in 1996, five years after it was offered to him, in order to improve the country's dreadful economic situation.

The establishment of UNSCOM began a cat and mouse game that continues to the present time. Despite Iraqi attempts to interfere with its work and deny it access to key facilities, UNSCOM discovered evidence of massive biological, chemical, and nuclear programs and destroyed vast amounts of material. More evidence became available in 1994 when the former head of Iraq's nuclear program defected to the West. In 1995 additional important information emerged with the defection of the head of Iraq's weapons program, who also was one of Hussein's sons-in-law. By 1998 UNSCOM had found twenty-one nuclear facilities whose existence Iraq had not admitted, warheads loaded with anthrax and other deadly biological agents, huge stores of chemical agents, missiles, and much more. But it also was becoming clear that Iraq was still hiding both information and materials to make weapons of mass destruction. Periodic bombing attacks by United States and British aircraft, including a four-day salvo in December 1998 that hit one hundred targets in Iraq, failed to get Hussein to honor commitments to allow UNSCOM to work without interference.

In fact, Hussein slowly appeared to be gaining the upper hand. By 1999 UNSCOM had left Iraq, without prospects of returning. This left the Iraqis free to pursue their nuclear, biological, and chemical weapons programs free of meaningful inspection and monitoring. In January 1999 the American representative at the Security Council summed up UNSCOM's last report by noting, "The report documents that Iraq has never really intended to cooperate with the UN, despite a history of agreements to do so."[5] Even worse, American experts feared that despite UNSCOM efforts and U.S. bombing, Iraq was as close to developing a nuclear weapon as it had been in 1991, before the Gulf War began, They also suggested it would take Iraq only half a year to rebuild the chemical and biological programs damaged by the December 1998 bombing.

The stalemate dragged on into the new century. In December 1999 the UN Security Council created a new inspection task force—the United Nations Monitoring, Verification, and Inspection Commission (UNMOVIC)—to replace UNSCOM. However, as of 2001, despite almost two hundred British-American bombing attacks on Iraqi military targets, Saddam Hussein had not allowed UNMOVIC into Iraq to do its work. The concern this raised in arms control circles was summed up by nuclear arms expert and former head of UNSCOM Richard Butler, who warned, "It would be folly not to reckon that he [Saddam Hussein] is back in the business of making weapons of mass destruction."[6]

The situation was grim for everyone but Saddam Hussein and a small group of his supporters. Iraq had pushed UNSCOM out of the country and not allowed UNMOVIC in, economic sanctions remained in place, the country was being periodically bombed, and everybody recognized that the government was still hiding information about its weapons programs and had the equipment and materials to resume those programs in the future. Meanwhile, most Iraqis continue to suffer from terrible economic conditions, but not because of UN sanctions. As oil prices rose beginning in 1999, so did Iraqi revenues. But that did not help ordinary Iraqis. In September 1999 the United States State Department reported that the Iraqi regime had enough revenues to buy additional food but refused to do so, or to distribute what was available to the needy. In fact, as the State Department reported in February 2001, those in power in Iraq were exploiting UN sanctions by diverting imported food to loyal government supporters and even smuggling it out of Iraq for resale elsewhere. Despite rising revenues—Iraq had sold more than $35 billion worth of oil under the UN food for oil program by the middle of 2000—the Hussein regime was letting months go by without ordering any medicine. Meanwhile, its smuggling operations involved much more than food. Each year millions of barrels of oil were leaving Iraq illegally, mostly by pipeline though Syria, on trucks crossing into Turkey, or on small ships able to hug the Persian Gulf coast and avoid detection by U.S. or other allied warships in the region. A reasonable estimate was that the Hussein regime earned $1 billion from smuggling oil in 2000, money it was free to use for any purposes it chose, including building weapons of mass destruction.

Few people had much hope. As one theater professor, who doubled as a taxi driver to make ends meet, observed:

Once we had fulfilling lives, but now we have dropped out of the world. Everything has changed, and we really don't understand why. All we can do is accept it. There is no alternative.[7]

The hard times, however, did not touch Hussein and those who keep him in power. Nor did the propaganda machine slow in its glorification of the Iraqi dictator. Thus in May 1999 the regime announced the opening of a newly built

Beaming, benevolent portraits seem to have become hallmarks of harsh dictatorships. Here a happy Saddam Hussein surveys a Baghdad street from a background showing an idealized cityscape.

lakeside resort city called Saddamint al-Tharthar 85 miles (142 kilometers) west of Baghdad. Ceremonies included Iraq's vice president giving Hussein a sword made of gold. Almost every brick in the city is engraved with Hussein's initials. In Baghdad, where poverty stalked the neighborhoods, rebuilding focused on luxurious new palaces and state guesthouses, as well as an assortment of new statues of Hussein. One of them, a 30-foot (10-meter) bronze casting in the city's center, depicted Iraq's dictator, in military dress with a pistol at his hip, thrusting his right arm upward as if he were signaling the start of a new attack.

Yet through all of Iraq's troubles, Saddam Hussein remains firmly in control of the country. His power is based on a small group of perhaps one hundred men who manage a vast network of about half a million soldiers, spies, and political loyalists. Among those closest to Hussein are his two sons, Udai and Qusai. Both are major political figures. Qusai, the younger brother, is the commander of the army's elite Republican Guards, the military pillar of the regime, while Udai heads Iraq's security service, which often carries out the regime's executions. Although there have been rumors of a behind-the-scenes power struggle between the two Hussein brothers, Saddam Hussein's power base remains solid. It has withstood many crises and British and American bombs. By contrast, Iraq's opposition movements are weak and divided. As long as Saddam Hussein stays in control, Iraq's future, it would seem, is unlikely to be much brighter than its recent past.

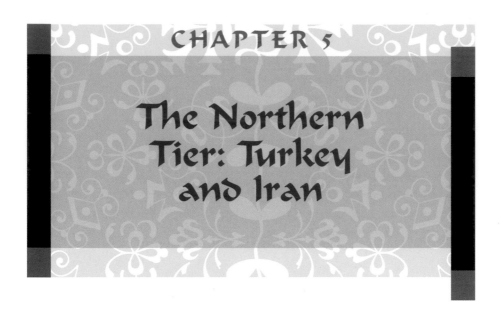

CHAPTER 5

The Northern Tier: Turkey and Iran

Turkey and Iran are the Middle East's two non-Arab but Muslim countries. They have large populations and are major regional military powers. However, as societies they have been moving in diametrically opposed directions in recent decades. Since the 1920s Turkey has been attempting to modernize as a secular state, with religion being a personal, private choice as in the West. In fact, most Turkish leaders consider the West to be the model they want their country to follow. Turkey has belonged to the North Atlantic Treaty Organization (NATO) since the early 1950s, wants to join the European Union (EU), and is friendly with Israel. Iran appeared to be on a course similar to Turkey's until the Islamic Revolution of 1979. Since then Iran has become an Islamic theocracy, bitterly anti-Western, a supporter of international terrorism, and committed to Israel's destruction. Far from seeking to emulate the West, Iran has militantly rejected everything Western and sought an Islamic alternative on which to build its future.

TURKEY

The Turks originated in central Asia and are relative new-comers to the Middle East. The earliest written account of Turkic-speaking tribes comes from China, where records first mention them around 1300 B.C. The first Turkic group to arrive in the Middle East were the Seljuks, who set up a state in Iran in the eleventh century. In 1071 Seljuk horse-men dealt the Byzantine army a devastating defeat at the Battle of Manzikert in what today is eastern Turkey, after which they took over much of Anatolia. Seljuk power lasted only about one hundred years. The Seljuks were over-whelmed and disappeared from history in the wake of the Crusades in the twelfth century and the Mongol invasion of the thirteenth century. This cleared the way for the rise of the Ottoman Turks, who in the thirteenth century had a tiny state in western Anatolia. Over the next two centuries, expanding from the same core region that in ancient times gave birth to the Hittite empire and which for centuries was the nucleus of the Byzantine Empire, they built one of the largest empires the Middle East had ever seen. When their empire gradually corroded and finally collapsed in 1918, the Turks rebuilt their national life in Anatolia as a modern nation state.

GEOGRAPHY, ECONOMY, PEOPLE

The Republic of Turkey is a rectangular-shaped country occupying a region of southwest Asia known as Anatolia, or Asia Minor, and a tiny corner of Europe called Eastern Thrace. It has an area of 300,948 square miles (779,452 square kilometers), about 12 percent larger than Texas. Turkey straddles one of the most strategic points in the world, where two narrow straits, the Bosporus and Dard-anelles, separate Europe from Asia. The Bosporus, on whose shores stands the city of Istanbul, links the huge inland

Black Sea to a smaller inland sea, the Sea of Marmara. The Dardanelles in turn connect the Sea of Marmara to the Aegean Sea, really a bay of the Mediterranean Sea. Ninety-seven percent of Turkey is in Asia. However, the 3 percent that lies in Europe includes most of Istanbul. For more than one thousand years before it became Istanbul the city was known as Constantinople, the capital of the Byzantine Empire and for many centuries one of the major centers of European culture. Turkey's small but important piece of European real estate makes it one of only three countries—Russia and Kazakhstan are the others—that boast territory in both Europe and Asia.

Turkey has about 5,800 miles (9,300 kilometers) of borders, almost three-quarters of which are seas. The Black Sea forms most of Turkey's long northern frontier. Its western tip, in the Balkans, fronts on Bulgaria, while its eastern edge, in the Caucasus, touches Georgia. Turkey's neighbor directly to the west is Greece, its longtime enemy. The Aegean Sea forms the rest of Turkey's western border; however, Greek islands just a few miles off the Turkish shore run the length of Turkey's coastline from Thrace to the Mediterranean Sea like a line of watchtowers. The Mediterranean Sea forms about half of Turkey's southern border. The remainder, moving eastward from the Mediterranean, fronts on Syria and Iraq. Due east of Turkey are Iran, Azerbaijan (with which Turkey shares a scant 5.5-mile, or 9-kilometer, frontier and to whose inhabitants the Turks are closely related), and Armenia, another longtime enemy.

Anatolia, the heart of the Turkish homeland, is a broad plateau bordered by narrow coastlines and ringed by several mountain ranges. The plateau averages about 3,000 feet (915 meters) in altitude. Its main lowlands are along the Aegean and Marmara coasts, a narrow coastal area on the Black Sea, a strip along the Mediterranean coast, and valleys along the banks of several rivers that flow into the Black, Aegean, Mediterranean, and Marmara seas. In the south, the plateau region is separated from the Mediterranean coast by the Taurus Mountains. In the northeast the Pontic Mountains ring the Black Sea coast. Farther west are the Koroglu Mountains. Anatolia rises in the east into a range of mountains

A snow-covered Mount Ararat sits in the distance, beyond the village of Dogubayazit, Turkey.

that eventually merges with the lofty Caucasus range. Turkey's highest peak, and the most dramatic sight in this region, is the gigantic snow-capped cone of Mount Ararat, an extinct volcano rising 16,945 feet (5,168 meters) above sea level. It was here, according to the Bible, that Noah's Ark came to rest after the great flood inundated the world; for two hundred years explorers have been combing Ararat's slopes in what thus far has been an unsuccessful search for remains of the ark. South of Ararat is Lake Van, a vast salt lake (1,419 square miles, or 3,675 square kilometers) that is the largest in Turkey. The rain and snow that in the eastern mountains feed the upper reaches of the Tigris and Euphrates rivers, both of which rise in Turkey and flow southward, the Tigris into Iraq and the Euphrates into Syria. The Kizil Irmak, the longest river inside Turkey, also rises in the eastern part of Anatolia. It then heads due west before pivoting toward the northeast and flowing into the Black Sea.

The interior of Anatolia is a vast semiarid grassland. Summers are dry and hot, while winters are cold and snowy. Ankara, Turkey's capital city of 3 million people, stands near the center of this region. A Mediterranean climate of mild rainy winters and hot dry summers predominates along the Aegean and Mediterranean coasts. The Black Sea coast gets rain during both its chilly winters and its mild summers. That coast, in particular its eastern section, is a lush well-watered region with Turkey's only dense forests. Rainfall here reaches almost 100 inches (2,500 millimeters) per year. In some places, where it generally rains every other day, the forest takes on the look of a jungle. A rich agricultural region, it is the source of almost all of Turkey's valuable tea crop and fully 70 percent of the world's hazelnuts.

Turkey's tiny European section is a fertile landscape of rolling plains with a Mediterranean climate. Most of Istanbul, Turkey's largest city (population 8 million), stands on its eastern edge overlooking the Bosporus. The rest of the city is on the Asian side of the strait.

Economy

Turkey began its modern history after World War I as a poverty-stricken, backward agricultural nation where 80 percent of the people earned their living working the land. Today Turkey has a growing industrial base and a standard of living that has risen significantly in the last generation. About 60 percent of the population lives in cities and towns. Sustained economic growth began in the 1930s when the government took control of many industries and used central planning to accelerate industrial development. Today state controls are being scaled back in order to increase efficiency and attract private investment. Although the state still owns many large enterprises, Turkey has a strong and rapidly growing private industrial sector. Textiles and clothing, which are almost entirely in private hands, are the leading industries and Turkey's most important exports, accounting for about 40 percent of Turkey's total exports. Other important industries are food processing, iron and steel, petroleum, and construction materials. Tourism has expanded and is a significant earner of foreign currency.

Another critical source is the money sent home by several million Turks working abroad. Most work in Western Europe; two million Turks live in Germany alone. The Turks are also justly famous as manufacturers of beautiful carpets, a tradition that predates their arrival in Anatolia to their days as nomadic tribesmen in Central Asia.

Turkish agriculture has lagged behind industry in modernizing. The lack of arable land, poor irrigation, and inefficient methods have limited production. Nonetheless, Turkey exports much of what it grows on the land. Cash crops such as cotton, tobacco, hazelnuts, sultanas (grapes grown for raisins and wine), and tea account for about a fifth of Turkey's total exports. Other important crops include corn, rye, wheat, barley, olives, and citrus fruits . Turkish farmers also raise large numbers of sheep, goats, and cattle. The country is a major producer of wool.

Turkey's natural resources include coal, chromium, lignite, iron, and a small amount of oil. It also has an abundance of the rarest resource in the Middle East: water. Turkey is modernizing its agriculture by expanding irrigation and providing the entire country with a clean and cheap source of electricity. The vehicle for these ambitions is the mammoth $32 billion Southeastern Anatolia Project, or GAP (from the initials of its Turkish name). In one of the largest public works projects in the world, the waters of the Tigris and Euphrates rivers are being harnessed by a network of twenty-two dams and nineteen hydroelectric plants. The project's largest structure and centerpiece, the Ataturk Dam on the Euphrates, is already completed. When the entire GAP project is completed in 2005, it will supply water to more than 9 percent of Turkey's land area, expanding the country's irrigated land by 40 percent, and produce one-fourth of the country's electrical power needs. One goal is to provide better opportunity on the land and keep some of Turkey's growing rural population in the countryside and out of its overcrowded cities. While all this sounds good for Turkey, Syria and Iraq are worried that Turkey's new dams will deny them water they badly need for development and to feed their growing populations. These conflicting national needs are a source of continual tension between Turkey and its southern Arab neighbors. In fact, between 1984 and 1998 the Syrian government, to pressure the Turks to provide Syria more Euphrates River water, allowed Kurdish rebels from Turkey to use bases in Syria.

People

About 99 percent of Turkey's 64.6 million people are Muslims, the vast majority of them Sunnis, with small numbers of Shiites and Alawites. Turkey's tiny Christian and Jewish communities account for about 0.2 percent of the population. The Armenian community of perhaps 50,000 is the country's largest Christian group. About 25,000 Jews still live in Turkey, one of the largest Jewish communities remaining in the Islamic world. However, despite its overwhelmingly Muslim population, modern Turkey is a secular state, the only Muslim country in the Middle East where Islam is not the state religion. Perhaps the single most important change that took place in Turkey with the collapse of the Ottoman Empire and establishment of the modern Turkish national state was secularization. Since the 1920s the government has promoted the idea of secular Turkish identity. Islam ceased to be the official religion of the state, civil law replaced Islamic law, the government took control of education and made it strictly secular, and a wide variety of other policies were introduced to limit the influence of Islam in public life. The growth of fundamentalist Islam in recent years has become the single most divisive issue in Turkish life.

The other deep division in Turkey is ethnic, and it has been the cause of serious and continuing trouble. About 20 percent of Turkey's population is Kurdish. The Kurds are an ancient Middle Eastern people who are related to the Persians and speak an Indo-European language. Turkey's 12 million Kurds occupy an awkward position in Turkish life. Most live in southeastern Turkey near the Syrian and Iraqi borders and adjacent to the Kurdish populations of those countries. Kurds constitute about 90 percent of the population of this section of Turkey, which is part of a larger region the Kurds call Kurdistan. At the same time, many Kurds also live in the cities throughout Turkey, where they have assimilated into

Turkish life and achieved success in a broad range of professions. However, there is a strong Kurdish nationalist movement in Turkey. It has deep roots that reach back to the founding of modern Turkey and Kurdish rebellions against the Turkish government in the 1920s and 1930s. Kurdish nationalists have a range of demands. There are many who would be satisfied with local and cultural autonomy. As one woman told a Western reporter:

> What we demand is our identity. We want to say on our identity cards that we are Kurds. We want schools and television stations in our language.[1]

That demand has been rejected by the Turkish political establishment, which fears that any concession to Kurdish demands for autonomy will quickly lead to secession. For many years the Turkish government refused to even admit that Kurds existed as a distinct ethnic group, calling them "mountain Turks." In 1981 a member of parliament received a year in jail for proclaiming, "There are Kurds in Turkey. I am a Kurd."[2] It still is illegal even to use the use the word Kurdistan (the name of the region where most Kurds live) or to suggest that Kurds deserve autonomy. By the 1980s, Kurds in increasing numbers saw independence as the only escape from Turkish oppression, and in 1984 the government's ironfisted attempts to suppress Kurdish nationalism led to open rebellion. The rebellion, which lasted until the year 2000 before being defeated, was waged by the Kurdistan Workers' Party (PKK). In fifteen years of bitter fighting more than 20,000 Kurds died and many more were driven from their villages. The PKK in turn killed hundreds of government officials and several thousand Turkish soldiers. The best guess is that more than 30,000 rebel Kurds, Turkish soldiers, and civilians lost their lives in the fighting. The stakes in this bitter dispute were raised even higher because Turkey's GAP water/hydroelectric project is being built entirely in the Kurdish part of the country. Although the rebellion is over, each side blames the other for the violence and death, and the basic issues between them remain unresolved.

THE OTTOMAN ERA

The Ottoman Empire began as a small state in western Anatolia that began to grow after the Mongol invasion of the thirteenth century. Its first expansion took place at the expense of the greatly weakened Byzantine Empire during the first quarter of the fourteenth century. The Ottomans were strengthened when many former Byzantine peasants in Anatolia converted from Christianity to Islam, their main incentive being to escape the crushing tax the Islamic Ottoman state imposed on non-Muslims. By the end of the century the empire extended deep into the Balkans. A key to Ottoman expansion was the army. Its elite core was the Janissaries, a force that in its heyday prior to 1600 was made up of Christian boys who had been kidnapped at a young age and converted to Islam. Completely cut off from their origins and heritage, the Janissaries were totally loyal to the Ottoman ruler, or sultan. Only after 1700 did they become corrupted; they then became less of a threat to the sultan's enemies than to the sultan himself and the Turkish state.

The Ottomans suffered a crushing defeat in 1402 at the hands of the Mongol chieftain Tamerlane, but recovered after Tamerlane's death in 1405. A new era of dramatic expansion followed. In 1453 the Ottomans shocked the Christian world when they conquered Constantinople and ended the thousand-year history of the Byzantine Empire. The majestic Hagia Sophia, for nine hundred years the largest Christian church in the world, was turned into a mosque, and Constantinople, the former center of the Greek Orthodox Christianity, became the capital of the Islamic Ottoman Empire. Expansion into Europe and across the Middle East continued into the sixteenth century. Eventually the Ottoman Empire sprawled from North Africa, the Arabian Peninsula, and the borders of Persia across the Fertile Crescent and Anatolia to Cypress and other islands of the Mediterranean Sea, the northern shores of the Black Sea, and the western fringes of the Balkans.

The Ottoman Empire reached both its political and cultural peak during the reign of Suleyman the Magnificent (1520–66). His reign saw the construction of some of the

Islamic world's most beautiful mosques; outstanding crafts-manship in gold, textiles, and other materials; and significant poetic and literary achievements. Suleyman also issued his famous Codex Suleymanicus, a synthesis of Islamic and secular law. At the same time, however, the seeds of decline were being planted. Endless court intrigues resulted in the murder of able princes to eliminate them from the line of succession. Even more damaging in the long run was Ottoman complacency regarding European technological progress.

The first serious European challenge to the Ottomans took place five years after Suleyman's death when naval forces from Spain and Venice defeated the Turkish navy in 1571 at the Battle of Lepanto. Still, the Ottoman military remained a formidable force; as late as 1683 a huge army surrounded and threatened Vienna. The city held, and the Ottoman defeat at Vienna became the beginning of the long period of decline that lasted for more than two centuries. By the early nineteenth century large pieces of the empire had been lost on all fronts, including the Balkans, where the Greeks finally won their independence. By mid-century the Ottoman armies clearly were no match for modern European forces, and the empire, wallowing in corruption and decadence, had become the "sick man of Europe." The attempt of army officers, the "Young Turks," to reverse the decline in the early twentieth century failed. The First Balkan War of 1912 reduced the Ottoman presence in Europe to the small slice of Thrace around Constantinople.

In 1914 the Ottoman Empire entered World War I on the side of Germany. Its lone major military victory of the war came in 1915 when it thwarted the British-led landing at Gallipoli and thereby defeated the Allied attempt to seize the Dardanelles. The hero of that battle was Colonel Mustafa Kemal, who after the war became the founding father of modern Turkey. Turkey's low point in the war also came in 1915 when its forces deported the Armenian population from several eastern provinces to prevent them from aiding Russian forces. While no exact figures exist, the best estimates are that at least one million Armenians were murdered or died from disease and starvation during that dreadful operation. The Armenian deportation is widely considered the first act of genocide of the twentieth century. Three years later, the war ended in defeat and dissolution of the Ottoman Empire.

MUSTAFA KEMAL ATATURK AND THE BIRTH OF MODERN TURKEY

The end of the war left the Turks, now bereft of their empire, in a struggle for national survival. The Treaty of Sèvres in 1920 gave them control of little more than northern Anatolia. Constantinople, still officially their capital, and the Bosporus and Dardanelles were under British occupation. It was at this point that Mustafa Kemal (later known as Mustafa Kemal Ataturk) emerged as a national leader. Between 1920 and 1923 Kemal abolished the Ottoman sultanate and declared Turkey a republic, defeated Armenian and Georgian forces in the east, forced Italian and French troops out of Anatolia, and signed a treaty of friendship with the Soviet Union that restored some territory to Turkey. In addition, in climactic battles fought in 1922, Turkish forces defeated Greece's attempt to annex western Anatolia. In the aftermath of the Turkish victory, about 1.5 million Greeks were uprooted from western Anatolia and resettled in Greece, ending a Greek presence there that dated from the eighth century B.C. Their forced migration was mirrored by that of 800,000 Turks who were forced from their homes in Greece and Bulgaria and resettled in Turkey. Kemal's victories were confirmed by the Treaty of Lausanne in 1923, which with minor subsequent adjustments established Turkey's current borders.

Mustafa Kemal had one overriding goal: to turn Turkey into a modern secular nation on the Western model. That required breaking the grip of Islam on Turkish life and confining it to the role religion played in the West: that is, to the realm of the private and personal. Kemal's energy and determination, and the scope of his reforms, were breathtaking. In 1923 a national assembly Kemal had convened three years earlier abolished the Ottoman sultanate and declared Turkey a republic. Kemal became Turkey's first president; he would be reelected three times and rule the country with dictatorial powers until his death. For most of that time Turkey was a one-party state run by Kemal's Republican People's Party (CHP according to its Turkish initials). The new regime also moved the country's capital from Constantinople to Ankara, a city in central Anatolia, yet another symbol of Turkey's fresh start. In 1924 the national assembly abolished the caliphate, the Islamic office left over from Ottoman times that made the sultan Turkey's religious as well as temporal ruler. The assembly also introduced a new constitution. It provided for a parliament elected by universal male suffrage.

Kemal broadened his battle against religion in 1925 when the government abolished all religious orders and Muslim courts. It made secular primary education compulsory for all children. Even the fez, the traditional Turkish cylinder-shaped hat, was forbidden as part of Kemal's determination to Westernize Turkey. In 1926 the government adopted the Swiss code of civil law. Civil marriage became mandatory. In 1928 Islam lost its status as the official state religion. Kemal also took the difficult step of banning the use of the Arabic script for writing Turkish and substituting the Latin alphabet, yet another effort to turn Turkey toward the West. The new system was in fact better suited to the Turkish language, but Kemal was taking no chances. A new law required all Turks under the age of forty to go to school to learn the Latin-based writing system. In 1930 Constantinople's name officially was changed to Istanbul, a name thought to be derived from two Greek words *stin poli*, meaning "in the city."

Under the Ottoman regime women had few rights; that changed when women were given the vote in 1934 and full legal equality with men in 1935. Another change implemented in 1934 required all Turks to follow the Western example and adopt surnames. The national assembly honored Kemal by giving him the name *Ataturk*, Turkish for "Father of Turks."

Westernization also meant economic development. Impressed with what he saw in the Soviet Union, Kemal was convinced that rapid growth was most quickly achieved by direct state intervention in the economy. In the 1930s the government therefore began a program of central planning and state ownership of major industrial enterprises. Following the Soviet model, but avoiding its disastrous extremes, Turkey introduced its first five-year economic plan in 1934.

In 1938, at the relatively young age of fifty-seven, Mustafa Kemal Ataturk died of liver disease. He was succeeded as president by his longtime second in command, Ismet Inonu. Under Inonu's leadership Turkey remained neutral for most of World War II, despite Allied pleas to join the desperate struggle against Nazi Germany. Turkey only declared war on Germany and Japan in February 1945, when the fighting in Europe was almost over. While the decision to remain neutral was questionable from a moral point of view—some Turks consider it shameful—the country did emerge from the most destructive war in history physically undamaged.

TURKEY AFTER WORLD WAR II

Turkey took two major steps in the immediate postwar era to link itself even more closely with the West. The first involved foreign affairs. Faced with pressure from the Soviet Union over control of the Black Sea straits, Turkey quickly chose sides in the Cold War, aligning itself with the Western democracies in their forty-five year struggle against the Soviet Union. Turkey came under the mantle of American protection in 1947 when the United States proclaimed the Truman Doctrine. It stated that Washington would protect countries threatened by Communist aggression or subversion. In 1950 Turkey sent soldiers to Korea to fight with American and other United Nations forces in defense of South Korea. In 1952 Turkey became a member of the North Atlantic Treaty Organization (NATO), the American-led defensive alliance formed in 1949 to protect Western Europe from Soviet aggression. More difficult, and still only partially completed, was the second step, in which Turkey attempted to move toward genuine democracy. That step ran up against stumbling blocks from the start. They included authoritarian attitudes among Turkey's political leaders, economic instability, the Kurdish rebellion, and, in the 1990s, the resurgence of Islamic fundamentalism.

Turkey's one-party system ended in 1946 when Celal Bayar and Adnan Menderes were allowed to form the Democratic Party. Other new parties followed. Nonetheless, the first postwar election, won by the CHP in 1946, was rigged. In 1950 the Democratic Party won Turkey's first free election. It governed for the next ten years with Bayar as president and Menderes as prime minister. However, in the wake of accusations of corruption and repressiveness, the military in 1960 overthrew the government. Bayar was imprisoned, while Menderes and two other ministers were hanged in 1961. That year the military returned Turkey to civilian rule under a new constitution designed to prevent the concentration of too much power in the executive branch. The Democratic Party was banned, but came to life again in the form of the Justice Party led by Suleyman Demirel, who throughout the 1960s and early 1970s was Turkey's leading politician.

Turkish political life, rocked by waves of economic hardship and social unrest, lurched through a series of crises during those years. In the early 1970s Bulent Ecevit, at the head of a revived CHP, emerged as a rival to Demirel. In contrast to the centrist Demirel, Ecevit became the leader of Turkey's moderate political left. During the 1970s each man served several terms as prime minister. Meanwhile, by the late 1970s increasing domestic turmoil and ineffective government brought the country to the brink of civil war. In 1980 the military again stepped in with a coup, banning all existing parties and arresting both Ecevit and Demirel. Reversing its 1961 position, the military wrote a new constitution that in the interests of maintaining order vested more power in the presidency. In 1983 the military permitted civilian political life to resume, but only under its tight supervision. A series of newly organized and named parties ran in parliamentary elections in the fall. The winner, led by former deputy prime minister Turgut Özal, was the conservative Motherland Party (ANAP), which ran with the generals' support. Özal served as prime minister until 1989 and as president from 1989 to 1993. He was responsible for far-reaching economic reforms that promoted free enterprise and economic growth.

Amid seemingly endless political maneuvering, Ecevit and Demirel returned to the political arena after a 1987 national referendum ended a ban the military had imposed on 200 politicians. Demirel headed the conservative True Path Party (DYP), while Ecevit led the leftist Democratic Socialist Party (DSP). Although several new politicians became significant figures in Turkish political life, Ecevit and Demirel would remain central players throughout the 1980s and 1990s. In fact, as the 1990s drew to a close, Ecevit and Demirel, by then the two old men of Turkish politics, were respectively the country's prime minister and president.

Perhaps the most interesting new actor on Turkey's political stage in the early 1990s was Tansu Ciller, the country's first prominent woman politician. Ciller became leader of the True Path Party in 1993 when Demirel, then prime minister, was elected Turkey's president. Ciller replaced Demirel as prime minister, thereby becoming the first woman to hold that office in Turkey's history and the first woman to do so in a Middle Eastern Muslim country.

The other important, and militant, new face was Necmettin Erbakan, leader of the Islamic fundamentalist Welfare Party. Erbakan rose to prominence during the first half of the 1990s as Turkey's most anti-Western major politician. During the municipal elections of 1994, in which his party was victorious in more than a dozen cities and towns including Instanbul and Ankara, he warned that "the Christians" of Europe wanted to oppress Turkey and likened them to infidels. While campaigning during the parliamentary elections of December 1995, he again bitterly attacked European influences as a threat to Muslims and said he wanted to abolish Turkey's secular constitution. The Welfare Party stunned most observers by finishing first in the parliamentary elections of December 1995 with 21.4 percent of the vote, narrowly edging out both Ciller's True Path Party and the Motherland Party. The Welfare Party rode a wave of sentiment among conservative Turks that modernization and secularism had brought to Turkey crass materialism and moral decay. At the same time, its electoral victory, even though it only amounted to a narrow plurality, caused immediate rumbling in the military, which considered itself the guardian of

Ataturk's secular revolution. After a swirl of political maneuvering, which included a failed attempt by the True Path and Motherland parties to work together, Erbakan cobbled together a coalition that included Ciller and the True Path Party. It survived for just over one stormy year. The military immediately criticized Erbakan's government for permitting schools to teach religious courses. An Islamic rally in a small town near Ankara caused further trouble when the local mayor said Turkey should adopt Islamic law. The guest of honor at the rally, the ambassador from fundamentalist Iran, urged the crowd to stand up to the "enemies of Islam."

In February 1997 the military demanded Erbakan enforce eighteen measures to protect secular state institutions from Islamic influence. These included closer supervision of Islamic financial institutions and the removal of Islamic fundamentalists from public offices. Erbakan temporarily defused the tension by agreeing to the military's demands, but soon the military and the government again were at odds about Islamic influence in Turkish state institutions. In June 1997 the Welfare Party's coalition fell apart and Erbakan was forced to resign.

The new government, built around the Motherland Party, was a fragile coalition. During the next eighteen months tension continued to build between secular and Islamic forces in Turkey. The government pushed antireligious policies that ranged from expelling seventy-three members of the armed forces for membership in Islamic organizations to strictly enforcing laws banning Islamic dress in public institutions, especially schools and universities. To cut down on the number of students attending religious schools, the government raised the minimum age for admission to Islamic schools from eleven to fourteen. In January 1998 a ruling dissolved the Welfare Party and banned Erbakan from politics for five years. Many of its members then joined the newly formed Virtue Party, a clone of the dissolved party. Islamic forces responded with several demonstrations, including one in Istanbul in February attended by ten thousand people.

Turkey's struggle to define itself inevitably extended into the realm of foreign affairs. The basis of its foreign policy was alignment with the Western democracies, formalized in

1952 with membership in NATO. At the same time, Turkey's place in the alliance was complicated by its strained and often hostile relations with Greece, its old adversary and a fellow NATO member. The most serious flash point in the 1960s and 1970s between the two countries was the status of the Turkish minority on Cyprus, a Mediterranean island-nation near the Turkish coast with an 80 percent Greek majority. In 1974, with Greek-Turkish relations on the island deteriorating, Turkey invaded Cyprus and occupied 40 percent of the island. Local Turks then proclaimed a "Turkish Republic of Northern Cyprus," which has received no international recognition besides Turkey's. Turkey and Greece also have territorial disputes in the Aegean Sea, where oil has been discovered.

Since the 1980s Turkey has attempted to cement its ties with the West by gaining membership to the European Union. For a long time it was unsuccessful, a major disappointment coming in 1997 when Turkey was not one of the five countries invited to begin the admission process. Turkey's rejection came in part because of economic concerns, but

A vendor in a small, local market in a section of Istanbul.

mainly for political reasons. The most important political issues were Turkey's role in the forceful partition of Cyprus and its human rights record, especially toward the Kurds.

Turkey was more successful in another arena farther to the east: the world of the newly independent Turkic states of the former Soviet Union. These states—Azerbaijan, Turkmenistan, Uzbekistan, Kazakhstan, and Kyrgyzstan—looked to Turkey as a model for nation building. The leaders of several of them also were concerned about Islamic fundamentalism and looked to Turkey for help in dealing with that problem.

If Turkey in many ways stands between Europe and the Middle East, within the Middle East it stands between Israel and the Islamic countries of the region. Turkey and Iran, both Muslim but non-Arab, were the only states in the region to recognize Israel shortly after the founding of the Jewish state. In the decades that followed those relations periodically cooled and warmed, as Turkey sought to remain on good terms with both Israel and the Arab world. In part because of its problems with Syria and Iraq, Turkey in the late 1990s established a close political and military relationship with Israel that included joint military exercises. In foreign affairs, as in domestic matters, Turkey's leaders based their policies on a secular view of their country's national interests. They joined NATO, opposed Islamic fundamentalism in Central Asia, and aligned Turkey with Israel as opposed to Syria and Iraq.

A secular orientation remained the bottom line in the late 1990s as it had been in the early 1920s. The fragile government installed after Erbakan's fall in mid-1997 collapsed at the end of 1998 in the wake of a corruption scandal. Its fall created the opening through which Bulent Ecevit returned to power. The military, which in 1980 had arrested Ecevit and charged him with "acts of treason," welcomed the return of the venerable leftist politician, who like the military itself was militantly anti-Islamic. He made this clear upon assuming the post of prime minister in January 1999 by telling parliament, "To all the problems we face, we shall seek solutions in the enlightened past of timeless leader Ataturk."[3] Another quality Ecevit brought at a time when Turkey was plagued with corruption scandals was a rare and unquestioned reputation for honesty.

Ecevit's immediate tasks were to crack down on Islamic activity and prepare his divided country for national elections. In February 1999 Ecevit received an enormous boost when Turkish commandos secretly went to Kenya and captured Abdullah Ocalan, the leader of the Kurdish rebellion in Turkey and the country's most wanted fugitive. Two months later Ecevit's Democratic Socialist Party won with a plurality of 24 percent of the vote in the parliamentary elections. All the other major parties lost strength; the Virtue Party took only 15 percent of the vote versus 21 percent won by Welfare in the 1995 election.

Although Ecevit appeared to have won a victory for secularism, the immediate aftermath of the election provided yet more proof that Turkey's secular-religious combat was far from over. When parliament met to take its oath of office on May 2, 1999, a thirty-one-year-old member of the Virtue Party named Merve Kavakci arrived wearing the traditional Islamic woman's head scarf. An uproar ensued. As part of the effort to keep Turkish public life secular, the government had long forbidden female university students, lawyers, civil servants, and judges from wearing head scarfs. Pro-secular members of parliament denounced Kavakci. Among them was Ecevit, who told his colleagues:

> No one may interfere with the private life of individuals, but this is not a private space. This is the supreme foundation of the state. It is not a place in which to challenge the state.[4]

When she refused to remove her scarf, Kavakci was not allowed to take the oath of office, which includes a vow to uphold the "principles and reforms of Ataturk." It was difficult to imagine Kavakci adhering to that vow in light of what Ataturk said about head scarfs in 1925:

> In some places I have seen women who put a piece of cloth or a towel or something like it over their heads and

hide their faces. Can the mothers and daughters of a civilized nation adopt this strange manner, the barbarous posture? It is a spectacle that makes the nation an object of ridicule. It must be remedied at once.[5]

The day after she was barred from taking the oath of office Kavakci defiantly announced her determination to take her place in parliament, head scarf and all. "I will cover my head in accordance with my religious beliefs," she said. "It is my personal choice."[6] Several days later the government stripped Kavakci of her Turkish citizenship, using a rarely enforced clause in Turkey's legal code.

While Kavakci's political career appeared over, at least in the short run, the bitter and growing debate over the place of Islam in Turkish life continued. Whereas Kavakci claimed her struggle was "for all women" and "to push for more democratic rights," secular Turks did not see it that way. As a philosophy professor at Istanbul University said of Kavakci and other Islamic politicians, "Their dream is to use democracy to bring an Islamic state."[7] While that statement probably was accurate, it could hardly be said that Turkey was entirely democratic. The country still had laws against "terrorism" that put people who spoke out on a variety of issues on the wrong side of the law and special "state security courts" to put them in jail. In April 1999 Turkey's highest-ranking judge boldly criticized the limits on free speech in his country:

> Although everyone knows that freedom of thought is vital to democracy, we have not been able to overcome obstacles that keep us from establishing it. Allowing people to hold opinions is not enough. They must be able to speak freely. The freedom to express one's thoughts is the basis on which all other freedoms are built.[8]

On no issue was debate more restricted than on the Kurdish rebellion, which by 1999 was fifteen years old. The rebels belonged to the Kurdistan Workers' Party (PKK), whose leader was Abdullah Ocalan. The Kurds began their rebellion in the face of restrictions on their cultural expression that went so far to ban them from speaking their language on the streets and playing their music. By 1999 those restrictions had been removed—the law against speaking Kurdish was repealed in 1991—but the Kurds still lived under oppressive conditions. Education in the Kurdish language was still forbidden. The government kept a tight military rein on the Kurdish region in the country's southeast. As one young Kurd told a Western journalist, "We speak with our eyes." An elderly man added, "You can see us, but you can't hear us. Our lips are sealed."[9]

During fighting that raged for more than fifteen years, Turkish soldiers destroyed three thousand villages, as well as forests where the Kurdish guerrillas tried to hide, and killed more than 20,000 Kurds. The Turks insisted that the Kurds had engaged in terrorism and that Ocalan was guilty of ordering thousands of murders. Aside from more than 30,000 victims on both sides, by 1999 the war was costing Turkey $8 billion a year—the total cost of the war was $100 billion—and tying down more than 200,000 soldiers. In February of that year Ocalan was captured. He was charged with treason and put on trial at the end of May. At his month-long trial Ocalan surprised most observers by calling for peace

One of the longest bridges in the world, the Bosporus Bridge in Turkey, connects two continents, Europe and Asia.

between the two sides. He accepted blame for some of the violence but also justified the Kurdish struggle. He said Kurds would be satisfied with cultural autonomy within a democratic Turkey. Finally, he asked that his life be spared so he could work toward the goals he had outlined.

Ocalan's appeal fell on deaf ears. In June the court found him guilty and sentenced him to hang. The United States and many European governments immediately urged the Turks not to carry out the sentence. Several Turkish intellectuals, including people close to the government, also publicly opposed the death sentence, which as of early 2001 had not been carried out. One newspaper columnist made perhaps the strongest case against carrying out the sentence when he wrote:

> Let us not hang him because he will become a symbol; because Turkey will then be isolated; because a democratic country does not act with vengeance; because terror then will never end; and because Turkey, to remain part of the democratic world, must realize that Kurds are living on their soil and respect their demand to protect their identity.[10]

More than a plea for mercy, the statement was an articulate summary of Turkey's eighty-year struggle to find its place as a member of in the modern democratic world.

The debate over Ocalan's fate took place against the background of dramatic events, both good and bad for Turkey, during the last half of 1999. In August the PKK agreed to a cease-fire and began withdrawing its fighters from the country. However, on August 17, an event that took less than a minute to unfold brought death and devastation to Turkey. A forty-five-second earthquake centered in the northern town of Izmit about 60 miles (96 kilometers) east of Istanbul killed more than 18,000 people. At least 50,000 more were injured and 350,000 left homeless. Many of the dead and injured had lived in newly constructed concrete buildings, which collapsed because they were cheaply built and could not withstand the shock caused by the quake. Ironically, older wooden houses, which were more flexible, stood up to the quake much better than the concrete structures.

Aside from the dreadful human toll, economic losses from the Izmit earthquake were measured in the tens of billions of dollars. This put a severe strain on Turkey's economy, which had prospered during most of the 1990s, growing at rates of 7 or 8 percent in most years, but which had been in a slump since late 1998. A second quake in the same region in November was not as powerful or destructive, but it still caused nearly a thousand deaths. Some better news came in the last month of the century, when on December 11 Turkey finally was invited to join the European Union. But the invitation, while welcome, was only the first step in a process expected to take several years. Nor was it unconditional. To achieve EU membership Turkey would be required to undertake major economic and political reforms, including easing restrictions of freedom of speech and improving its overall human rights record.

THE YEAR 2000 AND AFTER

The new century and millennium began with a new crisis involving Islamic fundamentalism. In January the government launched an offensive against a fundamentalist terrorist group called Hezbollah (but not connected to the group of the same name in Lebanon). The campaign bore quick results, including the death of Hezbollah's leader and the capture of his two closest aides. What followed, however, left the public in shock. Police discovered dozens of bodies, many mutilated by torture, beneath several Hezbollah hideouts. Attention focused in particular on one female victim, Konca Kuris, a popular author and lecturer who had been kidnapped in 1998. Kuris, described by her supporters as a Muslim feminist, had challenged traditional Muslim practices requiring the subjugation of women, arguing they distorted what the Koran actually said. A captured videotape revealed that Kuris had been tortured for weeks before her death.

The news of what Hezbollah had done was bad enough. Then the story became a major national scandal when evidence was uncovered that during the late 1980s and early 1990s government officials had provided Hezbollah with arms to attack Kurdish rebels in southeastern Turkey fighting for independence. These reports helped explain thousands of so-called "mystery killings" in the region that had taken the lives not only of active guerrillas, but of many Kurdish nationals, intellectuals, and businessmen. In the wake of these disturbing revelations, a shaken Prime Minister Ecevit promised operations against Hezbollah would continue until the organization had been wiped out.

Turkey received better news in February when the Kurdistan Workers' Party announced the end of its rebellion and promised to campaign for Kurdish rights by political and democratic means. In May, the parliament chose a new president, Ahmet Secdet Sezer, a former chief justice of Turkey's highest court known for his strong support for the rule of law, free speech, and democracy. Among Sezer's boldest stands prior to being chosen president was his call for the end of Turkey's ban on the teaching and broadcasting of the Kurdish language. As with all civilian politicians in Turkey, President Sezer had to deal with the military, which showed no signs being willing to reduce its role in Turkey's political life. Sezer's stands in favor of secularism certainly matched the military's point of view, but his advocacy of free speech and political reform, and especially his support of Kurdish rights, left him at odds with the generals who ultimately held the bulk of power in Turkey. In April 2001 Sezer visited Europe to advance Turkey's admission to the European Union. He promised to change Turkish law to correspond to European requirements. Whether he could get Turkey's generals and other skeptics in the general population to commit themselves to those promises was a question that remained to be answered.

IRAN

Today's Iranians are the descendants of the ancient Persians, builders of one of the greatest of all Middle Eastern empires more than 2,500 years ago. Persian roots in the Middle East go back another 1,000 years, to about 1500 B.C., when the Aryans, a nomadic Indo-European people, first settled on the Iranian plateau. Under their king Cyrus the Great, the Persians played a heroic role in the Bible when Cyrus allowed the Israelites to return to their homeland in the middle of the sixth century B.C.; under his successors Darius and Xerxes they played the role of villain a half-century later when they tried and failed to conquer the Greeks in the Persian Wars. In the fourth century B.C. the Persians were conquered by the Greek king Alexander the Great. Greek rule lasted less than a century. Beginning in the third century B.C. the Persians were ruled by the Iranian-speaking Parthians, who for several centuries managed to stand firm against the legions of the mighty Roman Empire. In the third century A.D. the Persians regained control of their country under the Sassanid dynasty. Centuries of warfare with the Byzantines weakened the Sassanids and left them vulnerable to conquest by the Muslim Arabs by 650. After the Arab conquest, the Persians gradually abandoned Zoroastrianism, their ancient native religion, for Islam, the religion of their conquerors.

In the centuries that followed the Arab conquest, Persian scholars, scientists, writers, poets, and artists contributed enormously to the development of Islamic civilization. However, unlike the cultures of many other Middle Eastern peoples, Persian culture and language survived Arab rule. They also survived the subsequent conquest and rule by the Seljuk Turks and Mongols. In 1502 the native Safavid dynasty took control of Persia. A vigorous Persian cultural revival followed. The Safavids made the Shiite version of Islam Persia's official state religion; ever since then the country has been the main bastion of the Shiite faith in the Islamic world. After a brief period of Afghan rule in the eighteenth century and two short-lived native dynasties, the Qajar dynasty ruled Persia from 1794 to 1925. During that period European powers increasingly intruded into the Middle East, and Persia became a pawn in the competition between the Russian and British empires. The main positive political development of that era occurred in 1906, when the weakened monarchy was forced to grant Persia a constitution and a parliament, or *Majlis*. The establishment of the Pahlavi dynasty in 1925 by a military officer named Reza Khan marked the beginning of modern Persian, or Iranian, history. A change in the country's name from Persia to Iran in 1935 was symbolic of that transition.

GEOGRAPHY, ECONOMY, PEOPLE

Iran is a rhombus-shaped country east of Anatolia with an area of 636,292 square miles (1,646,000 square kilometers), about a tenth larger than Alaska. Turkey and Iraq lie to the west, Pakistan and Afghanistan to the east. Iran borders on Turkmenistan in the northeast and Azerbaijan and Armenia in the northwest. In between, separating Turkmenistan and Azerbaijan, is Iran's long (about 440 miles, or 700 kilometers) Caspian Sea coastline. The Caspian Sea, the world's largest landlocked salt lake, is a rich fishing ground; more importantly, its waters cover rich oil deposits. To the southeast is the Persian Gulf, the epicenter of the richest oil deposits in the world. Due south, beyond the strategic Strait of Hormuz through which tankers take Persian Gulf oil en route to the world's industrialized nations, is the Gulf of Oman.

Most of Iran is a rugged semiarid plateau about 4,000 feet (1,200 meters) above sea level surrounded by high mountains. Two nearly uninhabited deserts, the *Dasht-e Kavir* (Salt Desert) and *Dasht-e Lut* (Barren Desert), cover much of the eastern part of the country. The salt swamps of the Dasht-e Kavir are so treacherous that they remain largely unexplored. The towering Elburz Mountains in the north, which include several active volcanoes, cut off the well-watered but swampy Caspian coastal area from the rest of the country. The northern slopes of the Elburz range are covered by dense forests that are protected by strict government limits on logging. Just south of the mountains in the shadow of Mount Damavand, a volcano that rises to 18,934 feet (5,771 meters), is Tehran (population 6.7 million), Iran's capital and largest city. The Elburz range extends into Iran's northwestern corner where it shelters Lake Urmia, Iran's largest lake.

The Zagros Mountains cut across southwestern Iran parallel to the Persian Gulf. Southwest of that range is the Karun River, one of the few rivers in Iran that flows all year long. The Karun River basin is Iran's largest fertile lowland. Less than 10 percent of Iran's land area is arable.

Iran has an extreme continental climate. Most of the country is hot and dry in summer and cold and dry in winter. Rainfall occurs mainly in the north along the Caspian coast and nearby mountains, where it falls all year long, and in the mountains of the northwest and west, where it is confined to the winter months. Temperatures reach 104°F (40°C) in the summer along the parched Persian Gulf coast. In areas where high altitude moderates the summer heat, winters are bitterly cold and mountain passes are blocked by snow. The melt-off from the snow is a vital part of Iran's limited water supply. Rainfall in Iran ranges from 50 inches (1,250 millimeters) in the western mountains to less than an inch (25 millimeters) in the eastern deserts.

Iran experiences occasional volcanic eruptions and severe earthquakes. The most recent major earthquake struck northwestern Iran in 1990, killing 40,000 people and injuring 60,000 more.

After Tehran, Iran's next two largest cities are Mashhad (population: 1.9 million), in the northeast, and Isfahan (population 1.25 million), about 200 miles (320 kilometers) south of Tehran. Qum (population 777,000), Iran's eighth-largest city, is more important than its size might suggest. It is Iran's religious center and the birthplace of the movement that in 1979 overthrew Iran's monarchy and established the current Islamic republic. Located about 65 miles (100 kilometers) south of Tehran, Qum is one of the seven cities holy to Shiites and in effect off-limits to non-Muslims.

Economy

Although Iran has a variety of natural resources, they are all overshadowed by oil. Oil first was discovered in Iran in 1908. Most of Iran's oil reserves of about 90 billion barrels, about 9 percent the world's known supply, are found in a 350-mile-long (560-kilometer) region that begins north of the Persian Gulf and runs about halfway down Iran's Persian Gulf coastline. That region falls largely within Khuzistan province, most of whose inhabitants are Arabs who follow the Shiite version of Islam. Oil accounts for about 90 percent of Iran's export earnings and provides the government with 80 percent of its revenue. Iran also has the world's second-largest reserves of natural gas, trailing only the former Soviet Union. If the modern oil industry provides Iran's most valuable export, an ancient craft provides its number-two export:

the world-famous and extraordinarily beautiful Persian carpets. Traditionally each meticulously woven carpet contains a flaw in its design in deference to the Islamic injunction that "only Allah [the Islamic word for God] is perfect." Iran also is the world's largest producer of nuts, and pistachios are its third most valuable export. Other exports include caviar—the tiny but very expensive eggs of the famed Caspian Sea sturgeon—and metal ores.

Iran's main agricultural areas are the Caspian coast, mountain valleys in the northwest, and the Karun River basin. Major crops, aside from nuts, include rice, wheat, barley, hemp, and citrus fruits. Agricultural progress has been held back by outdated methods, overworked soil, and inadequate irrigation. Iran's largest non-oil industry is textiles production, which includes rug weaving. Other major industries produce petrochemicals, weapons, processed foods, and machinery.

People

Only 51 percent of Iran's 69 million people are Persian, that is, native speakers of the Farsi (Persian) language. Most live in cities and towns, as does about 60 percent of the population as a whole, although Persians also live in mountain valleys in central Iran. Turkic-speaking Azerbaijanis account for about a quarter of the population; they are concentrated in Iran's northwest between the Caspian Sea and the Turkish border. In contrast to several other minority groups, the Azerbaijanis are well integrated into Iranian life. There are between 4 and 5 million Kurds in Iran, about 7 percent of the population. The Kurds, whose history in Iran, as elsewhere, has a long tradition of struggling for autonomy, live mainly in the western mountains near the Turkish and Iraqi borders. Their language—actually several dialects that often are not mutually understandable—is related to Persian. Two distant relatives of the Kurds—the Bakhtiari and the Lurs—live in Iran's southwestern Zagros Mountains and account for perhaps 4 percent of the population. Arabs are about 3 percent of the population, but their importance exceeds their numbers because they are concentrated near the Iraqi border in Khuzistan province, the center of Iran's oil industry. A variety of other ethnic groups whose loyalties are tribal or ethnic rather than national complete Iran's population mosaic. In addition, 2 million refugees, mainly Kurds from Iraq and Afghans, currently live in Iran.

About 99 percent of Iran's population are Muslims. Most of them, about 90 percent, are Shiites. Shiite religious solidarity has created a powerful unifying force for Iran, the only large Shiite island in the Sunni Muslim sea that covers most of the Middle East. The remaining 1 percent of the population includes Christians (mainly Armenians and Assyrians), Jews, Zoroastrians—perhaps 30,000 people still practice Iran's ancient native religion—and Baha'is. While most non-Muslim groups have the legal right to practice their religions, all suffer from some degree of discrimination and persecution. The Jewish community, which numbered 80,000 prior to the 1979 Islamic revolution, has shrunk to about 25,000 through emigration. It is subject to periodic attacks by the government, such as the arrest of thirteen Jews in 1999 for alleged "spying." Far worse off, however, are the 350,000 followers of the Baha'i faith. Iran's ruling clerics consider them deserters from Islam and they are denied all religious rights and are regularly subject to severe persecution. In 1999 a report prepared by the United States Department of State listed Iran as one of the most religiously repressive countries in the world.

MODERN IRANIAN HISTORY

The Pahlavi Dynasty (1925–1979)

Reza Khan began a new era in Persian history when he forced the last shah, or emperor, of the Qajar dynasty to go into exile in 1923. He abandoned the idea of turning Persia into a republic because of opposition from religious leaders. Instead, he had the Iranian parliament elect him shah and thereby founded the Pahlavi dynasty.

Reza Shah, as he was called after 1925, was a vigorous modernizer committed to following the example of Mustafa Kemal Ataturk in Turkey. Like Ataturk, Reza Shah ruled with dictatorial powers. Few aspects of Persian life escaped his attention. He reorganized and improved Persia's tax collection system and began construction of a railway to connect Tehran to the Persian Gulf and better tie the country together. He promoted industrialization under state ownership and control, a program that accelerated industrial development but also discouraged private initiative.

Although Islam remained Iran's official religion, Reza Shah introduced secular reforms designed to break the grip of Islamic clerics on Persian life. The state took control of religious schools. Reza Shah established a secular primary education system and in 1934 opened Tehran University, Persia's first university. A new legal system ended the control of religious courts over civil affairs. Other reforms ended legal discrimination against non-Muslims. One of the most important changes was the abolition of the special tax that non-Muslims had previously been forced to pay. Women also were given more legal rights. In 1935 the campaign for modernization was extended to clothing when the government banned the *chador*, the traditional garment that covered a woman's body from head to toe and most of her face. There also was an attempt to rid the Persian language of Arab words and influences.

Reza Shah promoted the development of Persia's oil industry with British help, but he resented British influence in his country. During the 1930s Reza Shah was strongly pro-German as he tried to counter British and Soviet influence in the region. In August 1941, two years after the beginning of World War II, Britain and the Soviet Union occupied Iran to end the shah's cooperation with Nazi Germany. They forced Reza Shah to leave Iran and abdicate in favor of his son, Mohammad Reza Shah Pahlavi. American troops joined the occupation in 1942.

The end of World War II brought unrest rather than genuine peace to Iran. The new shah's first problem was to get the Soviet Union to withdraw its forces from northern Iran, which was achieved in 1946 due to American pressure on the Soviets. The next challenge to the shah came from militant Iranian nationalists led by Mohammad Mossadegh, who became Iran's prime minister in 1951. Mossadegh nationalized Iran's oil industry by seizing control from the previous owners, mainly British (and some American) companies. He also wanted to limit the power of the shah so that parliament, not the shah, would be the real ruler of Iran. Mossadegh's nationalization policies got him into trouble with Western powers whose oil companies had lost property in Iran. In 1953 he was overthrown in a coup organized the American Central Intelligence Agency (CIA). The shah, who had left the country earlier in 1953, returned to his throne with American backing and increased power. However, part of Mossadegh's legacy lived on when Iran's oil industry remained nationalized. American and European oil companies still made out well when the shah negotiated deals that allowed them to manage Iran's oil industry while earning large profits.

After being restored to his throne, the shah gradually consolidated his power and moved Iran firmly into the Western camp during the Cold War. At the same time, the economic gap between rich and poor grew, as did social unrest and political criticism of the shah. Critics of his rule and the concentration of wealth and power in Iran called it "the one thousand family regime." In the early 1960s, the shah responded with a broad program of modernization and social reform he called the "White Revolution." The cornerstone of the program was land reform. The government bought millions of acres from Iran's large landlords and distributed them to landless peasants, along with lands owned by the royal family. Within three years, 1.5 million tenant farmers became landowners. There were improvements in education and health care and profit sharing for factory workers. In 1963 women received the right to vote.

While the "White Revolution" had many supporters, it also had powerful opponents, including landowners and Islamic religious leaders. The Islamic leaders were especially opposed to granting women rights and to other measures, such as the introduction of a secular calendar, that undermined their authority. Leftist groups wanted more radical change and opposed the shah's dictatorial methods. In 1963 there were violent riots against the shah and his policies led by a militant Islamic cleric, the Ayatollah Ruhollah Khomeini. The shah reacted to the riots, and to all other dissent, with force. Khomeini was arrested and eventually exiled from Iran.

The shah meanwhile used his growing oil revenues for a variety of expensive and prestigious projects, such as building a subway for Tehran. He spent billions on modern American weapons to make Iran the most powerful military power in the Persian Gulf region. Iran was a steadfast American ally, aside from Israel and Turkey the most consistently pro-American country in the Middle East. As long as oil revenues grew and the standard of living rose in Iran, despite great inequalities, the shah was able to maintain a strong base of support. Those who did not support his regime were silenced by his dreaded secret police, the Savak. However, after 1975 oil prices fell, government revenues declined, and the shah had to cancel many projects. This hurt businesspeople and the middle class. Rapid population growth meant numerous young people entering the labor force who could not find jobs. Peasants who had received their own land often could not make a living on their small farms. Opposition to the shah swelled.

The shah's repressive policies had the effect of channeling much of that opposition into the hands of Islamic militants like Khomeini, who continued to agitate against the shah from outside the country. One reason was that in Iran's oppressive political environment there were few places Iranians could gather for political discussions. Practically the only places Iranians, especially the young, could meet undisturbed were in mosques and religious clubs controlled by Islamic leaders. This was because security forces were reluctant to move against religious institutions.

The shah also offended Iranian nationalist sentiments by inviting thousands of foreign civilian and military experts into Iran. If nothing else, their high standard of living, which few Iranians could match, intensified discontent. So did runaway corruption that extended throughout the government and reached the royal family. By the late 1970s antigovernment riots and government repression were becoming increasing violent and bloody. The regime faced a wall of opposition that extended across the political spectrum from the pro-Communist left to the militant Islamic right. Discontent and disorder had reached the point where they had become a threat to the shah's power.

The collapse came with shocking suddenness. The most effective opponents of the regime were supporters of the Ayatollah Khomeini, who thundered against the shah from his base of exile in France. In late 1978 the shah's regime, once so vigorous and still heavily armed with the most modern weapons, simply crumbled. On January 16, 1979, the shah, who unknown to the public was suffering from cancer, announced he was leaving the country to go on "vacation." He would never return.

By February 1 Khomeini was back in Iran. Now it was the turn of the secular nationalist and radical left opponents of the shah, who had been cheering his departure, to experience their own rapid and bitter defeat. The shah's secular opponents were divided into many groups, ranging from democrats to Communists. None of them had a broad or solid social base. In contrast, the Islamic forces were tightly organized. They could count on the strong religious convictions of millions of Iranians and had a dynamic and charismatic leader in Khomeini. Within ten days of his arrival in Iran, Khomeini was in control of the country. He appointed a provisional government, but real power lay with a fifteen-member Islamic Revolutionary Council that Khomeini had established while in exile. Bands of armed "Revolutionary Guards" were organized to counter the army, which Khomeini did not control, and intimidate any opponents. It took Khomeini and his supporters only three months to sweep aside anyone who wanted a secular regime. Protests from democratic groups against the perfunctory trials and immediate executions of hundreds of officials of the fallen regime were ignored.

At the end of March 1979 Iranians voted in a national referendum that asked a single question: Did they want an Islamic republic? There was good reason to doubt the official figures that 92.5 of eligible voters cast ballots and of those 92.8 percent voted for an Islamic republic. But it did not matter. As of April 1, 1979, a monarchy that traced its roots back 2,500 years to Cyrus the Great was gone. In its place was the Ayatollah Khomeini's newly declared Islamic Republic of Iran, the first Islamic state of that type in history.

The Islamic Republic Under Khomeini (1979–1989)

The year 1979 was one of revolutionary change and continuous turmoil. Khomeini and the Islamic clerics began a process of rapid and thorough Islamization of Iranian society. They banished programs and music from radio and television and closed down newspapers that did not support the Islamic revolution. Women were forced to wear traditional Islamic clothing, including the veil, that covered their entire bodies. Banks, factories, and other businesses were nationalized. Political parties of all kinds were crippled. The only political organization that managed to survive the onslaught as a viable opposition was the *Mujahrdeen Klaq* (People's Holy Warriors), a group that was both Marxist and Islamist. It declared armed resistance against the Khomeini regime.

The new constitution, while providing for a parliament and a president to govern the county, placed all power firmly in the hands of Iran's Muslim clergy. The ultimate power was Khomeini himself, who became the country's spiritual leader—or supreme leader—for life. His powers included control of the armed forces and Revolutionary Guard, the right to declare war, and the authority to dismiss the president. His successor after his death would be chosen by the Assembly of Experts, an elected body of about eighty Islamic clerics. A twelve-member Council of Guardians that included specialists on Islamic law appointed by the supreme leader supervised the work of the parliament. Its job was to make sure all laws were consistent with Islamic teaching. The council also had the power to invalidate laws passed by parliament and determine who could run for president. The Sharia (Islamic law) became the law of the land in personal, criminal, and property matters, and the Shiite version of Islam became the country's official religion. Iran, in short, was being turned into a totalitarian Islamic society, although not without resistance. Tens of thousands of Iranians fled abroad. They included many wealthy people and supporters of the shah, but also many of the country's most highly educated citizens. The departure of thousands of educated and business people helped cripple the economy. Iran continued to be rocked by demonstrations by workers and farmers hurt by economic decline, battles between rival political factions, political assassinations, and executions.

While all this was happening, on November 4, 1979, a group of radical students invaded the U.S. Embassy and seized sixty-six American hostages. Thirteen were released, but the Khomeini regime, which had labeled the United States the "Great Satan" and Iran's number-one enemy, refused to secure the release of the remaining captives. The United States broke diplomatic relations and imposed an economic boycott on Iran. A rescue attempt in April 1980 failed, badly embarrassing U.S. president Jimmy Carter. The crisis dragged on for 444 days until January 20, 1981, when Carter left office and Ronald Reagan was inaugurated as president. Iran then released the hostages, but American-Iranian relations remained in a bitterly deep freeze.

The end of the hostage crisis brought Iran little relief. Although the country held presidential and parliamentary elections in 1980, they were tightly controlled and the results were a foregone conclusion. The successful presidential candidate was a former adviser to Khomeini, Abolhassan Bani-Sadr. Bani-Sadr, who had studied economics, sociology, and Islamic law as a university student, was a relative moderate in the context of Iranian politics. He lasted in office barely eighteen months, until Khomeini engineered his removal in June 1981, after which Bani-Sadr fled to France. By 1981 political life was turning increasingly violent. In June a bomb killed seventy-four of Iran's leading Islamic politicians; the next month another bomb killed the country's president and prime minister. The Khomeini regime responded with a full-scale attack on the Mujahrdeen Klaq, killing between five to six thousand people over the next several years. By 1985, at least seven thousand political opponents of the regime of various stripes had been executed.

The worst crisis of the Islamic Republic's first decade erupted in September 1980 when Iraq invaded Iran. The Iraqi dictator Saddam Hussein feared the Iranian revolution might spread to his country. He calculated that an attack while the Khomeini regime was young and still relatively weak would cause its collapse. Hussein also hoped to use the turmoil in Iran to seize full control of the Shatt-al-Arab, a tidal river on the Iran-Iraq border, and the oil-rich province of Khuzistan, a region populated by Arabs. The Iraqis enjoyed early victories, but then the Iranians regrouped. Their soldiers, fired by religious faith, fought with suicidal devotion and in 1981 and 1982 drove the Iraqis back. At that point Khomeini refused an Iraqi peace offer. He demanded that Iraq first remove Hussein from power and pay Iran $150 billion in war damages. The war continued, turning into a bloody stalemate that dragged on for a total of eight years. Both sides attacked the other's cities, oil production facilities, and even oil tankers of neutral nations in the Persian Gulf. The Iraqi use of chemical weapons against Iranian troops was especially devastating and terrifying.

By 1988, defeats on the battlefield and soaring combat deaths finally convinced Khomeini to make peace. He said having to make peace with Iraq was like being forced "to drink the poison cup." Neither side made any gains in the long war. At least half a million soldiers on both sides were dead and two million people were injured. The war left Iran physically exhausted and financially bankrupt.

Iran's war with Iraq was forced on it by Iraqi aggression. At the same time, Iran could have ended the war in 1982 rather than 1988 had Khomeini not turned it into what amounted to a Shiite religious crusade. That crusade in fact dominated Iran's relations with the rest of the outside world. Khomeini denounced the regimes of the Arab states surrounding Iran for betraying Islam and proclaimed the goal of exporting the Iranian revolution to the entire Muslim world. Some of the worst tensions were with Saudi Arabia and the other Arab Persian Gulf states. Relations with Saudi Arabia neared rock bottom in 1987, when 275 Iranian pilgrims to Mecca, Islam's holiest city, died during rioting there.

Khomeini meanwhile bitterly denounced the West, especially the United States, the country he called the "Great Satan." To drive the point home, Iranian children regularly chanted "Death to America" in elementary schools. Iran became a leading supporter of international terrorist groups, mainly Arab groups in the Middle East, but also radical groups in Europe. Aside from the United States, a special target of hatred was Israel. The Khomeini regime financed a long list of murderous attacks against Israel by various Arab terrorist organizations, as well as attacks against Jewish communities elsewhere in the world. It also violently opposed any attempt, regardless of the source, to promote peace between Israel and Arabs. Egypt therefore was subject to scathing Iranian denunciations for signing a peace treaty with Israel in 1979. Nor did Iran's position change after Khomeini's death in 1989. In 1999, twenty years after Egyptian president Anwar Sadat made peace with Israel, Tehran honored one of Sadat's assassins by naming a street after him.

The Islamic Republic After Khomeini

The Ayatollah Khomeini died on June 6, 1989. Hundreds of thousands of people attended his funeral as the Islamic Republic mourned the passing of its founder and spiritual leader. Khomeini left his successors a revolution that was deeply entrenched, but also a country badly debilitated by war and burdened with a shattered economy. Their urgent task was to restore Iran to physical health, while simultaneously maintaining the dominance of Islamic values and the spirit of the Islamic revolution they had imposed on Iranian society with such great effort and at such great cost to the Iranian people.

The day after Khomeini's death Iran's Assembly of Experts elected the Ayatollah Ali Khamenei as the country's supreme leader. A former student of Khomeini, Khamenei served as Iran's president from 1981 until his election as supreme leader. His replacement as president was another cleric, Ali Akbar Hashemi Rafsanjani, until then speaker of the Iranian parliament. Shortly after Rafsanjani's election the post of prime minister was abolished and its powers transferred to the president.

Although Iran's supreme leader and president were both Islamic clerics, there were differences between them that reflected a larger division among the Islamic clerics who ruled Iran. Compared to the new supreme leader, Rafsanjani was relatively moderate and pragmatic. He wanted to focus on economic reform and slightly tone down Iran's militant foreign policy in order to improve relations with Western Europe. Rafsanjani did not, however, intend to forsake the goal of spreading Iran's Islamic Revolution or reduce hostility to the United States or Israel. In any event, while the president generally was more popular with the Iranian people than his archconservative rivals, it was the conservatives who controlled the key levers of power and ultimately determined policy.

Rafsanjani's attempts to reform the economy were thwarted by impersonal and uncontrollable market forces as well as by conservative clerics. The fall in oil prices on international markets reduced government revenues and hurt the Iranian economy. Periodic protests testified to hardships endured by ordinary Iranians who had no other way of expressing their discontent. There were riots in several cities protesting cuts in state subsidies for basic goods in 1994. In 1995 the government, strapped for cash, doubled the price of petroleum products. This led to other price increases and, in April, to serious riots in the poor sections of Tehran.

The gulf between the relative moderates and the archconservatives among Iran's ruling clerics widened as a result of the presidential election of 1997. One of the four candidates approved by the Council of Guardians—it rejected 234—was Sayed Mohammad Khatami, a respected cleric with relatively moderate views. Khatami won the election with more than 69 percent of the vote and received especially strong support from women, young people, and the business community. Khatami's election was clear evidence that the conservative clerics who still held the important reins of power were increasingly out of touch with the people they ruled, especially with the younger generation. A publisher in Tehran explained the appeal that translated into so many votes:

> Everybody was depressed. It seemed that laughing was forbidden. Khatami had a huge open smile. He showed he cared about people.[11]

After his election Khatami spoke openly about the need for economic reform and fewer restrictions on the lives of the people. Yet despite his popularity he could do little of substance because of conservative opposition. The conservatives flexed their muscles in 1998 by bringing corruption charges against a key Khatami ally, Gholamhossein Karbaschi, who had been the mayor of Iran for eight years. Despite Khatami's efforts—he did succeed in getting the prison term reduced and an additional penalty of sixty lashes changed to a fine—Karbaschi began serving a two-year prison term in 1999. (He was pardoned by Khamenei and released from prison in January 2000.) Conservatives also dominated the 1998 elections to the Assembly of Experts. This was hardly a surprise since the candidates were carefully screened by the Council of Guardians, which disqualified virtually all moderates.

Whatever his problems at home, President Khatami was determined to improve Iran's relations with the outside world and end what in effect was two decades of self-imposed isolation. To that end he traveled abroad. In the fall of 1998 Khatami addressed the United Nations General Assembly in New York. In March 1999 he became the first Iranian leader in two decades to set foot in Europe when he visited Italy and met with Pope John Paul II at the Vatican. In May, he visited three Arab states, beginning with Syria, Iran's only ally in the Arab world, and finishing with Saudi Arabia and Qatar, with whom relations had been poor for years. The trip ignited an angry debate among Iran's Persian Gulf Arab neighbors. The United Arab Emirates (UAE), which had a long-standing territorial dispute with Iran over three small islands in the Persian Gulf, strongly criticized the Saudis for warming up to Iran. The UAE feared any Saudi-Iranian reconciliation with Iran would come at its expense.

Nor did Khatami's foreign visits allay concerns about other Iranian intentions that went far beyond the Persian Gulf. Iran was known to have extensive programs to develop biological, chemical, and nuclear weapons. It also was developing long-range guided missiles with ranges as long as 2,400 miles (3,600 kilometers) capable of carrying nuclear warheads. Iran was seeking technological assistance for these programs from various sources, including China, North Korea, and Russia. Russia's decision to sell Iran reactors for a nuclear power plant was of particular concern to the United States because those reactors might advance Iran's nuclear weapons program. Iran's effort to hire Russian scientists for their weapons programs also was worrisome. There was no doubt that Russian experts, lured by the promise of large salaries, were in Iran working to build weapons of mass destruction and guided missiles. A reasonable estimate was that advanced missiles might be operational by 2002 and nuclear warheads five years after that. Given Iran's militancy and its extensive support of Islamic terrorist groups, its ambitious weapons programs worried countries throughout the Middle East, and beyond it as well.

The Post-Khomeini Generation

In the spring of 1999 three couples in their twenties were strolling along a river high in the mountains overlooking Tehran. Nearby others were enjoying the lush scenery and clear mountain air that provided a welcome escape from the tension and pollution of Iran's capital city. Suddenly a stranger walked up to one of the young men and asked accusingly:

> What are you doing? Why are you holding that woman's hand? Are you afraid someone will steal her?[12]

This incident said a great deal about the condition of Iran's twenty-year-old Islamic revolution as it faced its third decade, and a new millennium. The man who accosted the young couples was acting with the approval of Iran's conservative clerics. His actions reflected their determination to make sure all citizens behave according to strict Islamic practices. In this case, the couples, just by holding hands, had violated rules against men and women displaying affection in public. On the other hand, the reaction of the couples reflected how difficult that is going to be. The young people said nothing in public; that would be too dangerous. But in private they expressed anger and resentment at the Islamic clergy that was interfering in their lives and not allowing them to enjoy themselves.

That attitude was widespread among the two-thirds of the Iranian population that was twenty-five or younger, too young to remember the shah and life before the Islamic Republic. Many were simply fed up with the dreary and humorless life the Islamic authorities continue to impose on them. They secretly went to underground merchants to rent or buy bootleg tapes of banned American movies, such as *Big Momma's House* or *Hollow Man*, or special television programs such as the annual Academy Awards. As of mid-2000, the going price to rent a tape in Tehran was the equivalent of about $1; the same tape could be bought for about $8. Bootleg audio-cassettes of music by performers ranging from Britney Spears and Madonna to the Backstreet Boys sold for about a dollar. Also popular were exiled Iranian artists living in places like Los Angeles. They included a famous singer named Googoosh, one of Iran's superstars before the 1979 Islamic revolution whose music combined Western styles with Persian traditions. Silent for twenty-one years before she left Iran in 2000, her performances in the United States were smuggled into Iran on audio-cassettes and compact discs, where they then reached across the generations. As a political scientist once imprisoned under the shah observed about his students:

> The younger generation has no attachment, no feeling for the revolution. When I teach the revolution, many of my students just look out the window and watch the clock. They say: "What about us? You had your revolution and your war. What's in it for us?" And I can't tell them the answer.[13]

A young man in his late twenties, who had been lashed as punishment for being the lead singer in a rock band, went further. He dared to compare the Islamic Republic to the United States and to Iran before the revolution:

> We have no money and no amusement. I haven't seen America but have heard only good things about it, that you have freedom and an easy life there. Like we hear how it was in the Shah's time—a free and easy life. We loved the Shah. But we don't like this regime. This is not true Islam. . . . I wish we could go back to the old days. If only there could be a disco.[14]

One of the most serious results of this frustration was growing drug addiction. Iran's border with Afghanistan, a major producer of opium, was an open tap for the flow of drugs. By 1999 Iran had an estimated 1.2 million drug addicts; 60 percent of the country's prison inmates were jailed for drug possession. Many of the drug addicts were jobless young men. In Islamshar, a town just south of Tehran, one young man in his twenties explained to an American reporter why there were so many drug addicts in his town:

> Look at all of us. We're all jobless. We have nothing to do. We try to do a little bit of business here and they arrest us as hooligans. That's why there are so many addicts here. It's the despair.[15]

Many young women also were deeply dissatisfied with life in Iran. The irony of this was that the regime's problems with women were in part the product of a policy that had improved their lives: providing educational opportunity. Under the Islamic Republic the literacy rate among women more than doubled to 74 percent. Whereas a third of university students were women before the revolution, by 1999 half were. One-third of all Iranian doctors were women and women were active in many other professions. Yet the regime insisted they cover their entire bodies and their hair in public, live under laws that allow men to have several wives, and endure other forms of legal and social discrimination. Behind closed doors, especially in the cities, it was different: Many women wore makeup, fashionable and even sexy Western clothing, and danced to Western music. The Islamic Revolution was kept outside. One twenty-two-year-old student, who prefers to wear T-shirts and jeans indoors, expressed support for President Khatami but also added:

> We have an expression: whatever we have woven becomes threads instead of cloth. The Islamic regime has failed to win the loyalty of the children of the revolution.[16]

Khatami himself understood that Iran's Islamic revolution was in trouble. At the same time, notwithstanding his pre-

Iranian girls on a day trip to a park in 2000

sumed moderation, he was entirely loyal to it and part of the Islamic power structure. In 1999, in a speech marking the revolution's twentieth anniversary, he warned the Iranian people:

> Poisonous winds are blowing inside and outside the country. And enemies are attempting to separate you from the revolution.[17]

Yet disillusionment had reached beyond the young generation to people who remembered the shah and what they considered a better life. While the youth complained about freedom they could only imagine, older people, worn down by two decades of economic privation, bitterly remembered better times. "We haven't had a good meal in 20 years," a thirty-seven-year-old farmer told a Western journalist. "I don't care about the revolution. The problem is we can't live."[18] After twenty years, Iran's ruling clerics still firmly controlled the reins of power. But they no longer controlled what people were thinking, certainly a "poisonous wind" for any dictatorial revolution.

The dissatisfaction of the young generation burst into the open in the summer of 1999. In July students at Tehran University protested against the slow pace of reform in general and new restrictions on freedom of the press in particular. The government responded with a violent raid on the student dorms by police and militant Islamic vigilantes that left dozens of people wounded and more than twenty people hospitalized. The student demonstrations then spread quickly to eighteen cities involving tens of thousands of participants, and the regime responded with further violence. The student protesters loudly proclaimed their allegiance to President Mohammad Khatami and his program of reform, and no doubt meant what they said. Yet in reality their movement had become the most serious domestic threat in twenty years to Iran's Islamic Republic. When President Khatami finally spoke out five days after the protests began, it was not as a reformer. Echoing the remarks he made a few months earlier, he took pains to distance himself from the students, who he said were led by people with "devilish aims." The protests, he added, were "intended to attack the foundations of the system and lead the country into anarchy."[19]

Khatami's statement underscored that the Ayatollah Khamenei and the Islamic clerical power structure were calling the shots. In the end, the regime's use of force and the threat of severe punishment brought the student protests to an end after nine days. Nor did Khatami's reelection in June of 2001 with 77 percent of the vote have any noticeable effect on the ultraconservative clerics who controlled Iran. Left unsettled was whether an entire generation, and especially its educated elite, would continue to bend to the will of religious extremists who insisted that demands for basic human freedoms had no place in Iran.

The year 1999 ended with a highly publicized trial, which in December resulted in a five-year jail term for a popular and respected reformist Islamic cleric named Abdullah Nouri. A newspaper editor and close adviser to President Khatami, Nouri had insisted that religious hard-liners had betrayed Iran's 1979 revolution by placing themselves above the law. For that and other comments urging moderation, he was found guilty of insulting Islam and defying its beliefs, of spreading lies and "sowing confusion," and of insulting the Ayatollah Khomeini, who held an almost godlike status among Iran's conservative Islamic hard-liners.

After the Millennium

The first major event of the new century and millennium in Iran was the election of a new parliament. The election was viewed as something of a showdown between President Khatami and his fellow reformers and hard-line conservative clerics loyal to supreme leader Ayatollah Khamenei. Prior to the election, the Council of Guardians, the powerful supervisory body made up of twelve clerics and Islamic lawyers and a bastion of conservative power, disqualified more than four hundred candidates nominated by reform groups. This interference did little good. When the smoke cleared after two rounds of voting, the larger and decisive round in March and a smaller round in May, reformers had won more than two-thirds of the seats. Of course, real power lay with Khamenei and the Council of Guardians, not the weak parliament or president, and Khamenei made this clear when he began a crackdown on the press in April. By August, more than twenty reformist newspapers had been closed and more than a dozen journalists jailed. They included Ibrahim Nabavi, generally regarded as Iran's best political satirist and cartoonist, who was sent to prison without the benefit of a trial.

The conservatives meanwhile were pushing their offensive on other fronts as well. In July a judge convicted ten Jews of spying for Israel, sentencing them to terms of four to thirteen years. By then the defendants—who included a rabbi, two university professors, and a youth sixteen years old when the case began—already had spent fifteen months in jail. The charges clearly had been trumped up, and Western observers immediately criticized the verdict, pointing out the complete lack of evidence and the failure to give the defendants a fair trial. The trial and verdict shook Iran's dwindling Jewish community and seemed likely to accelerate emigration of Jews from Iran, where their situation clearly was increasingly insecure. However, the main target of the entire affair probably was President Khatami, or at least his foreign policy. In particular, hard-liners wanted to undermine Khatami's efforts to improve relations with the West, a policy opposed by supreme leader Khamenei and the rest of the conservative establishment. In December 2000, President Khatami and the reformers received another blow when the conservatives drove Ataollah Mohajerani, the moderate minister of culture, from office. A supporter of greater freedom of the press and artistic expression, Mohajerani had survived an attempt to remove him in 1999 when he made a dramatic speech to parliament laced with Persian proverbs. But a year later pressure on him was too great to resist, and he resigned his position.

As 2001 began, hard-line Islamic conservatives clearly were in charge in Iran, and they showed no sign of compromising with the reformers. But in three consecutive elections—the presidential election of 1997, the parliamentary elections of 2000, and the presidential election of 2001—more than two-thirds of the electorate had sided with those calling for change. Iran faced a quandary from which there seemed to be no easy way out.

CHAPTER 6

The Arabian Peninsula: Saudi Arabia, Yemen, Oman, Kuwait, United Arab Emirates, Qatar, Bahrain

The Arabian Peninsula is a arid plateau of about 1 million square miles (2.6 million square kilometers) that looks like a gigantic boot. It juts out in a southeasterly direction from the Fertile Crescent toward the Gulf of Aden and the Arabian Sea, flanked by the Red Sea on the west and the Persian Gulf and Gulf of Oman on the east. Its enormous oil resources, the largest in the world, make what otherwise would be a barren backwater one of the most valuable pieces of real estate in the world.

As its name suggests, the Arabian Peninsula is the ancient homeland of the Arab people who today form a majority of the population of the Middle East. It is also the birthplace of Islam, the youngest of the world's three major monotheistic religions and the religion of most Middle Easterners. The peninsula has rarely been under the control of a single power. Ancient Middle Eastern empires from the Egyptian to Persian, daunted by its enormous deserts, stopped their conquests at its northernmost fringe. Alexander the Great, Europe's first empire builder, who conquered the Persian Empire, stayed away completely. Even the mighty Roman Empire was limited to a tiny toehold on the peninsula's northwestern corner. The Ottoman Turks tried to grab it all, but failed. The peninsula was unified by the Arabs themselves shortly after the founding of Islam in the seventh century, but only for a short time. Several parts became independent when the Arabs expanded their conquests and moved their capital from Medina, in the western part of the peninsula, to Damascus, in what today is Syria.

Today seven countries occupy the Arabian Peninsula: Saudi Arabia, Kuwait, Bahrain, the United Arab Emirates (UAE), Qatar, Oman, and Yemen. All except Yemen are traditional Arab monarchies whose rulers wield absolute power. The ruling families not only select the monarch himself— either a king, emir (prince), or sultan—but occupy virtually all key positions of power. While there may be advisory councils, some of whose members are elected (in Kuwait's case an elected parliament), and possibly constitutions, these institutions exist at the whim of the ruler. Political parties are illegal. In essence, the monarchies of the Arabian Peninsula have less in common with modern nation-states than they do with ancient or feudal principalities. As such, they are among the world's most fragile political entities.

Fragile or not, the six monarchies of the Arabian Peninsula are enormously wealthy. They control about half of the world's known oil reserves and in three cases (Saudi Arabia, Kuwait, and the UAE) are using up their resources at a slower rate than producers elsewhere in the world. In 1981, Saudi Arabia, Kuwait, the UAE, Bahrain, Qatar, and Oman formed the Gulf Cooperation Council (GCC). The GCC's main purpose was to promote regional security. It also worked to encourage economic cooperation. The GCC's members often are called the Gulf states.

In three of the Gulf states—Kuwait, Qatar, and the UAE— noncitizens, mainly foreign Arabs and south Asians, make up most of the workforce and the overwhelming majority of the population. All six states were hurt by low oil prices that have prevailed, aside from a few exceptional years, from the late 1980s through mid-1999. They were forced to cut their budgets, which supported extravagant welfare states for their citizens. In December 1998 Saudi Arabia's Crown Prince Abdullah warned, "The boom days are over, and they will not come back."[1] Crown Prince Abdullah's warning was at least partially premature. In March 1999 the Gulf states met their comembers of the Organization of Petroleum Exporting Countries (OPEC), the eleven-nation cartel whose member nations control three-quarters of the world's known oil reserves. OPEC's members agreed to cut oil production by about 5 percent, and with less oil available on international markets prices rose quickly, tripling over the next eighteen months. While this huge price increase did not quite bring back the "boom times" of twenty years earlier, it did provide a huge income windfall for the oil-producing Gulf states. Beyond that, their enormous oil reserves remained a guarantee of continued great wealth for a long time to come.

SAUDI ARABIA

Saudi Arabia is a land of contrasts and contradictions. The driest country in the world, its sands hold the world's largest pools of oil. Although it forbids the practice of any religion other than Islam, it depends on non-Islamic countries for protection against its powerful Islamic neighbors. Ruled by a fundamentalist Islamic regime, it nonetheless is threatened by subversion from even stricter fundamentalist movements. Despite billions of dollars spent on the most modern armaments, it is militarily weak. Although its economy has modernized, its political system remains traditional. While it constantly imports Western technology and expertise, it desperately tries to keep out Western ideas and cultural influences. And despite enormous oil revenues and a relatively small population, in recent years it has been unable to balance its budget.

GEOGRAPHY, ECONOMY, PEOPLE

Geography
Saudi Arabia has an area of approximately 865,000 square miles (2,240,000 square kilometers), about one-third the size of the United States. It occupies about 80 percent of the Arabian Peninsula, virtually all of it desert. Saudi Arabia's northern neighbors are Kuwait, Iraq, and Jordan. Coastlines along the Gulf of Aqaba and the Red Sea form its western border.

To the south are Yemen and Oman, and to the east are the United Arab Emirates (UAE), Qatar, and the Persian Gulf. Saudi Arabia's desert borders with Yemen, Oman, and the UAE remain undefined. Saudi Arabia for many years shared two "neutral zones," one with Iraq and the other with Kuwait. In 1975 Saudi Arabia and Iraq divided their zone. The neutral zone shared with Kuwait was divided in 1966, but revenues from oil resources are shared.

There are no permanent rivers in Saudi Arabia. Its parched *Rub al-Khali* (Empty Quarter) desert in the south, an area as large as Texas, can go without rain for ten years. Northern regions get some rain, usually between 4 and 8 inches (100 to 200 millimeters). Summer temperatures in the interior reach 129°F (54°C); the coastal areas are not much cooler and extremely humid. Winters are mild, although northern and central regions can see nighttime temperatures drop below freezing.

In addition to the Empty Quarter desert, Saudi Arabia has four other main regions. The largest is the barren central plateau, called the Nejd. It varies in altitude from 2,000 feet (600 meters) in the east to about 5,000 feet (1,520 meters) in the west. The rugged northwest region along the Red Sea—there is almost no coastal plain—is called the Hejaz. The Asir region extends down the Red Sea coast from the Hejaz to the border with Yemen. It features Saudi Arabia's highest mountains, gets more rain than any other part of the country, and has a fertile, but narrow, coastal plain. Saudi Arabia's barren Eastern Province along the Persian Gulf is the site of its enormous oil fields.

The two most important cities in Saudi Arabia are Mecca (population 618,000) and Medina (population 500,000). Located in the Hejaz, they are Islam's two holiest cities. Mecca, the birthplace of the Prophet Mohammad, is Islam's holiest site, the place to which every Muslim is supposed to make a pilgrimage, or *hajj*, once in his or her lifetime. Riyadh (population 3.5 million), in the Nejd, is the country's capital and largest city. Jiddah (population 1.4 million), on the Red Sea coast about 50 miles (80 kilometers) west of Mecca, is Saudi Arabia's administrative capital.

A street scene in Jiddah, a port city on the Red Sea

Economy

When the twentieth century began, Saudi Arabia's economy was based on camel raising by nomads, limited farming, fishing and shipping along the coast, and a little commerce. Taxes on pilgrims making the *hajj* was an important source of income. Altogether, it added up to a very meager living for most of the population. Everything changed with the discovery of oil in 1938. Large-scale production began after World War II. In 1969 revenues reached $1 billion. They reached $25 billion in 1975 and hit a peak of $110 billion in 1981, after which they declined along with world demand.

Modern Saudi Arabia's economy is completely dominated by and dependent on oil. After oil was discovered in Saudi

Arabia, its resources were developed by the Arabian-American Oil Company (Aramco), a consortium of American oil companies. The Saudi government received a percentage of the profits. Between 1973 and 1980 the Saudi government bought 100 percent of Aramco; in 1988 it changed the company's name to the Saudi Arabian Oil Company.

Saudi Arabia's fourteen major fields contain one-fourth of the world's reserves, almost 300 billion barrels, and it is the world's largest producer and exporter of oil. Oil revenues make up three-quarters of government revenues—Saudi Arabians pay no taxes—and almost 95 percent of all export earnings. Revenues, however, have fluctuated, depending on the world price of oil, which in recent decades has jumped above $40 per barrel and sunk as low as $10. Depending on a variety of economic and political factors, Saudi production of oil in recent decades has ranged from between 5 and 10 million barrels per day. During the second half of the 1990s the government's annual oil revenues ranged from about $38 to $55 billion. Saudi Arabia also has other mineral resources, including significant deposits of natural gas.

Saudi Arabia has played a central role in the Organization of Petroleum Exporting Countries (OPEC). OPEC is dominated by Middle Eastern oil-producing countries and has tried to maintain a high price for its members by controlling production. Usually Saudi Arabia has played a moderating role in OPEC, trying to avoid excessive price increases. Saudi reasons for moderation reflect self-interest. Stable prices are the best way to generate the long-term revenues the kingdom needs for economic development. The Saudis calculate moderate oil prices also will help ensure that the industrialized nations are not encouraged to develop alternative sources of energy that eventually might replace oil. At the same time, the Saudis have supported using oil as a political weapon. They played a central role in the Arab oil boycott of the United States after the U.S. supported Israel in the 1973 Arab-Israeli war (Yom Kippur War).

Oil revenues have paid for a generous program of social services that includes free education and medical care for all Saudi citizens. Gasoline and electricity prices are kept low by government subsidies. Oil has made millionaires and

even billionaires out of princes in the Saudi royal family and other well-connected Saudi businessmen. It has paid for huge construction projects that have transformed Saudi Arabia's old cities and created entirely new ones, and for the building of expensive modern factories that now produce petrochemicals, steel, and cement.

Oil revenues also have financed the construction of more than thirty plants to desalinize (take the salt out of) seawater. These plants currently supply Saudi Arabia with more than 70 percent of its drinking water.

Oil revenues also pay for an expensive project to extract underground fossil water for use in agriculture. Fossil water is underground water left over from many thousands of years ago when the local climate was wetter. The problem is that, like oil, this water is not renewable. The Saudis are using it to irrigate newly developed wheat fields. They now grow all the wheat they need, and even export some. But Saudis are eating and selling wheat that is the world's most expensive to produce. It would be much more economical for the country to import the wheat it needs. Instead, largely as a matter of pride, the Saudi government subsidizes the wheat so it can find customers at home and abroad. Meanwhile, nobody is certain when the irreplaceable fossil water will run out, although twenty-five years is a good guess. Other Saudi crops, grown on oases or on the limited fertile land in the Asir region, include dates, tomatoes, barley, and bananas. With its rapidly expanding population, Saudi Arabia must import about two-thirds of its food.

While the Saudi government has used its oil revenues to develop the country, it has also wasted vast sums of money. Extravagant public projects—the use of fossil water for farming is an example—poor planning, wildly opulent palaces, and other perks for a royal family with four thousand princes have drained the government treasury. Eighty percent of the country's budget regularly has gone to pay salaries of public sector employees. Because the government controls the oil industry and so many other businesses, private enterprise accounts for only 35 percent of the country's gross domestic product. War has been another large expense.

The Saudis spent more than $25 billion to support Iraq during the Iran-Iraq War. The Gulf War cost them another $65 billion. Foreign-made weapons for the Saudi military cost tens of billions more. These expenses, combined with reduced oil revenues in the 1980s and 1990s, led to budget deficits, forcing the Saudi government to cut expenses and undertake other reforms. In 1999 the budget deficit reached almost $10 billion and forced the Saudi government to borrow abroad. Higher oil prices wiped out most of the deficit in 2000, but it remained uncertain if the budget could be balanced in 2001.

These problems aside, Saudi Arabia is still fabulously rich in oil. It has large investments abroad and a growing industrial base. These assets give it an economic future that most countries would find enviable.

People

Saudi Arabia did not take a census until 1974. Current estimates put the total population just over 20 million. That number includes more than 5 million foreigners, mainly workers who are vital to keeping the economy running. Some are technical experts from the United States, Western Europe, and various Arab states whose skills are vital to the oil industry and other modern businesses. Most are unskilled or manual laborers, mainly from Egypt, Yemen, and south and southeast Asia, who do the jobs that Saudis are unwilling to do. Most employed Saudis work for the government.

About 85 percent of Saudi citizens are Sunni Muslims who belong the ultraconservative Wahhabi sect. The rest are Shiites, including a large percentage of the population of the oil-rich Eastern Province. Ninety percent are ethnic Arabs. Today less than 10 percent of the Saudi population follows the traditional Arab nomadic way of life. About three-quarters of the people live in urban areas.

Saudi Government and Society

Saudi Arabia is an absolute monarchy. It has no legislature and political parties are banned. Since its founding in the 1920s it has been ruled by its founder, King Abdel Aziz al-

Saud (usually called Ibn Saud), and four of his forty-four sons: Saud (1953–64), Faisal (1964–75), Khalid (1975–82), and Fahd (1982–present). As of the year 2000, the current ruler, King Fahd, was seventy-eight years old and seriously ill. His likely successor is his half brother and yet another son of Ibn Saud, Crown Prince Abdullah, who has effectively ruled the country from behind the throne of his half brother Fahd since 1997. That Saudi Arabia is the world's only country named for a family is a reflection of the absolute power that family holds.

The king governs by royal decree and appoints all important government officials. However, he does not make his decisions without consulting his cabinet, leading members of the royal family, and religious authorities. The king also must have the support of key members of the royal family. The most important government posts such as minister of defense or commander of the military are held by royal princes. In 1964, after a long struggle, leading members of the royal family forced the woefully incompetent King Saud to abdicate in favor of his brother Faisal. Still, there is no other major country where power is held by so small a group that rules by traditions dating from a tribal past. In 1992 King Fahd issued what is called the Basic Law of Government, which serves as Saudi Arabia's first constitution. He also established a Consultative Council that began operation in 1993. These measures created some political window dressing for the monarchy but did nothing to alter or limit its power.

Saudi society operates under tight religious control. In the eighteenth century, the House of Saud, ruler of a section of the Nejd, adopted the strict fundamentalist doctrine of the Wahhabi sect. The Wahhabis believed Islam had been corrupted over the centuries and wanted all Muslims to return to what they considered a pure form of worship. They opposed all luxuries, decoration of mosques, and vices such as coffee and tobacco. Wahhabi influence grew along with the power of the House of Saud, which in the 1920s won control over most of the Arabian Peninsula.

Today in Saudi Arabia the public worship of any faith other than Islam is forbidden. Non-Muslims may not approach within 15 miles (24 kilometers) of Mecca and may only visit the outskirts of Medina. All forms of public entertainment are banned, including theaters and movies, as are alcoholic beverages. The only exceptions are an annual folklore festival and sporting events such as camel racing and soccer. The special religious police, the *mutaween*, enforces Islamic orthodoxy. Even non-Muslims must be careful not to run afoul of the mutaween, whose official name once was the Committee for the Propagation of Virtue and the Prevention of Vice. In Saudi Arabia the Sharia (Islamic law) is the law of the land. This contrasts with the situation in other Arab countries, where the Sharia is only the *basis* of law, a formulation that allows modifications and alternatives to the Sharia's harsh punishments. Those punishments—including death for adultery, amputation of the hand for theft, floggings for various crimes, and public executions—are enforced in Saudi Arabia.

The strict observance of Islamic law, reinforced by tribal and customary law, also severely limits the status of women in Saudi Arabia. In legal cases a woman's testimony is worth only half a man's and her share of a family inheritance is only half a man's. Women make up less than 6 percent of the labor force. Women are strictly segregated from men in business and public life. All workplaces, restaurants, and schools are segregated by sex. City buses have separate sections for women, and women may not travel without a male relative on intercity buses or trains. There probably are few jokes about women drivers in Saudi Arabia, since women there are not allowed to drive.

Women have made some progress in Saudi Arabia. Today half of all Saudi women are literate, versus only 2 percent forty years ago. Girls account for close to half the children in Saudi schools. Educated Saudi women want to work and participate in public life, and have said so openly. But they face strong conservative resistance; in fact, the enforcement of public segregation has been stricter in recent years.

Saudi Arabia lagged behind the times for many years in yet another important way: Slavery was not legally abolished there until the 1960s.

MODERN SAUDI ARABIAN HISTORY

Saudi Arabia was one of the Arab states that emerged from the wreckage of the Ottoman Empire after World War I. Between 1919 and 1926 Ibn Saud defeated a series of rivals to unify about 80 percent of the Arabian Peninsula under his rule in what was called the Kingdom of the Hejaz and Nejd. The last unsuccessful challenger was the leader of the Hashemite family, Hussein Ibn Ali, great-grandfather of Jordan's King Hussein. Saud formally changed the country's name to the Kingdom of Saudi Arabia in 1932. Although Saudi Arabia officially was neutral in World War II, Ibn Saud was one of the few Arab leaders to strongly favor the Allies. His country became a charter member of the United Nations and immediately lined up with the West during the Cold War.

Saudi Arabian history since World War II is primarily a story of the regime's search for security against both internal and external enemies. Internally, the House of Saud has tried to keep the general population quiet by using oil revenues to give them a high standard of living. It has sought the support of prominent Sunni clerics to limit the influence of Islamic fundamentalists critical of the royal family for its friendship with the West and its luxurious lifestyle. It has also tried to keep Western influences from penetrating Saudi society. When all else has failed, it has resorted to force and repression to keep order.

Externally, the Saudis generally have opposed radical Arab regimes. They have resorted to bribery in the form of foreign aid to win the acceptance of countries with secular regimes such as Egypt, Syria, and Iraq. The Saudis also have tried to settle intra-Arab disputes in order to keep the Middle East stable and to build bridges between conservative Arab regimes. They have sought support and bought weapons from the Western democracies, while keeping them at arm's length to avoid criticism from fellow Arabs, whether nationalist or Islamic. From the 1940s onward Saudi Arabia lined up with the rest of the Arab world against Israel's right to exist. It joined the rest of the Arab world in denouncing Egypt's 1979 peace treaty with Israel. The Saudis also provided generous aid to the Palestine Liberation Organization until the PLO supported Iraq after its 1990 invasion of Kuwait. However, since 1993 they have supported the PLO–Israeli peace process. At the same time, that support has been qualified by a declaration by the country's chief religious leader that any peace with Israel, in the tradition of the Prophet Mohammad, must be temporary. Meanwhile, during the 1980s and 1990s the main external threats were its powerful neighbors Iran and Iraq.

The Sons of Abdel Aziz al-Saud (Ibn Saud)

Ibn Saud died in 1953 and was succeeded by his son Saud. During Saud's reign there was considerable tension between Saudi Arabia and the radical Nasser regime in Egypt. Wasteful and incompetent, Saud was pushed aside in favor of his brother Faisal in 1964. Under Faisal, Saudi Arabia in 1967 strongly supported Egypt, Syria, and Jordan in their unsuccessful war against Israel. While Faisal's reign was relatively stable, there were several rumored coup attempts, the most serious of which occurred in 1969. During 1973 Saudi Arabia led the Arab boycott against the United States for supporting Israel against Egypt and Syria during the Yom Kippur War of 1973. The boycott lasted until 1974. The next year Faisal was assassinated by one of his many nephews and succeeded by his brother Khalid.

Khalid's reign saw the first serious Islamic fundamentalist outburst against the Saudi regime. It occurred in 1979 when several hundred Sunni Muslim fundamentalists seized control of the Grand Mosque in Mecca. It took two weeks and hundreds of casualties before Saudi authorities retook the mosque. In early 1980, sixty-three fundamentalists, including several Egyptians and Yemenis, were publicly beheaded for their part in the incident. Khalid's reign also saw Saudi oil revenues start to decline as world prices fell, a development that marked the beginning of the kingdom's long-term budgetary problems.

Khalid died in 1982 and was succeeded by yet another brother, King Fahd. It was during Fahd's long reign, which still continues, that Saudi Arabia faced its most serious security threats yet. The Iranian revolution, with its militant Shiite fundamentalism, was not welcomed in Saudi Arabia.

The Grand Mosque in the Holy City of Mecca, in Saudi Arabia

When Iraq attacked Iran, the Saudis backed Iraq, notwithstanding their fear of Iraq and Baghdad's role as the aggressor in the war. They urged the rest of what they called the "Arab nation" to do likewise. Saudi-Iranian tensions gradually increased. They reached a deadly flash point in July 1987 when there was a bloody confrontation between Iranian pilgrims making the hajj and Saudi authorities at Mecca's Grand Mosque. More than four hundred pilgrims died, including almost three hundred Iranians. In 1988, the year the Iran-Iraq war ended, Saudi Arabia broke diplomatic relations with Iran.

Soon a new tiger, an Arab one, was at the gate. It was Iraq, the beneficiary of billions of dollars of Saudi aid during the Iran-Iraq War. In 1990 Iraq invaded and overran Kuwait, the small oil-rich state squeezed between Iraq and Saudi Arabia. There was little doubt that Iraqi dictator Saddam Hussein had designs on Saudi territory and oil. Saudi foreign policy lay in ruins. All the aid it had given Iraq had not bought security. Despite billions of dollars of high-tech Western weapons, the Saudi army was no match for Iraq's battle-hardened forces.

King Fahd had to call for Western troops to protect his country from Saddam Hussein and Iraq. Eventually more than 500,000 foreign troops, mainly Americans but also Europeans and contingents from Egypt, Syria, and several other Arab states, arrived in Saudi Arabia. In the Gulf War that followed that coalition routed Iraqi troops from Kuwait. However necessary from a military point of view, the entire operation infuriated the Saudi regime's fundamentalist critics, who feared and loathed the West. It also demonstrated Saudi Arabia's inability to defend itself. In addition, in the wake of the Gulf War the Saudis broke relations with Yemen, Jordan, and the PLO as punishment for supporting Iraq. They also ended the $6 million monthly stipend they had been giving the PLO since 1989 and expelled thousands of Palestinian and about 800,000 Yemeni workers from the country.

Toward the Year 2000

During the 1990s the main threats to the Saudi monarchy came from internal Islamic fundamentalist circles. It was to broaden the monarchy's base of support in the face of mounting fundamentalist criticism that King Fahd in 1992 announced a new Basic Law and had established a Consultative Council. These steps had no noticeable effect on the fundamentalists, who in 1993 announced the formation of a Committee for the Defense of Legitimate Rights (CDRL). When the government disbanded the organization two weeks later, it moved its operations to London, immediately causing tension between Riyadh and London. In 1994 Osama bin Laden, a billionaire Saudi fundamentalist and one of the world's most notorious terrorists, announced his support for the CDRL. King Fahd tried another approach to counter fundamentalist influence in 1994 by appointing a Supreme Council of Islamic Affairs. Its job was to ensure that the country's policies were consistent with Islamic principles. At the same time, the government arrested more than

150 Islamic militants and clerics on charges of sedition. The next year Fahd reshuffled his cabinet to bring in some younger experts. However, he left the most important ministries, including defense, internal affairs, and foreign affairs, in the hands of royal princes.

These measures did not solve the problem. In November 1995 a car bomb set by Sunni Muslim extremists exploded outside the headquarters of the Saudi Arabian National Guard, killing seven foreigners, including five Americans. Four Saudis were executed for the crime in April 1996. Two months later, another bomb killed nineteen American soldiers and wounded nearly four hundred at the U.S. military's Khobar Towers housing complex near the city of Dhahran. This time Shiites linked to Iran were responsible. American officials criticized the Saudi investigations of both incidents as being designed to withhold critical information rather than reveal it. It took until June of 2001 for the U.S. to indict thirteen Saudis and a Lebanese for the crime.

Saudi Arabia faces another serious threat, the combination of its outdated and brittle political system and the age of its leaders. The twenty-five surviving sons of Ibn Saud are getting old. As of the year 2000, King Fahd was seventy-eight years old and seriously ill. Crown Prince Abdullah, his half brother, heir apparent, and the man actually in charge since the mid-1990s, was 77. The prince next in line was 76. Behind them were several brothers in their sixties. After them stood a long line of grandsons. Everything is complicated by a Saudi law allowing the king to name his own successor, which conflicts with the tradition that the eldest surviving brother of the founding king should inherit the throne, as well as the obvious necessity, sooner or later, for a younger generation to begin leading the country. As one Western diplomat noted about the remaining sons of Ibn Saud who might become king, "What you have is a bunch of leaders who, even if they had lots of determination, would just be plain old."[2] Saudi Arabia should have no trouble coming up with another aging leader after King Fahd and Crown Prince Abdullah die. The challenge will be to update its political system so it will have effective leadership in a world that shows little mercy to those who lag behind.

KUWAIT
GEOGRAPHY, ECONOMY, PEOPLE

Kuwait is a gravelly patch of desert dotted with a few oases and some salt marshes at the northwest corner of the Persian Gulf. Its area of 6,880 square miles (17,818 square kilometers) makes it slightly smaller than New Jersey. Kuwait's ten offshore islands include Bubiyan (the largest) and Warba, which sit astride the Shatt-al-Arab and until recently were claimed by Iraq. In fact, Iraq at times has claimed all of Kuwait and tried unsuccessfully to annex the country in 1990, an act of aggression that led to the Gulf War. A neutral zone along Kuwait's border with Saudi Arabia was divided in 1969 in an agreement that provided for the two countries to share revenue from the zone's oil deposits. Kuwait has direct borders with only two neighbors: Iraq to the north and west and Saudi Arabia to the south. Its eastern border is the Persian Gulf. Still, its proximity to Iraq means Kuwait must get along in a dangerous neighborhood. Furthermore, not far across a sliver of Iraqi territory and beyond a slice of the Persian Gulf is Iran, whose Islamic Revolution constitutes another serious threat to Kuwaiti security.

Kuwait gets very little rain, and most of that comes in the form of sudden cloudbursts between October and April. It must import or desalinize most of its drinking water. Six huge oil-powered plants desalinize water from the Persian Gulf. Kuwait's desalinated water is expensive, $2 per cubic meter, about ten times the cost of water in Chicago, but Kuwaiti consumers do not feel the pain because the government absorbs approximately 90 percent of the cost.

Sand and dust storms lash Kuwait throughout the year, especially in the spring. The summers are brutally hot, although not as humid as in other parts of the Persian Gulf region. Winters are mild.

Kuwait is rich because of its geology. Its sands cover almost 100 billion barrels of oil, more than 9 percent of the world's total resources. Only Saudi Arabia, Iraq, and possibly the United Arab Emirates have larger oil deposits than Kuwait. Its economy is totally dependent on oil and income from foreign investments bought with oil profits. Oil and refined petroleum products account for almost all of Kuwait's exports and 75 percent of government revenues. Oil refining is the country's main industry. Aside from fish caught in offshore gulf waters, Kuwait must import all its food.

Kuwaitis and Non-Kuwaitis

A highly unusual and fundamental characteristic of Kuwait's population is the ratio of Kuwaitis to foreign nationals. Since its oil boom, foreigners have done most of the work in Kuwait, especially the difficult or unpleasant jobs. The share of foreigners living in Kuwait passed 50 percent around 1970; soon more than two-thirds of the population was non-Kuwaiti. The largest single foreign group was Palestinians, who in 1990 numbered 400,000, a figure about four-fifths as large as the Kuwaiti population. Additional foreign workers came from other Arab states, Iran, Pakistan, and India, while skilled personnel to manage the oil industry generally were Americans or Europeans.

In 1991, after invading Iraqi forces were expelled from Kuwait, the government decided to reduce the number of foreign workers in the country. Most Palestinians were expelled, accused by the Kuwaiti government of supporting the Iraqi occupiers and collaborating with them. Only about 20,000 were allowed to remain. Workers from other countries also were forced to leave, and restrictions were placed on foreign workers attempting to enter the country. Still, Kuwaitis remained a minority in their own country. As of mid-1998, about 1.9 million people lived in Kuwait. Of those, more than 1.1 million, about 60 percent, were foreigners.

Currently, Arabs—Kuwaiti and non-Kuwaiti—account for about three-quarters of Kuwait's total population. The largest non-Arab groups are south Asians (9 percent) and Iranians (4 percent). Islam is the country's official religion. About 90 percent of Kuwait's inhabitants are Muslims, with Sunnis outnumbering Shiites by more than two to one. Christians, Hindus, and Parsis together account for most of the remaining people. Virtually the entire population lives in urban areas, the largest of which is Kuwait City, the capital (population 265,000).

One reason such a low percentage of the country's population is Kuwaiti is that it is extremely difficult for outsiders to become citizens. Many descendants of families that have lived in Kuwait for generations are denied citizenship. Once they become citizens, naturalized Kuwaitis may not vote for twenty years; before 1995 the wait was thirty years.

Oil Wealth and Financial Problems

Kuwait's enormous oil revenues and the additional revenues from foreign investments enabled the government to provide the population with extensive social benefits. All Kuwaiti citizens receive free education and all residents, including foreigners, enjoy free health care. Most Kuwaiti citizens who work hold government jobs at excellent salaries. Among the many benefits and subsidies Kuwaitis receive is a $230,000 interest-free mortgage when they marry. However, in the 1990s Kuwait experienced some economic problems. The total damage from the Gulf War and Iraqi occupation was a staggering $170 billion. Furthermore, like the other oil-rich Persian Gulf states, Kuwait was hurt by the decline of world oil prices. Low oil prices reduced government revenue and made it increasingly difficult for Kuwait to maintain its opulent social welfare system. The financial squeeze was made worse by falling income from Kuwait's investments abroad, whose value declined from about $100 billion to $40 billion because of the huge cost of rebuilding after the Gulf War. During the 1990s Kuwait therefore had a string of budget deficits, although they shrank as oil prices rose after mid-1999. By 2001 the Kuwaiti government was confident it could balance its budget and even show a surplus despite a projected spending increase of 10 percent.

The financial problems of the late 1990s left some Kuwaitis, especially the rapidly growing segment of the population under twenty, concerned about the future. Most young Kuwaiti citizens had grown up in a world of luxurious entitlements and expected to continue to enjoy them. As one perplexed Kuwaiti youth asked in early 1999, while fellow teenagers raced their expensive sports cars along the seacoast, "With all our oil, why should life be harder for us than it was for our parents?"[3] Since Kuwait still has a per capita income of $23,000, one of the highest in the world, that complaint probably seems unreasonable to most non-Kuwaitis. But it may be a cause of domestic trouble in the future if oil prices fall and budget troubles return.

MODERN KUWAITI HISTORY

Kuwait means "little fort" in Arabic, which is what Kuwait City was into the early 1920s, when it was still surrounded by a mud wall. The city dates from a settlement established in the early eighteenth century by arrivals from the central part of the Arabian Peninsula. The al-Sabah family, which rules Kuwait today, was selected around 1760 by local settlers to manage local affairs and handle their relations with the Ottoman Empire. In this pre-oil era, the local economy was based on pearling, fishing, and trade. In 1899 Kuwait's reigning sheikh put his domain under British protection, mainly to resist Ottoman claims to his territory. Oil exploration began in 1934; the first major strike was made within four years. Full independence came in 1961, at which point Iraq claimed sovereignty over Kuwait. The Iraqis dropped that claim, at least temporarily, in 1963, the year Kuwait joined the Arab League. A constitution adopted in 1962 provided for an elected parliament that has the power to pass laws, an institution unique among the Persian Gulf monarchies. Real power, however, remained with the ruling prince, or emir, who appoints the country's ministers and can dissolve the assembly and suspend the constitution. In 1977 the emir dissolved parliament for the first time. He reinstituted it four years later with reduced powers. The emir also dissolved parliament in 1986 and 1999.

In the decades after independence, Kuwait used its oil wealth to build modern air-conditioned cities, roads, power plants, hospitals, harbor facilities, and much more. In 1975, it took full control of its oil resources from foreign oil companies. Kuwait went through an economic crisis in 1982 when its stock market collapsed amid shady deals, causing billions of dollars in losses. In foreign affairs, it tried to guarantee its security by providing millions of dollars of aid to poorer, but militarily more powerful, Arab states such as Egypt and Syria. Kuwait gave Iraq billions of dollars in aid during the Iran-Iraq War (1980-88), in part because it feared Iran, but also as protection money to Iraq. The strategy did not work. In August 1990, deeply in debt and tempted by its small neighbor's oil resources, Iraq invaded and annexed Kuwait. The ruling family and much of the Kuwaiti elite fled the country. During the six-month occupation that followed, Iraqi forces carried out a campaign of plunder, murder, torture, and rape. The country was liberated by an American-led coalition of European and Middle Eastern nations in February 1991. Before they retreated, the Iraqis set fire to more than five hundred oil wells, causing devastating environmental destruction.

Kuwait Since the Gulf War

At enormous cost, Kuwait repaired and rebuilt the physical destruction the Iraqis left behind. During 1991 and 1992 it signed agreements with the United States, Britain, and France to protect itself from foreign aggression. Foreign residents considered potentially subversive, particularly Palestinians, were expelled. But Kuwait remains insecure, largely because of its antiquated political system. There is internal opposition to the absolute power of the emir and the royal family. Some opponents call for democratic reform, most prominently a secular group formed in 1997 called the National Democratic Rally. It is the only political organization in Kuwait whose leadership includes a woman. More serious opposition comes from conservative Islamic forces. They demonstrated their strength in 1992 by winning a majority in parliament and again in 1997 when a majority of the parliament demanded that the Sharia (Islamic law) become the *sole* rather than *a* source of Kuwaiti law. Conservative Muslims also opposed a decree issued in May 1999 by Kuwait's ruler, or emir, Sheikh Jaber al-Ahmad–al Sabah, granting voting rights to Kuwaiti women. However, the decree required the approval of parliament, which narrowly rejected it in November. The emir responded the next month by choosing a woman, a member of his family who advocates full political rights for women, to be Kuwait's undersecretary of education. But that did little to solve the voting issue. Another setback occurred in 2001, when Kuwait's highest court rejected a suit—brought by a man on behalf of his wife—seeking to give women the vote.

It thus remains to be seen whether the court will extend suffrage to women and whether that in turn will be part of a larger process of modernizing Kuwait's political system. Nor is it certain that political reform will contribute to Kuwait's future stability.

BAHRAIN

Bahrain is an archipelago in the Persian Gulf just off the Saudi Arabian coast. Its 273 square miles (707 square kilometers) make it about one-fifth the size of Rhode Island, or about 3.5 times the size of Washington D.C. Only six of its 35 islands are inhabited. Bahrain, the main island and by far the largest (240 square miles, or 620 square kilometers), is connected to two of the other major islands by causeways. A additional causeway 16 miles (25 kilometers) in length connects Bahrain to Saudi Arabia and the mainland. The country's capital, Manama (population 145,000), is at the northern end of Bahrain island. About a third of the country's 616,000 inhabitants are foreign nationals, mainly south Asians, Iranians, and foreign Arabs. Almost all are Muslims, with Shiites outnumbering Sunnis by at least three to two. The al-Khalifa family, which has ruled Bahrain since the 1780s, is Sunni. The tension between the Sunni-dominated government and Bahrain's Shiite majority has been a constant problem in the politics of the country.

Although Bahrain island has a typical desert climate, its strategic location along ancient trade routes, good harbors, and freshwater springs attracted settlers as far back as the Bronze Age five thousand years ago. In more recent times, during the seventeenth and eighteenth centuries, it was contested by Persians and Arabs until an Arab tribe expelled the Persians in the 1780s. The island was under British protection from the 1820s until 1971, when the British withdrew from the sheikhdoms of the Persian Gulf. After unsuccessful negotiations with what was then called the Trucial States (today the United Arab Emirates) and Qatar, Bahrain chose to become an independent state.

In the 1930s oil was discovered in Bahrain, which became the Persian Gulf's first oil exporter during that decade. Bahrain's early start enabled it to modernize its economy before its neighbors and develop into an banking center during the oil boom years of the 1970s. The government also provided an extensive network of social services that included free education and medical care. The downside of Bahrain's early start is that its oil deposits are relatively small and running out. Soon it will not be able to count on oil to sustain its economy.

Currently, oil production and processing produce 60 percent of Bahrain's export earnings and a similar percentage of government revenue. Bahrain's efforts to diversity its economy have included building a large aluminum plant and a shipyard. The government, hoping to expand Bahrain's status as a financial center, has worked hard to attract foreign banks. However, although many banks have come, declining oil prices reduced revenues from the banking sector.

Bahrain also faces environmental problems. Along with its diminishing oil reserves, groundwater resources are being depleted, and Bahrain, once famous as a green island in the midst of a desert region, has lost much of its vegetation. Desertification is a serious problem. Oil spills have polluted Bahrain's coastline, offshore coral reefs, and sea vegetation.

Bahrain was ruled from 1961 to 1999 by Emir Sheikh Isa bin Sulman al-Khalifa. He was succeeded at his death in March 1999 by his forty-nine-year-old son Hamad, in a smooth transition of power. Like his father, Sheikh Hamad rules as an absolute monarch. All major political posts are held by members of the emir's family. The country briefly had an elected national assembly, but the emir abolished it in 1975. Political parties are banned. The tight lid on political life in Bahrain has meant that discontent, especially among the Shiite community that has borne the brunt of Bahrain's economic slowdown in the 1980s and 1990s, has boiled beneath the surface.

Bahrain's problems intensified after Iran's Islamic Revolution. Iran renewed some of its old territorial claims on Bahrain, and several plots to overthrow the government linked to the Khomeini regime were uncovered in the 1980s.

The 1990s brought violent clashes between government security forces and Shiite protesters. Violence in 1996 included several bombings in the capital. That year saw Bahrain's first execution, of a Shiite convicted of murdering a police officer in 1995. Shortly thereafter, the government announced it had uncovered yet another Iranian plot to overthrow the government. Adding to Bahrain's problems were long-standing territorial disputes with neighboring Qatar. The most important disagreement concerned the Hawar islands, just off the Qatari coast in a region believed to contain valuable oil and natural gas deposits.

In order to diffuse political tensions, in 1992 the emir announced the formation of a thirty-member Advisory Council. In 1996 he enlarged the council to forty members. Significantly, at about the same time the emir expanded his security forces. Overall, these measures were not an adequate response to Shiite complaints for improved economic conditions and a role in the country's political life. The regime also faced discontent from young educated people who resented economic hard times and were frustrated with the regime's unwillingness to make real political reforms. These pressures probably were the reason that Emir Hamad decided to hold a referendum on the establishment of a two-house parliament. It would have an elected lower house with full law-making powers and an upper house appointed by the emir. In mid-February 2001, on the eve of the election, the sheikh announced the freeing of nine hundred political prisoners. The referendum marked another milestone, as it was the first time women were allowed to vote in Bahrain. The vote itself confirmed a foregone conclusion, for more than 98 percent of the electorate supported the emir. Exactly what the voters would get after the election remained unanswered, as Emir Hamad announced that it would take two or three years to introduce the system and that it would be done under the supervision of Bahrain's crown prince. Bahrain has sought security in agreements with the United States and Britain and has maintained close ties with Saudi Arabia. However, it would be a mistake to take Bahrain's long-term stability for granted.

UNITED ARAB EMIRATES

The United Arab Emirates is a federation of seven sheikhdoms formed in 1971 when the British withdrew from the Persian Gulf region. It is dominated by Abu Dhabi, by far its largest and the richest member. Abu Dhabi has about 85 percent of the UAE's approximately 32,000 square miles (83,600 square kilometers) of territory and 40 percent of its estimated 2.3 million people. Most important, it has the bulk of the UAE's estimated 98 billion barrels of oil—almost 10 percent of the world's total reserves—and huge deposits of natural gas. The other two UAE sheikhdoms with oil deposits are Dubai, the second largest in both area and population, and Sharjah, the third ranking in both categories. The other members—Ras al-Khaimah, Ajman, Fujairah, and Umm al-Qaiwain—are smaller, poorer, and largely dependent on the wealthier emirates for protection and support.

The UAE stretches for almost 750 miles (1,200 kilometers) along the Persian Gulf coast. It also has a short coastline beyond the Strait of Hormuz along the Gulf of Oman.

A camel race in the United Arab Emirates, with camels specially bred for speed

Like its neighbors, it is largely desert where summer temperatures exceed 120°F (48.9°C). The UAE's southern border with Saudi Arabia remains undefined, and it has a territorial dispute with Iran over several tiny Persian Gulf islands. The UAE's eastern neighbor is Oman, where another undefined border runs through the desert. Abu Dhabi, the capital (population 928,000), and Dubai (population 674,000) are the UAE's largest cities.

The UAE was formed by its members as protection against powerful neighbors, particularly Saudi Arabia and Iran. Its federal structure is rickety, mainly because it was layered over the existing sheikhdoms, which continued to exist under their ruling families. A federal Supreme Council elects the UAE's president, who since independence has been Abu Dhabi's emir, Sheikh Zayed bin Sultan al-Nahyan. A forty-member Federal National Council appointed by the various emirs is an advisory body. Abu Dhabi and Dubai have veto power over federal policy, but within each sheikhdom the ruling emir's power remains absolute. Since 1971 there has been constant tension between Abu Dhabi, which wants to strengthen federal institutions, and Dubai, supported by several of the smaller emirates, which wants federal powers to remain limited. One result is that the provisional constitution established in 1971 has not been made permanent. Instead, it has been periodically renewed. The federal budget is not financed by taxation but by contributions from the individual sheikhdoms.

If the UAE does not resemble a nation politically, it does so even less demographically. As of 1998, about 75 percent of the population was made up of foreign nationals, mainly workers from Pakistan, Bangladesh, Iran, and other Arab countries. Even including foreign Arabs, non-Arab residents outnumber Arabs in the UAE. During the mid-1990s foreigners made up about 90 percent of the labor force. That percentage may have declined slightly since the passage of a 1996 law designed to force some of them out of the country by limiting their employment opportunities. About 80 percent of the total population is Sunni Muslim. Shiites make up about 16 percent. A smattering of Hindus and Christians are found among the foreign workers.

Prior to the discovery of oil, the economy of the UAE sheikhdoms depended on trading, fighting, and pearling. During the nineteenth century pirating was a major source of income, until the arrival of the British. After their treaties with local rulers, the "pirate coast" became known the Trucial Coast. Oil was discovered in 1958 and led to rapid modernization and dramatic improvement in social services provided by the local governments. The oil industry and massive construction also brought in the foreign laborers who today make up the majority of the population.

The UAE suffered a severe financial and embarrassing diplomatic setback in 1991 when the local Bank of Credit and Commerce (BCCI) collapsed. The bank, mostly owned by Abu Dhabi's ruler Sheikh Zayed, was linked to international drug dealers, arms merchants, and Third World dictators. Its officers were convicted of extensive fraud and other illegal activities. Billions were lost worldwide, with Sheikh Zayed, who was victimized by his own bank, among the largest losers. The bank itself was liquidated in 1996.

During the 1990s the UAE's main focus was security. In 1992 Iran began asserting its territorial claims over three disputed Persian Gulf islands, warning the UAE it would have to cross a "sea of blood" to make good its claims. In 1994 the UAE followed the example of several other Gulf states by signing a military cooperation agreement with the United States. That year Sheikh Zayed ordered that a wide range of crimes—including murder, theft, adultery, and drug offenses—be tried in according to Sharia in religious courts rather than in civil courts. At the same time, the UAE has called for cooperation among Arab states to combat militant Islamic fundamentalists.

On the economic front, the UAE has been broadening its economic base. It has built plants to produce steel, aluminum, and chemicals. It has also established itself as a trading center from which more than 350 companies operate. The country's per capita income, which at $28,000 in the early 1980s was the world's highest, in 1999 stood at $22,000, still one of the world's highest. It is politics that remains the problem. The UAE will face a serious political challenge when Sheikh Zayed, age eighty-one, dies. Until then, however, it is likely to maintain its stability.

QATAR

Qatar occupies a thumb-shaped peninsula that juts out from Saudi Arabia for about 100 miles (160 kilometers) into the Persian Gulf. It is a parched landscape of 4,247 square miles (11,000 square kilometers) whose highest hills barely rise 130 feet (40 meters) above sea level. Beneath the peninsula's barren western hills are buried 3.7 billion barrels of oil. Just off the northeast coast beneath the shallow waters of the Persian Gulf is the North Field, one of the largest natural gas fields in the world that holds 4 percent of the world's total reserves. The exploitation of oil since its discovery in 1949 has turned Qatar from one of the world's poorest countries into one of the richest.

Qatar borders on Saudi Arabia and the UAE in the south. Just offshore is Bahrain, with which Qatar has a several territorial disputes. Less than 100 miles away across the Persian Gulf is Iran, which all the Gulf states, especially the smaller ones, consider a security threat. Three-quarters of Qatar's about 725,000 residents are foreign nationals who do most of the country's work. They come mainly from south Asia, Iran, and other Arab states. More than 92 percent are Muslims, the overwhelming majority of them Sunnis. Most native Qataris belong to the strict Wahhabi sect. There are some Christians and Hindus among the foreign residents. About 80 percent of the population lives in and around Doha (population 340,000), Qatar's capital and main port.

Oil is the liquid spine of Qatar's economy. It accounts for 70 percent of export earnings and two-thirds of government revenues. Oil production is expected to last at its current level for twenty-five years. While Qatar has tried to diversify its economy by building plants that produce steel, chemicals, and cement, the real guarantor of its future is the North Field. The gigantic field is half the size of Qatar itself. Once Qatar's oil runs out, it will be able to produce natural gas in huge quantities for a century.

Qatar's rulers, the al-Thani family, arrived in the region in the late eighteenth century and became its ruling family about one hundred years later. They signed agreements for British protection in the nineteenth century, but lived under

Ottoman occupation from 1872 until 1915. New agreements with Britain made Qatar a British protectorate until 1971. When the British left, after failed negotiations with sheikhdoms that ultimately formed the UAE, Qatar declared its independence in late 1971. The al-Thanis continue to rule the country as absolute monarchs.

Although one family rules Qatar, the country's politics in the twentieth century has been disorderly. Every ruler has been deposed or forced to abdicate. A year after independence, the free-spending and ineffective ruling emir was overthrown in a bloodless coup by his cousin Khalifa bin Hamad al-Thani. He presided over an era of prosperity and modernization, especially during the oil boom years of the 1970s. At the same time, he focused on security concerns, especially after the Gulf War. In 1992 the emir rejected an appeal by fifty leading citizens for democratic reforms, responding instead by briefly jailing some of them. During 1992 and 1993 he signed a series of security agreements with the United States, Britain, and France.

While these agreements did protect Qatar, they did not keep the emir in power. In 1995, Emir Khalifa was deposed by his son Hamad. As soon as he came to power, Hamad made it clear that he intended to make some changes and follow independent policies, some of which have not been popular with the conservative and insecure rulers of the other Gulf states. In foreign affairs, he took the lead in trying to improve relations with Iraq and Iran. He also was involved in on-again, off-again trade discussions with Israel. In April 1996 Israeli prime minister Shimon Peres made an official visit to Qatar. In domestic affairs, the emir announced in 1997 that Qatar would hold municipal elections in which women would be allowed to vote. That precedent-breaking election took place in March 1999.

Emir Hamad's most far-reaching innovation, in the sense that it literally reaches 22 Arab countries, was the founding in 1996 of Al Jazeera, the first (and still the only) television station in the Arab world to broadcast news without government censorship or bias. The Arabic-language station has become a sensation in the Arab world, winning a wide audience among the Arab public but also widespread anger from

Arab governments, including Saudi Arabia. When asked about the reaction of Arab governments the emir commented:

> What a headache. It's caused no end of problems, but all the same I think of it as a kind of oxygen, invigorating our thinking. I tell my children, if you want to know the issues of real importance in the Arab world, watch Al Jazeera.[4]

One of the station's reporters added that the station has "put Qatar on the map."[5] Whether that will help or hurt the emir, who has his share of opponents, remained an open question.

OMAN

Thousands of years before anyone cared about petroleum, Oman grew rich as a source of frankincense, a fragrant tree resin used as incense and in embalming that was one of the most valuable products in the ancient world. In the early nineteenth century Oman was the most powerful state on the Arabian Peninsula. Its rule extended to the island of Zanzibar off the east African coast and to a small part of the south Asian coastline in what today is Pakistan. At the start of the twentieth century, however, Oman's fortunes had declined and it was a poor country that depended on Britain for protection. Oman became independent in 1951, but as late as 1970, three years after oil production began, it had only 6 miles (9.5 kilometers) of paved roads.

Oman's ruling dynasty has held power since the mid-eighteenth century. Its ruler from 1932 until 1970, Sultan Said ibn Taimur al Said, banned travel and trade and tried to keep the country isolated from the outside world. He even forbade the use of bicycles and sunglasses. A new era began in 1970 when Sultan Said was overthrown by his son Qaboos, who still rules Oman. Today Oman has 3,500 miles (5,600 kilometers) of paved roads, hospitals and health clinics, generous social benefits, a school system with almost 500,000 students, a medical school, and a telephone network that allows calls anywhere in the country for ten cents.

Oman faces the Arabian Sea and the Gulf of Oman. It has an area of 199,500 square miles (309,500 square kilometers). A tiny part of the country, separated from the main part by about 20 miles (32 kilometers) of UAE territory, is at the tip of the Musandam Peninsula. It overlooks the strategic Strait of Hormuz, through which oil tankers must pass to take Persian Gulf oil to customers worldwide. Altogether, Oman has more than 1,000 miles (1.600 kilometers) of coastline, including a fertile plain along the Gulf of Oman. Muscat (population 250,000), Oman's capital and largest city, is on that plain. Immediately to the west and southwest of the coast region are mountains; beyond them to the west and south is a desert plateau that covers the bulk of the country. The Dhofar region in the far south, watered and cooled by summer monsoon rains, has more moderate temperatures than the rest of the country.

The Wahiba Sands in eastern Oman are a region of dunes stretching along the coast of the Arabian Sea. Visitors often find the windswept shapes quite striking.

Oman has a population of about 2.3 million people. That figure includes at least 400,000 non-Omanis, the vast majority from south Asia, who make up about half of the labor force. Foreign workers hold most of the nongovernment jobs and do the bulk of the country's unskilled labor. They work long hours at low salaries while native Omanis occupy high-paying government jobs in offices that usually close in mid-afternoon. About three-quarters of all native Omanis are Muslim Arabs who belong to the small Ibahdi sect. Most of the rest are Sunnis.

Oman's economy is dominated by oil, which provides 75 percent of all export earnings and government revenues. The country has about five billion barrels of oil, which is expected to last for only about twenty more years. Attempts to encourage other industries and diversify the economy before that happens have had limited success. Oman's other natural resources include natural gas, gold, and copper. Agriculture and fishing, the traditional occupations of Oman before the oil boom, are still important parts of the economy. Sur, Oman's main fishing center on the Gulf of Oman, once had another, less savory, business: From the seventh to nineteenth centuries it was a center of the slave trade than ran from East Africa to the Middle East and India.

Sultan Qaboos has been an effective ruler during the three decades he has been in power. He defeated a rebellion by radical Arab groups in the 1970s. While retaining his absolute power, he appointed a Consultative Council in 1981 and increased its membership and expanded its range of activities in 1991. He introduced a major reform in 1994 when he announced that women could serve in the council. Two were appointed, out of a total membership of eighty. That same year the sultan's security forces arrested more than two hundred Islamic militants in an effort to curb the rise of Islamic fundamentalism in Oman.

Oman has followed an independent foreign policy under Sultan Qaboos. It was the only Arab state in the Middle East to support Egypt's peace treaty with Israel in 1979. In 1994 Israeli prime minister Yitzhak Rabin visited Oman; his successor, Shimon Peres, made an official visit in 1996. However, at the end of the year Oman announced it was "freezing" all ties with Israel because of what it said was lack of progress in the peace process with the Palestinians. Meanwhile, Oman has attempted to assure its security through cooperation and military ties with the United States. During the Gulf War, American soldiers used weapons the United States had been storing in Oman since the 1980s.

Despite three decades of prosperity and stability, Oman has serious problems. Sultan Qaboos, at age fifty-nine, is very popular, but is unmarried and childless, raising the question of succession. Oman's growing population—half of which is under fifteen—means it will be difficult for young Omanis entering the workforce to find the high-paying jobs they want. An increasingly well-educated population is likely to demand political reforms that go beyond advising or consulting and would limit the sultan's absolute power. Islamic fundamentalists are another potential challenge to the regime. In short, like the other Gulf monarchies, Oman faces an uncertain future.

YEMEN

The world's first famous Yemenite was the Queen of Sheba, who according to the Bible about three thousand years ago journeyed from her kingdom in the southern part of the Arabian Peninsula to Jerusalem to visit the Israelite king Solomon. The other kingdoms that rose and fell in what today is Yemen drew their wealth from trade, especially the export of frankincense and myrrh, fragrant tree resins that were highly valued in the ancient world. By the seventh century A.D., when the population converted to Islam, the region was in decline. After Islam split into Sunni and Shiite sects, many Shiites fleeing Sunni persecution elsewhere in the Arab world fled to the highlands of Yemen. The Shiite Rassid dynasty ruled parts of northern Yemen from 897 until it was overthrown in a revolution in 1962. Foreigners, including the Fatamids of Egypt, Ottomans, Portuguese, and British also controlled different parts of Yemen for varying periods of time. In 1728 a local Sunni dynasty took control of part of southern Yemen, establishing a division of the country between north and south that lasted until 1990.

Yemen has an area of 205,335 square miles (531,869 square kilometers). It includes the former Yemen Arab Republic (North Yemen) and the People's Democratic Republic of Yemen (South Yemen). Yemen borders on only two countries, Saudi Arabia in the north and Oman in the east. The border with Saudi Arabia still has not been exactly defined. The Red Sea is Yemen's western border, while the Gulf of Aden and the Arabian Sea form its southern frontier. Two African countries, Eritrea and Djibouti, are just across the strategic Bab al-Mandab strait that connects the Red Sea to the Gulf of Aden.

Yemen has the most varied geography and climate on the Arabian Peninsula. Most of its interior is desert where summer temperatures reach 130°F (54°C); conditions are especially brutal in the east where the Empty Quarter begins. The country's coastal region is a semidesert about 40 miles (64 kilometers) wide. Aden (population 400,000), the country's main port and second-largest city, whose history dates back 2,500 years, stands on the coast by the Gulf of Aden astride the major sea route between India and Europe. Yemen's northwestern highlands and mountains between the coast and the interior desert are the wettest part of the Arabian Peninsula, getting as much as 20 inches (500 millimeters) of rain a year. They are also the highest part of the peninsula, with some peaks rising to more than 12,000 feet (3,660 meters) above sea level. Some fertile farmland is found in this region, although farmers must depend on rainfall that often is irregular. Sanaa (population 926,000), Yemen's capital and largest city, is in the highlands. Yemen also controls two strategically placed islands: Perim in the Bab al-Mandab strait and Socotra in the Gulf of Aden.

Yemen has a population of about 17 million, making it the second most populous country on the Arabian Peninsula after Saudi Arabia. The Saudis in fact were not enthusiastic about Yemen's unification because they feared a united Yemen might someday challenge their dominant position on the peninsula. About 90 percent of all Yemenis are Arabs; there is a significant Afro-Arab population in the western coastal regions opposite Africa. Northern Yemen is almost entirely Muslim; some Christians and Hindus live in the south. The Muslims are approximately equally divided between Shiites, who are concentrated in the north, and Sunnis, most of whom live in the south. This has been a divisive factor in Yemen's history. Tribal loyalties are another divisive force in Yemeni society. An important part of Yemen's population, and its economy, are the hundreds of thousands of citizens who work abroad. Most of them work in the oil-rich Gulf states and regularly send part of their earnings home to help relatives.

Unlike the other countries of the Arabian Peninsula, Yemen is a poor country, one of the twenty poorest countries in the world. It has only begun to exploit its oil deposits, which were not discovered until the mid 1980s. Yemen's per capita income is only about $400, and more than half the workforce is involved in agriculture or fishing. Yemen's economy was badly hurt after the Gulf War when Saudi Arabia, in retaliation for Yemen's sympathy for Iraq, expelled about 800,000 Yemeni workers. On the positive side, since the 1980s oil income has financed new schools, roads, hospitals, and other projects. Along with Yemen's natural gas deposits, Yemen's oil reserves provide the basis for an improved economy in the future.

At the same time, oil money may not be able to overcome the impact of khat, a widely used narcotic drug. Yemenis have been chewing khat for a thousand years. Addiction to khat, in fact, may be Yemen's most serious social problem. About 80 percent of Yemen's men, 60 percent of its women, and a growing percentage of children under ten years regularly chew khat. Farmland that once produced cotton, fruits, and vegetables increasingly is used to grow the drug. North Yemenis in particular chew khat on a regular basis. The habit is a serious drain on the incomes of people who cannot afford it; many Yemenis who make less than $100 per month admit they spend half their income on khat. The drug not only induces lethargy that saps the ability to work, but keeps people away from their work. As one Yemeni economist noted:

> In the West, you work from 9 to 5. We claim to work from 8 to 2, but many people knock off at noon to be sure to get to the khat markets while they can buy the freshest

leaves. So we lose at least four hours work every day, and if we continue like that, we'll stay poor forever.[6]

In 1999 Yemen's president, Ali Abdullah Saleh, himself a khat chewer for many years, announced a campaign to end khat chewing, which he called a "social evil." He is likely to find the job difficult. Many Yemenis seem to agree with a government official who told a Western reporter, "Without khat, Yemen is nothing." Beyond that, few Yemenis believe that President Saleh practices what he preaches. As the speaker of Yemen's parliament put it, "After all those fine words, he's still chewing khat."[7]

If Yemen is to prosper, it must first achieve political stability. So far, that has not been possible. Both of the two independent Yemeni states were unstable while they existed. North Yemen was a backward monarchy until the revolution of 1962. The Yemen Arab Republic (YAR) that succeeded it was rocked by civil war until 1967 and then by military coups and assassinations until Lieutenant General Ali Abdullah Saleh took power in 1978. Meanwhile, a second Yemeni state came into being in 1967 when the British, who had conquered Aden and its surrounding territory in 1839, withdrew from South Yemen. That state, the only Marxist regime in the Arab world, was called (after 1970) the People's Democratic Republic of Yemen (PDRY). South Yemen was no more stable than North Yemen. The two countries fought a border war in 1979 and eyed each other warily thereafter. Unity finally came in 1990, after South Yemen lost its main supporter when the Soviet Union collapsed. General Saleh became the newly formed Republic of Yemen's first president.

Unity brought continued political infighting rather than stability. Yemen's sympathy for Iraq during the Gulf War crisis of 1990–91 increased tensions with Saudi Arabia and the other Gulf states and cost Yemen foreign aid. In 1994 a civil war broke out when former South Yemen leaders tried to secede. Within two months General Saleh and the former North Yemen leadership were victorious. Over the next few months Saleh reinforced his position by having Yemen's legislature reelect him president and revise the constitution to strengthen his powers. Meanwhile, there were growing tensions between Saleh's secular political party, the General People's Congress (GPC), and the main Islamic group, Yemeni Congregation for Reform (YIP). The YIP opposed Saleh's decision to grant women the vote and the right to run for office prior to the 1997 parliamentary elections. Those elections, won by the GMC, appeared to be generally fair, marking a first for the Arabian Peninsula. Saleh then appointed an economist from the former South Yemen as the country's prime minister in an attempt to overcome divisions that did not end with the conclusion of the civil war. In September 1999 Yemen held its first presidential election in which voters cast ballots directly for the candidates. While Saleh won with more than 96 percent of the vote, the opposition, with considerable justification, denounced the election as a sham. The main opposition party, which was not permitted to field a candidate, called for a boycott of the vote.

Yemen is a country that has generally attracted little attention outside the Arabian Peninsula, but that suddenly changed on October 12, 2000, when a small rubber boat pulled alongside the U.S. Navy destroyer *Cole* as it was refueling in the port of Aden. At least two Islamic fundamentalist terrorists were on board the rubber boat, and they were on a suicide mission whose goal was to kill Americans. At 12:15 P.M., an enormous explosion tore a huge hole, 20 by 40 feet (6 by 12 meters), in the side of the *Cole*. Seventeen U.S. sailors died and thirty-nine were injured. It was the worst terrorist attack against American military forces since nineteen airmen were killed in the bombing of their barracks in Saudi Arabia in 1996. U.S. officials uncovered evidence that the attack on the *Cole* was carried out by the organization headed by Osama bin Laden, the Saudi Arabian billionaire whose headquarters are in Afghanistan. In 1998, bin Laden's operatives had carried out two deadly bombing attacks on U.S. embassies in Africa; on September 11, 2001, in the deadliest terrorist act ever, they would crash two passenger airliners into New York City's World Trade Center and another into the Pentagon in Washington, D.C., killing well over 6,000 people.

Several months after the *Cole* incident, in February 2001, the citizens of Yemen went to the polls to vote in municipal elections and on a referendum Saleh had put on the ballot.

Saleh claimed the referendum was to advance what he called Yemen's "democratic experience." In reality, it was on constitutional amendments to extend the presidential term from five to seven years, extend the term of the parliament from four to six years, and create a second house of parliament appointed by the president. Rather than make Yemen more democratic, the amendments were intended to strengthen the power of Saleh and his ruling party. Not surprisingly, the voters approved the amendments by a majority of more than 77 percent. Equally unsurprising was the violence that accompanied the election. Tribal clashes of various sorts that caused the postponement of the voting at 140 polling stations also left more than twenty people dead.

Yemen thus began the new century and millennium as a troubled country. It remained poverty stricken. Its secular government was under a growing challenge from Islamic forces. One radical group, the Aden-Abyan Islamic Army, was disrupting the country with a campaign of violence, including car bombings in cities. The regime itself, despite the 1997 parliamentary election and some degree of political freedom, at its core was a military dictatorship with a reputation for corruption. Very rapid population growth was certain to be a heavy anchor on efforts to promote economic development. So was violence having nothing to do with politics in a country where 16 million people owned a total of 50 million guns. Some of those guns were used to kidnap Westerners working in or visiting Yemen—more than one hundred during the 1990s—who were then held for ransom. All of these factors added up to a problematic future.

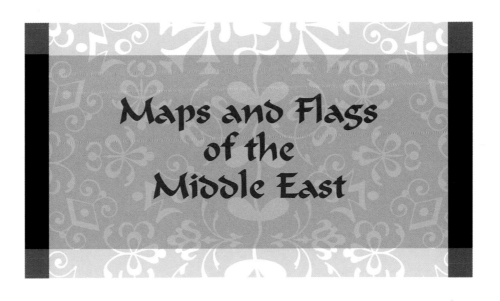

Maps and Flags
of the
Middle East

Map #1 Political map of the Middle East

Map #2 Geographical map of the Middle East

Flags of the countries in the Middle East

BLACK SEA

ITALY

BULGARIA

ALBANIA

Sea of Marmara

Istanbul

GREECE

Ankara

TURKEY

Anatolia

Kizil R.

Adana

Rhodes

Crete

CYPRUS

Tarabulas

Beirut

MEDITERRANEAN SEA

LEBANON

ISRAEL

Dama

Suez Canal

Tel Aviv

Jordan R.

Dead S

Tripoli

Benghaz

Alexandria

Jerusalem

Amman

Cairo

Port Said

Suez Canal

Elat

JORD

LIBYA

EGYPT

Nile R.

RED SEA

Aswan

SUDAN

THE MIDDLE EAST

BLACK SEA

Sea of
Marmara

Bosporus

Dardenelles

AEGEAN
SEA

PLATEAU
OF ANATOLIA

Kizil R.

Lake Tuz

TAURUS MTNS.

Crete

MEDITERRANEAN SEA

Lake Tiberias

Jordan R.

Dead

Nile Delta

Gulf of Sidra

Negev
Deser

Sinai
Peninsula

Gulf of Suez

Gulf of A

Libyan Desert

Strait
of Tiran

Nile R.

Hb

RED

Sahara Desert

Lake Nassar

Nubian
Desert

**THE
MIDDLE
EAST**

Egypt

Over the centuries many flags have flown in Egypt, but its present tricolor dates from the Arab Liberation Movement of 1952, which overthrew the Egyptian monarchy. The central emblem, added in 1984, features the eagle of the medieval hero Saladin, an emblem found on the Citadel in Cairo, which he created.

Israel

The *talith*, or prayer shawl, traditionally worn by Jewish men inspired the blue stripes in the flag that was used by the Zionist movement from the 1890s on. The ancient Jewish symbol known as the Star of David appears in the center. The modern State of Israel officially adopted the flag following its independence in 1948.

Palestinian Authority

The Arab Revolt Flag, first displayed in Palestine in 1918, has continued to be considered as the national flag of Palestinians. Today it is flown widely by the Palestinian Authority and private citizens in the Gaza Strip and West Bank as a symbol of their aspiration for national independence and self-government.

Libya

Historically, many countries have had monochromatic (one-color) flags, although they are no longer in favor. Libya in 1977 chose to celebrate its Green Revolution by selecting that color for its flag. Libya today is mostly desert, but it hopes to become a source of agricultural products as it was in the time of the Roman Empire.

Syria

Traditional Muslim colors—red, white, green, and black—were chosen by Arab nationalists just before World War I. Variations of the current flag of Syria have been used to represent it since 1917. The present design—also used from 1958 to 1961—was selected in Syria in 1980 to distinguish it from the similar flags of Egypt and Iraq.

Lebanon

Following World War I, France ruled Greater Lebanon, where the cedar tree had been a familiar symbol since biblical days. The current national flag was chosen in 1943 at the time the independence of Lebanon was proclaimed. Red and white were colors featured in earlier military flags.

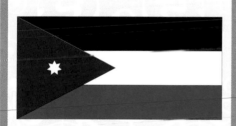

Jordan

When the territory now constituting the Kingdom of Jordan was recognized by the British, the Arab Revolt Flag of 1917 with an 7-pointed star added to its triangle was already in use. The star had been added by King Abdullah to distinguish his banner form similar flags then flown in Syria, Iraq, and the Hejaz.

Iran

Since the 19th century the colors green, white and red have been considered the national colors of Iran. The lion and sun symbol of early flag designs was replaced in 1979 following the country's Islamic Revolution. The repeated inscription, "God Is Great" and the central logo reflect the religious fervor of the current regime.

Iraq

The traditional call to prayer of the Islamic *muezzin*, "God Is Great," was added to the national flag of Iraq as an inscription by Saddam Hussein during the Gulf War (1991). The pan-Arab colors and the three stars of the flag date from 1963 and stand for the unity of Arab lands, which Iraq has long championed.

Turkey

Red was the traditional color of those Turkic people who, having migrated from Central Asia, invaded the Anatolian Peninsula to found the Ottoman Empire. The crescent and star symbol had long been used in that area and is frequently associated with Islam. The current flag dates from 1936, after the establishment of the Turkish Republic.

Saudi Arabia

The strict Wahhabi religious reformers who united most of the Arabian Peninsula in the 19th and 20th centuries emblazoned their battle standards with the Muslim statement of faith: "There Is No God But Allah and Mohammad Is the Prophet of Allah." The sword reflects the militancy of their religious convictions.

United Arab Emirates

Seven small semi-independent territories on the southern shore the Arab Gulf agreed to unify in 1971, following the withdrawal of British troops. The new flag for the UAE featured stripes of green for fertile fields, white for pure intentions, black for the past, and red for the blood they were willing to shed for freedom.

Bahrain

Two versions of the national flag of Bahrain are officially recognized. The red flag with a simple white vertical stripe at the hoist is less often displayed than a similar design featuring a zigzag division between the two colors. The flag was adopted in 1933.

Yemen

Yemen obtained independence from the British in the 1960s. In 1990, North Yemen and South Yemen united, reducing their national flags to a common design of three stripes in the traditional Arab national colors and omitting other symbols they had used previously.

Oman

For centuries the national flag of Oman was plain red, a color associated with the Kharijite sect. Modernization of the country, begun in 1970, saw white and green added to the flag to represent peace and the nation's Green Mountains. The coat of arms at the hoist combines traditional Arab swords, a dagger, and belt.

Kuwait

Following Kuwaiti independence in 1961, a red flag with the national name in white Arabic script was replaced by the present national flag design. The new flag combined the four colors long associated with Arab dynasties, as chosen before World War I by young Arab

Qatar

Like most Arab Sheikhdoms along the Arab Gulf, Qatar traditionally used red flags, but in the early 19th century the British introduced white as a symbol of peace. The maroon color was probably chosen to distinguish it from the flag of neighboring Bahrain.

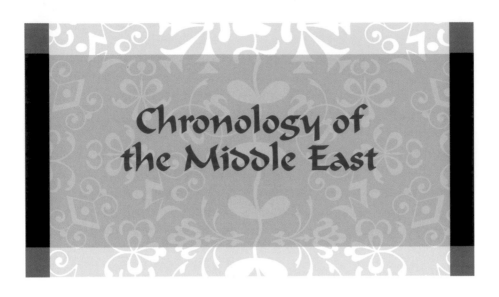

Chronology of the Middle East

Ancient Times to 1800

9000-8000 B.C.
- Development of agriculture.

8000 B.C.
- Jericho and Catal Huyuk develop as world's first cities.

3500 B.C.
- Sumarians in Mesopotamia develop the world's first system of writing.

3100 B.C.
- Egypt united as the world's first country; Old Kingdom: 3100–2258 B.C.

2400 B.C.
- Sargon of Akkad conquers neighboring states in Mesopotamia and creates world's first empire.

2000–1786 B.C.
- Middle Kingdom era in Egypt.

1800 B.C.
- Beginnings of Judaism, world's first monotheistic religion.

1750-332 B.C.
- New Kingdom era in Egypt.

14th century B.C.
- Religious reforms of Egyptian pharaoh Akhenaton.

1200 B.C.
- Phoenicians perfect world's first phonetic alphabet of twenty-two letters.

11th and 10th centuries B.C.

- United Israelite kingdom with Jerusalem as its capital.

7th century B.C.

- Beginnings of Zoroastrianism in Persia.

6th century B.C.

- Cyrus the Great rules Persia; allows exiled Israelites to return to Judea.

334–323 B.C.

- Conquests of Alexander the Great.

4th century B.C.– 4th century A.D.

- Greek and Roman dominance of Middle East.

2nd and 1st centuries B.C.

- Rome extends power to the region; Alexandria library burns and 500,000 irreplaceable papyrus scrolls are destroyed.

1st century A.D.

- Birth of Christ (possibly 4 B.C.) and origins of Christianity.

1st and 2nd centuries A.D.

- Two unsuccessful Jewish revolts against Rome; Romans destroy the Jews' Second Temple after the first revolt in A.D. 70; in the wake of the second revolt (132–135), the Romans either kill or exile from Judea most of its Jewish population and rename the region Syria Palestina.

5th century

- Beginning of Coptic Church in Egypt.

7th century

- Founding of Islam and the beginning of Islamic conquests; Mesopotamia, Persia, and Egypt all conquered by 650.

10th century

- Fatamids rule Egypt and found Cairo in 969.

11th–13th centuries

- Crusader era.

1071

- Seljuk Turks defeat Byzantines at Manzikert.

1250–1517

- Mamluke rule in Egypt; Mamlukes defeat Mongol invaders in Syria in 1260.

14th century

- Rise of the Ottoman Empire.

1453

- Ottoman Turks conquer Constantinople.

16th century

- Safavid dynasty makes Shiite version of Islam official religion in Persia.

1520–1566
- Reign of Ottoman sultan Suleyman the Magnificent.

1571
- Spanish and Venetian navies defeat the Turks at Lepanto.

1728
- Yemen divided into two countries; division lasts until 1990.

1798–1801
- French occupation of Egypt; Rosetta Stone found in 1799.

1800–1945

1840s
- Beginning of the Baha'i faith in Persia.

1861
- French intervene in Lebanon to save Christians from massacres by the Druze; establish Mount Lebanon district for Lebanese Christians.

1869
- Suez Canal opened.

1881–1903
- First large wave of Jewish immigration to Palestine from Russian Empire.

1882
- Great Britain occupies Egypt.

1897
- First Zionist Congress.

1899
- Kuwait under British protection.

1905–1914
- Second large wave of Jewish immigration to Palestine from Russian Empire.

1908
- Oil discovered in Persia.

1911
- Italy seizes Libya from Ottoman Empire.

1914–1918
- World War I. Ottoman Empire dismantled after the war.

1915
- Ottomans, led by Colonel Mustafa Kemal (after 1934: Mustafa Kemal Ataturk), thwart British invasion at Gallipoli.
- Ottoman genocide against the Armenians.

1917
- Balfour Declaration promises Jews a national home in Palestine.

1919–1926

- Ibn Saud conquers most of the Arabian Peninsula and creates Saudi Arabia (a name adopted in 1932).

1920

- Supreme Council of the League of Nations, at the San Remo Conference, gives Britain the Mandate for Palestine, defining Palestine as including land on both sides of the Jordan River; mandate confirmed by the League in 1922.
- Treaty of Sèvres limits Turkey's territory to northern Anatolia.

1922

- Egypt officially independent.
- Turks defeats the Greeks and drive them from Anatolia.
- Britain detaches all territory west of the Jordan River, three-quarters of Palestine's total area, from its mandate to create Transjordan.

1923

- Treaty of Lausanne: Turkey (with minor differences) achieves current borders.
- Kemal has Turkish national assembly abolish the Ottoman sultanate and declare Turkey a republic.

1924

- Turkish national assembly abolishes the Ottoman caliphate.

1925

- Pahlavi dynasty takes power in Persia.

1927

- Oil discovered in Iraq.

1928

- Islam disestablished as Turkey's official religion.

1930

- Turks rename Constantinople Istanbul.

1932

- Iraq independent.

1933–1939

- Large wave of Jewish immigration to Palestine, as Jews flee persecution in Nazi Germany.

1935

- Persia's name changed to Iran; government bans the chador.

1936

- Farouk becomes king of Egypt.

1938

- Ataturk dies.
- Oil discovered in Saudi Arabia; oil pumping begins in Kuwait.

1939–1945

- World War II.

1941

- Britain and the Soviet Union occupy Iran. U.S. joins the occupation in 1942.
- Syria officially independent (actual independence in 1946, when the French leave the country).
- Lebanon officially independent.

1943

- Lebanese "National Covenant" sets the basis for the ethnic/religious division of power in the government according to the census of that year. It remains in force until 1989.

1945–Present

1946

Iran
- U.S. successfully pressures the Soviet Union to end its occupation of northern Iran.

Turkey
- U.S. sends aircraft carrier to eastern Mediterranean to back Turkey against Soviet pressure.

Jordan
- Kingdom of Transjordan independent with Abdullah as king.

1947

Palestine Mandate
- Britain announces it will leave Palestine. UN votes to divide Palestine into a Jewish state and an Arab state, a decision the Jews accept and the Arabs reject.

1948

Israel
- Declares independence.
- War of Independence; Israel defeats five invading Arab states (Egypt, Syria, Jordan, Iraq, Saudi Arabia). War lasts until 1949.

1950

Jordan
- Abdullah annexes eastern Jerusalem and the West Bank, grants its residents Jordanian citizenship (having expelled all Jews in 1948), and changes the name of the country to the Hashemite Kingdom of Jordan. The international community does not recognize the annexations.

Turkey
- Sends soldiers to Korea to help the United States defend South Korea against North Korean aggression.

1951

Jordan
- Abdullah assassinated by Islamic fanatic opposed to the king's peace talks with Israel.

Libya
- Becomes independent.

Iran
- Mohammad Mossadegh becomes prime minister.

1952

Egypt
- Military officers overthrow King Farouk and declare Egypt a republic.

Jordan
- Hussein ibn Talal named king; he officially takes the throne on his eighteenth birthday in 1953.

Turkey
- Joins the North Atlantic Treaty Organization.

1953

Iran
- Mossadegh overthrown by U.S.-sponsored coup; shah returns from exile.

1954

Egypt
- Nasser emerges as Egypt's undisputed leader.

1956

Egypt
- Nasser officially becomes president after running unopposed in election.

- New constitution.
- Nasser seizes Suez Canal.
- Suez War with Britain, France, and Israel.

Israel
- Suez War.

1958

Egypt/Syria
- Establishment of the United Arab Republic (UAR), which is dissolved in 1961.

Lebanon
- U.S. Marines land to protect government from pro-Nasser Muslim forces.

Iraq
- Military coup overthrows King Faisal and abolishes monarchy; entire royal family is executed.

United Arab Emirates
- Oil discovered in Abu Dhabi.

1960

Turkey
- Military coup ends civilian rule.

1961

Turkey
- Civilian rule restored under a new constitution.

Kuwait
- Becomes independent.

1962

Egypt
- Nasser intervenes in civil war in Yemen with 50,000 soldiers. Egyptian troops will fight in Yemen for more than five years.

Iraq
- Baath Party seizes power, but is overthrown nine months later by pro-Nasser military officers.

Kuwait
- Adopts constitution with parliament, which the ruling emir suspends in 1977, 1986, and 1999.

Yemen
- North Yemen monarchy overthrown; Yemen Arab Republic established.
- Egypt intervenes in civil war with 50,000 troops.

1963

Iran
- Women receive the right to vote.

1964

Palestinians
- Palestine Liberation Organization founded.

1967

Israel/Egypt/Syria/Jordan
- Nasser orders UN peacekeeping force out of the Sinai Peninsula; blockades Israeli port of Elat by closing the Strait of Tiran to Israeli shipping; moves troops and tanks to Israeli border; signs military alliances with Syria and Jordan; proclaims intention to destroy Israel.
- Six-Day War. Israel defeats its opponents and occupies eastern Jerusalem including the Old City, Sinai Peninsula, the West Bank and Gaza Strip, and the Golan Heights.

Yemen
- Britain leaves Aden colony (South Yemen), which becomes People's Democratic Republic of Yemen.

1968

Iraq
- Baath Party again seizes power. Saddam Hussein becomes the power behind the scenes by early 1970s.

1969

Israel/Egypt
- War of Attrition along Suez Canal (continues until 1970).
- Golda Meir becomes prime minister.

Palestinians
- Yasir Arafat becomes head of the PLO.

Libya
- Military coup ends the monarchy and brings Muammar Qaddafi to power.

1970

Egypt
- Nasser dies; Anwar Sadat becomes president.

Jordan
- King Hussein's army crushes the PLO during "Black September" fighting and drives Palestinian militias from the country.

Lebanon
- PLO and armed Palestinian militias, having fled Jordan, establish themselves in southern part of the country.

Oman
- Qaboos bin Said overthrows his father and becomes ruler. Oman begins economic development.

Syria
- Hafez al-Assad takes power.

1971

Syria
- Assad "elected" president with 99.2 percent of the vote.

Qatar
- Becomes independent.

1973

Israel/Egypt/Syria
- Yom Kippur War; Israel again defeats Egyptian and Syrian forces but at extremely high cost in casualties.

Libya
- Qaddafi declares "cultural revolution" against "non-Islamic thinking."

1974

Palestinians
- Arab League officially recognizes PLO as sole representative of the Palestinian people.

Turkey
- Invades Cyprus and sets up "Turkish Republic of Northern Cyprus."

1975

Lebanon
- Civil War begins and lasts until 1989.

Iraq/Iran
- Agreement on division of the Shatt-al-Arab waterway.

Saudi Arabia
- King Faisal assassinated.

1976

Israel
- Yitzhak Rabin becomes prime minister.
- Rescue of Israeli and Jewish hostages at Entebbe.

Libya
- Qaddafi publishes first part of his *Green Book* (parts two and three published respectively in 1978 and 1979).

1977

Egypt/Israel
- Sadat declares willingness to make peace with Israel and visits Jerusalem.

Israel
- Menachem Begin becomes prime minister after Likud defeats Labor in parliamentary elections.

1978

Israel/Egypt
- Camp David Accords.

Israel/Lebanon
- Israeli army invades southern Lebanon to attack PLO bases.

1979

Israel/Egypt
- Israel/Egyptian peace treaty.
- Arab League suspends Egypt, most Arab countries sever diplomatic relations with Egypt, Egypt ousted from several Arab economic and financial institutions.

Iraq
- Saddam Hussein takes power openly as president.

Iran
- Shah flees the country.
- Ayatollah Khomeini comes to power as leader of Islamic Revolution.
- Monarchy is abolished; Iran declared an Islamic Republic.

- Iranian students overrun U.S. embassy and seize hostages; hostage crisis lasts until 1981.

1980

Iraq/Iran
- Saddam Hussein repudiates the 1975 agreement on the Shatt-al-Arab waterway and invades Iran, launching Iran-Iraq war.

Turkey
- Military again seizes power; installs new constitution with more powerful presidency.

1981

Egypt
- Anwar Sadat is assassinated by Islamic fundamentalists for making peace with Israel.
- Hosni Mubarak becomes president.

Israel/Iraq
- Israeli air raid destroys Iraqi nuclear reactor before it is loaded with nuclear fuel and stymies Iraqi plans to develop nuclear weapons.

Libya
- American and Libyan warplanes clash over the Gulf of Sidra.

Iran
- Opponents of the regime kill seventy-four leading

Islamic politicians in bombing attack.

1982

Israel/Lebanon/Palestinians

- Lebanon War: Israel sends its army into Lebanon to destroy PLO bases. PLO forced to leave Lebanon and relocate headquarters in Tunisia. Beginning of costly Israeli military presence that lasts until 1999.
- Christian Lebanese militia forces allied with Israel murder hundreds of Palestinians in two refugee camps near Beirut.

Syria

- Assad has Syrian army destroy Hama, the stronghold of the Islamic fundamentalist Muslim Brotherhood, killing an estimated 20,000 people.

1983

Turkey

- Civilian rule restored, but under tight military supervision.
- Motherland Party, with military support, wins parliamentary elections; Turgut Özal becomes prime minister (and serves until 1989, when he becomes president).

Lebanon

- Shiite suicide bombers attack U.S. and French military bases, killing 241 U.S. Marines and 59 French soldiers.

1984

Egypt

- Trial and execution of Sadat's murderers.

Israel

- Operation Moses (rescue of 8,000 Ethiopian Jews and transporting them to Israel) begins and lasts until 1985.

1985

Israel/Lebanon

- Israel withdraws from most of southern Lebanon to narrow security zone along the Israeli-Lebanese border.

1986

Libya

- American warplanes bomb Libya after its agents are tied to a terrorist nightclub bombing in Europe that kills several American soldiers.

1987

Saudi Arabia

- More than 400 pilgrims in Mecca for the hajj, including 275 Iranians, are killed during rioting at the Grand Mosque.

Palestinians/Israel

- Start of first intifada (uprising) against Israeli occupation of the Gaza Strip and West Bank.

1988

Libya
- Pan American Flight 103 bombed in midair over Lockerbie, Scotland, with 270 lives lost; Libyan agents are implicated.
- UN imposes sanctions on Libya that last until 1999.

Jordan
- King Hussein renounces all Jordanian claims to the West Bank.

Iraq
- Kurdish village of Halabje attacked by Iraqi military using poison gas bombs: 5,000 people are killed and 10,000 injured.

Iraq/Iran
- War ends in stalemate, with Shatt-al-Arab divided as before. Iraq uses chemical weapons to get Iran to accept an end to the fighting.

1989

Egypt
- Readmitted to the Arab League.

Jordan
- First parliamentary elections since the 1950s.

Lebanon
- Taif Agreement ends Lebanese civil war but leaves Syria in control of the country, with more than 30,000 troops occupying key areas.
- Syria orchestrates the election of Elias Harawi as Lebanon's president.

Iran
- Ayatollah Khomeini dies; Ayatollah Khamenei succeeds him as supreme leader.

1990

Iraq/Kuwait
- Iraq's Saddam Hussein invades Kuwait and annexes it to Iraq. Diplomacy fails to get Hussein to withdraw.
- UN imposes trade embargo on Iraq.
- UN authorizes "all necessary means to force Iraq from Kuwait."

Iran
- Earthquake in the northwest kills 40,000 people.

Yemen
- Country reunited for the first time since 1728 as Republic of Yemen.

1991

Israel
- Operation Solomon brings 15,000 Ethiopian Jews to Israel.

Iraq/Kuwait
- Gulf War (also called Operation Desert Storm in the U.S.): most countries of the region involved.

Iraq

- Military forces driven from Kuwait, but not before setting hundreds of oil well fires and causing an environmental disaster in the Persian Gulf region.
- UN Security Council requires that Iraq give up all chemical and biological weapons, as well as all materials for developing nuclear weapons. UN Special Commission on Iraq (UNSCOM) formed to find and destroy Iraq's capabilities to make these weapons.
- Hussein regime begins removing Kurds from city of Kirkuk and surrounding territory in order to "Arabize" that oil-rich region. About 200,000 are forcibly removed by 2001.

Egypt

- Islamic fundamentalists begin attacks on Coptic Christians.

United Arab Emirates

- BCCI bank scandal leads to billions of dollars in losses for investors.

1992

Egypt

- Islamic fundamentalists begin attacks on foreigners, government officials, and intellectuals.
- Boutros Boutros-Ghali becomes UN Secretary-General.

Jordan

- King Hussein treated successfully for cancer in the United States.

Lebanon

- First parliamentary elections in twenty-one years.

1993

Egypt

- Islamic fundamentalist group Holy War tries to blow up the World Trade Center in New York City.

Israel/Palestinians

- Oslo Accords signed in Washington, D.C.

Turkey

- Suleyman Demirel becomes president.
- Tansu Ciller becomes Turkey's first woman prime minester.

1994

Israel/Palestinian Authority

- Cairo agreement fills in various details of Oslo Accords.
- Palestinian Authority established according to Oslo Accords.
- Israel hands over control of Jericho and Gaza Strip to the PA.

Israel/Jordan

- Israel-Jordan peace treaty signed.

Yemen

- Civil war, won by North Yemen side.

1995

Israel/Palestinian Authority
- Oslo II agreement signed in Washington, D.C. Israel withdraws from six more West Bank towns.

Israel
- Prime Minister Rabin assassinated by extremist opposed to the peace process.

1996

Israel

- Benjamin Netanyahu elected prime minister.

Palestinian Authority
- Palestinian Council elected: al-Fatah, led by Arafat, wins a majority.
- Arafat elected president of the PA with 87 percent of the vote.

Iraq
- Saddam Hussein accepts UN "oil for food" program.

Turkey
- Welfare Party, an Islamic fundamentalist group led by Necmettin Erbakan, wins election and takes power (until 1997).

Saudi Arabia
- Islamic fundamentalists bomb U.S. military residence at Khobar Towers, killing nineteen American airmen.

Qatar
- Al Jazeera television station is founded.

1997

Israel/Palestinian Authority
- Hebron Protocol signed: Israel withdraws from most of that city.

Iran
- Sayed Mohammad Khatami is elected president with almost 70 percent of the vote.

Yemen
- Parliamentary elections are reasonably fair, a first for the Arabian Peninsula. However, the presidential election in 1999 is a sham.

1998

Israel/Palestinian Authority
- Wye River Memorandum signed: agreement calls for additional Israeli withdrawals in return for anti-terrorist efforts by the PA and amendment of the PLO charter to eliminate clauses calling for Israel's destruction.
- Palestinian National Council votes to approve a letter to President Bill Clinton stating that twenty-four articles in the PLO Covenant calling for Israel's destruction have been either "nullified" or "modified." Vote is conducted without discussion.

Jordan
- King Hussein again ill with cancer.

Iraq
- U.S. and British warplanes bomb Iraq for four days to force compliance with agreements regarding UNSCOM, but without success.

Turkey
- Military bans Welfare Party; it is reorganized as the Virtue Party.

1999

Egypt
- Mubarak elected to fourth term as president with 94 percent of the vote.

Israel
- Ehud Barak elected prime minister.

Jordan
- King Hussein dies; succeeded by his son Abdullah.

Iraq
- UNSCOM leaves, having been unable to complete its mission.
- UN Security Council replaces UNSCOM with new inspection group, the United Nations Monitoring, Verification, and Inspection Commission (UNMOVIC), but Hussein refuses to allow it into Iraq.

Turkey
- Bulent Ecevit returns to power as prime minister.
- Commandos capture Abdullah Ocalan, leader of the Kurdish rebellion, in Kenya.
- Virtue Party member Merve Kavakci banned from parliament for wearing a traditional Islamic woman's head scarf.
- Kurdistan Workers' Party accepts a cease-fire.
- Catastrophic earthquake near the northern town of Izmit kills at least 18,000 people, injures more than 50,000, and leaves 350,000 homeless.
- Invited to join the European Union, but invitation conditional on major political and economic reforms.

Kuwait
- Emir grants women the right to vote, but parliament refuses to approve the measure, leaving Kuwaiti women without suffrage.

Qatar
- Women are permitted to vote and run for office in municipal elections for the first time.

2000

Israel/Palestinian Authority
- Failure of Camp David peace talks.

- PA launches "second" intifada.

Syria
- Hafez al-Assad dies; his son Bashar becomes president.

Turkey
- Police discover dozens of bodies of people murdered by the Islamic fundamentalist group Hezbollah (not connected with the group of the same name in Lebanon). Among the victims is Konca Kuris, a popular woman author and critic.
- Kurdistan Workers' Party formally announces the end of its rebellion.
- Ahmet Secdet Sezer chosen president by parliament.

Yemen
- Islamic fundamentalists controlled by Osama bin Laden blow up a bomb alongside the U.S. destroyer *Cole*, killing seventeen U.S. sailors and injuring thirty-nine.

2001

Israel
- Ariel Sharon elected prime minister.
- Hamas suicide terrorist murders twenty-one young Israelis outside Tel Aviv disco.

Israel/Palestinian Authority
- Cease-fire designed to end the second intifada signed, but violence continues.

Iran
- Khatami reelected president with 77 percent of the vote.

Libya
- Scottish court convicts one Libyan agent for the midair bombing of Pan American Flight 103 over Lockerbie, Scotland, which cost 270 lives. A second agent is acquitted.

Kuwait
- Country's highest court rejects a suit intended to win women the right to vote.

Encyclopedia

Abdullah ibn Abdel Aziz al-Saud (1923–)

Crown Prince and First Deputy Prime Minister of Saudi Arabia. The second oldest of the surviving sons of Saudi Arabia's founder, Abdullah is expected to become king when the current ruler, King Fahd, Abdullah's older brother, dies. With Fahd seriously ill, Abdullah in effect has held the reins of power in Saudi Arabia since 1997.

Abdullah ibn Hussein (1962–)

King of Jordan. Just before his death in February 1999, King Hussein passed over his brother, Crown Prince Hassan, and selected his eldest son Abdullah as his heir. The British-educated Abdullah pledged to continue his father's policies, including promoting peace between Israel and its Arab neighbors. A career military officer for eighteen years, Abdullah could count on the strong support of the army as he began his reign. A few months after ascending the throne, the king showed his determination to be in touch with the pulse of his country when he twice donned disguises—once posing as a television reporter and the other time as a taxi passenger—to travel around Amman and experience directly how ordinary Jordanians lived. Whether he was successful was another matter. Two years into his reign there was grumbling among many Jordanians that Abdullah was too Western and pushing too hard to modernize a country where traditional values still ruled.

Abu Dhabi City
Capital of the United Arab Emirates. Abu Dhabi has the same name as the UAE's largest member sheikhdom and the island on which it is located. It was founded around 1760 and remained a small trading and pearling center until the oil industry developed in the 1960s. It is now a modern city with sleek office buildings, hotels, and an international airport. Consistent with traditional Muslim attitudes regarding the mixing of the sexes, Abu Dhabi City has a government-run beach reserved exclusively for women.

Alexandria

Located on the Mediterranean coast just east of the Nile delta, Alexandria was founded by Alexander the Great in 332 B.C. Under the Greek Ptolemaic dynasty it was Egypt's capital and most important city, a major port and trading center and, with its great library of 500,000 volumes and university, the intellectual center of the Hellenistic world. (The library, with its priceless ancient knowledge, was destroyed by fire in the first century B.C.) The remains of the magnificent Pharos lighthouse, one of the ancient Seven Wonders of the World, lie under water just offshore. Alexandria was where seventeen-year-old Cleopatra was crowned queen of Egypt in 51 B.C. and where, as part of her political scheming, she later charmed the Roman leaders Julius Caesar and Mark Antony. Beginning in the first century Alexandria was a center of the newly founded Christian religion. It was reduced to the status of Egypt's second city in the tenth century when Egypt's Fatamid Arab rulers founded their new capital at Cairo. Alexandria enjoyed a renaissance in the nineteenth century as the cosmopolitan home to large Greek, Italian, French, and English communities. Their departure after the 1952 revolution ended that era of pluralistic vibrancy. Today Alexandria, still Egypt's second-largest city, is a major port and industrial center.

Ankara

Ankara, the capital of Turkey, was a commercial center in Hittite times 3,800 years ago. Later it was the capital of a Roman province. In 1402 Ankara was the scene of the crushing defeat the notorious Tamerlane dealt the Ottoman Turks. The city was in decline in the nineteenth and early twentieth century and had a population of only 60,000 when Mustafa Kemal Ataturk made it the base of his nationalist movement in 1920 and then Turkey's capital in 1923. Today it is Turkey's second-largest city as well as an industrial and cultural center. It is also home to the *Anitkabir*—the mausoleum of Mustafa Kemal Ataturk.

Amman

Capital of Jordan. Amman and its surroundings probably have been inhabited for almost nine thousand years. Just outside the city is one of the Middle East's largest Neolithic (c. 6500 B.C.) archeological sites. From the third century B.C. until the Arab conquest in A.D. 635 the city was called Philadelphia; the Arabs changed its name to Amman. About half of Jordan's population lives in and around Amman, a far cry from 1948 when it was a dusty town of 25,000 on the edge of the desert. Much of the city's commercial dynamism is due to its Palestinian residents, who came to the city as refugees after the 1948–49 and 1967 Arab-Israeli wars. After the 1991 Gulf War hundreds of thousands of Jordanians and Palestinians expelled from Kuwait settled in Amman.

Arab-Israeli Conflict

The Arab-Israeli conflict dates from the late nineteenth century, when Arabs began to oppose Jewish immigration into what was then called Palestine. After 1948, when Israel became an independent country, that opposition translated into the Arabs refusing to accept Israel's right to exist and attempting to destroy the Jewish state. The Arab refusal to accept Israel's right to exist remains the core issue of the conflict. The Arab states most directly involved in the Arab-Israeli conflict have been Egypt, Syria, Jordan, Lebanon, Iraq, Saudi Arabia, and Libya. Iran, Muslim but not Arab, has been among Israel's most militant foes since its Islamic Revolution of 1979. The Palestinian Arabs formed several dozen organizations [See "Palestinian Organizations"] to oppose Israel, mainly through terrorist attacks and guerrilla warfare. The most important of them is the Palestine Liberation Organization (PLO), founded in 1964.

The Arab-Israeli conflict has produced four wars between Israel and one or more Arab states: Israel's War of Independence (1948–49), which the Arabs call the Palestine War, in which Israel fought Egypt, Syria, Jordan, Iraq, and Lebanon; the Suez War (1956) between Israel and Egypt (in which Britain and France also fought against Egypt); the Six-Day War (1967), in which Israel fought against Egypt, Syria, and Jordan; and the Yom Kippur War of 1973, which the Arabs call the Ramadan War, in which Israel fought Egypt and Syria.

The term "war" sometimes is attached to two other large-scale military confrontations. Israel and Egypt also fought a series of battles along the Suez Canal during 1969–70 known as the War of Attrition. Israel's attempt to drive Palestine Liberation Organization forces from Lebanon in 1982 is called the Lebanon War. There also have been countless incidents of violence, mainly involving terrorist attacks against Israelis by Palestinian guerrillas and retaliation against Palestinian bases by the Israeli military.

Arab-Israeli peacemaking efforts have been based on two United Nations Security Council Resolutions, each adopted in the wake of a major war: Resolution 242 and Resolution 338.

UN Resolution 242 (November 1967) called for Israel to "withdraw from territories" occupied during the Six-Day War of 1967 and for all countries in the area to be guaranteed the right to live in peace within secure and recognized boundaries. Resolution 242 contained ambiguities, among them a lack of precision about the extent of Israel's withdrawal. However, Israel could point to what the resolution did not say. It did not include the word "the" or the word "all" before "territories," nor did it call for a withdrawal to the lines of June 5, 1967. These omissions had been deliberate, as several diplomats involved in drafting the resolution pointed out. This enabled Israel, which was determined not to return to its insecure 1967 borders, to maintain that under Resolution 242 it would not be obligated to withdraw from all the territories taken during the war, an interpretation supported by the United States. Israel also insisted that it was not obligated to evacuate any territories except as part of a general peace agreement, since that was the implied goal of Resolution 242. Not surprisingly, the Arab states interpreted the resolution far differently. They insisted that Israel must withdraw from all territories occupied during the war; at the same time, they expressed no interest in peace. (Syria rejected Resolution 242 entirely.) In fact, at a summit meeting the previous September, the Arab League had responded to Israeli peace proposals with what came to be called the three "noes": no peace, no negotiations, no recognition. UN Resolution 338 (October 1973) called for direct negotiations between Israelis and Arabs to implement Resolution 242. However, Arab leaders refused, as they had since 1948, to deal directly with Israel until Egyptian president Anwar Sadat broke ranks and went to Jerusalem in 1977. That visit led to negotiations that produced the Camp David Accords of 1978 and the Egyptian-Israeli peace treaty of 1979.

The first groundbreaking agreement between the Israelis and Palestinians was the Declaration of Principles of 1993, usually called the Oslo Accords. Negotiated by Israel and the PLO, the Oslo Accords set up the Palestinian Authority. That agreement was followed by the Israeli-Jordanian peace treaty of 1994. A second major Israeli-Palestinian agreement signed in 1995, called the Taba Agreement, but better known as Oslo II, expanded on the 1993 Declaration of Principles. There also have been four narrower agreements focusing on specific Israeli withdrawals from West Bank and Gaza territory in return for Palestinian commitments to Israeli security requirements: the Cairo Agreement of 1994, the Hebron Protocol of

1997, the Wye River Memorandum of 1998, and the Sharm al-Sheikh agreement of 1999.

While these agreements represented progress, they fell far short of a comprehensive Middle East peace. As of mid-2001, many of the most difficult issues between Israel and the Palestinians remained unresolved and peace negotiations have broken down. Most of the Arab world, as well as Iran, continued to be hostile to Israel, and several heavily armed states, including Iraq, Syria, and Libya, formally remained at war with the Jewish state.

Arab League (League of Arab States)

The Arab League was founded in 1945 by Egypt, Syria, Lebanon, Transjordan (present-day Jordan), Iraq, Saudi Arabia, and Yemen. Since then more than a dozen new members from the Middle East and North Africa have joined. Its most influential member has been Egypt, with the exception of the decade (1979–89) when it was suspended from the League for making peace with Israel. The League has tried to promote Arab cooperation in political, economic, and cultural matters. These efforts have enjoyed limited success, largely because of rivalries that divide the Arab states. Various sessions and summit meetings have been boycotted over the years by different members, especially radical states such as Libya, Syria, and Iraq. One of the League's most notable successes was to defend newly independent Kuwait against threats from Iraq in 1961.

The one area where the League maintained unity for decades was in its opposition to Israel. Several member countries jointly attacked Israel in 1948 in an unsuccessful attempt to destroy the Jewish state in its infancy. The League then established an economic boycott of Israel. Aside from banning all trade with Israel, the boycott was extended to companies worldwide that did business of any kind with Israel. This "secondary" boycott went beyond refusing to do business; it included requiring companies to reveal if they had Jewish shareholders, employees, or directors. The boycott finally began to erode in the mid-1980s when several Arab states stopped observing some of its provisions, but it has not been ended.

Iraq's invasion of Kuwait in 1990 and the Gulf War in 1991 deepened old divisions in the League and caused some new ones. When in March 2001 the League finally held its first summit meeting in more than ten years, the only unifying theme its members could find was hostility to Israel. There were a number of harsh anti-Israel speeches, the most strident being Saddam Hussein's, which ended with the line, "May God damn the Jews."[1] Yet the bitter rift between Iraq and Kuwait was not bridged, which made it impossible for League members to unify around an effort to lift UN sanctions against Iraq.

Arafat, Yasir (1929–)

President of the Palestinian Authority. Arafat was born in Cairo, where his father had moved from a small town in what today is the Gaza Strip. He became involved in Palestinian Arab student politics while at Cairo University, graduated as a civil engineer, served in the Egyptian army, and worked as an engineer in Kuwait. In the late 1950s he co-founded the *al-Fatah* ("Conquest") guerrilla organization, which began terrorist operations against Israel in 1965. It also became the strongest Palestinian organization confronting Israel. Arafat became head, or chairman, of the Palestine Liberation Organization, which al-Fatah came to dominate, in 1969. Under Arafat's leadership the PLO became the world's largest and most active terrorist organization, carrying out attacks primarily against Israel, but also against Jordanian and American targets (including American diplomats) in the Middle East and Europe.

After years of calling for Israel's destruction, Arafat finally publicly accepted its right to exist in the 1990s. Under his leadership, the PLO in 1993 negotiated the Oslo Accords, which became the basis for subsequent Israel-Palestinian peace negotiations. However, since then, when speaking to Arab audiences, Arafat repeatedly has compared the Oslo Accords to Mohammad's peace treaty (the Khudaibiya treaty) with a Jewish tribe on the Arabian Peninsula. The treaty was only temporary. Slated to last for ten years, it was broken by Mohammad after two, at which point he attacked and conquered the Jewish tribe. Arafat also has continued to call for *jihad*, or holy war, against Israel.

At the same time, Arafat has met face-to-face with every Israeli prime minister since Yitzhak Rabin as he doggedly pursues his life-long goal of an independent Palestinian state. Key Israeli leaders have changed their views of Arafat over time. Once they considered him their country's permanent enemy with whom no negotiations were possible. After the 1993 Oslo

Agreement they viewed him as a moderate within the Palestinian ranks who was prepared to negotiate a viable peace agreement. However, in July 2000 Arafat rejected extensive concessions made by Israeli prime minister Ehud Barak during negotiations in the United States, and al-Fatah played a prominent role in Palestinian attacks against Israelis that followed the breakdown of negotiations. These developments caused many prominent Israelis who had believed it was possible to work with Arafat to conclude that he was not prepared to conclude a genuine peace with them.

al-Assad, Bashar (1965–)

President of Syria. Assad became Syria's president after the death of his father, Hafez al-Assad, in June 2000. An ophthalmologist by training who was not involved in politics, Bashar Assad did not become his father's heir apparent until his older brother was killed in a car accident in 1994. At that point Assad was called home from London, where he had been studying for two years, given an officer's appointment in the army, and set on a course to gather the power he would need to succeed his father. Not surprisingly, he advanced quickly in the army, reaching the rank of colonel in 1999. That same year he was put in charge of an anticorruption drive that removed a number of high-ranking politicians from office. Unlike his father, Bashar Assad has traveled widely and has an extensive knowledge of the world beyond Syria; he is fluent in both English and French. Assad has been his country's most visible and important advocate of computer literacy as head of the Syrian Computer Society since 1994. Bashar Assad's education and travels do not seem to have made him more tolerant than his father. That became clear in May of 2001 when, in welcoming Pope John Paul II to Syria, Assad made a speech that included extremely crude anti-Semitic remarks.

al-Assad, Hafez (1930–2000)

President of Syria, 1971–2000. Assad was Syria's dictator for three decades, making him among the most durable Middle Eastern leaders. He was born into a prominent family of the minority Alawite sect in a country with a Sunni majority.

Trained as an air force pilot, Assad entered politics and served as minister of defense and commander of Syria's air force before becoming president. Once he was in charge, he relied on Soviet aid and military equipment to build up Syria's armed forces, in effect making Syria a Soviet client state until the Soviet Union collapsed in 1991. Assad dealt with Islamic opposition to his secular regime by brutally suppressing the fundamentalist Muslim Brotherhood

in 1982. Assad's health became problematic after he suffered a heart attack in 1983. Subsequent efforts by Assad's younger half brother Rifaat to position himself to become Syria's next president nearly led to civil war. Assad died in June 2000 and was succeeded by his son Bashar.

Ataturk, Mustafa Kemal (1881–1938)

Founder and first president of the Turkish Republic. Mustafa Kemal was a World War I military hero who led Turkey's revival after the war. He was committed above all else to Turkey becoming a modern secular state based on the Western model and fought Islamic influences in public life at every turn. His secularist and modernizing principles are known as kemalism. Mustafa Kemal took the surname Ataturk, "Father of Turks," in 1934. He and his principles are still mentioned in Turkey's current constitution.

Baghdad

Baghdad, the capital of Iraq, was founded in the eighth century when the Arab Abbasid dynasty ruled the region. The city originally was built inside circular walls on the west bank of the

Tigris River, which explains why it was called the Round City. Eventually the city expanded beyond those walls and to the east bank of the Tigris. Baghdad reached a glorious peak as the Arab world's cultural and intellectual center under the Abbasids in the eighth and ninth centuries. It stood astride major east-west trade routes and was one of the richest cities in the world. The city then declined as Abbasid rule weakened. Centuries of stagnation followed after the Mongols sacked the city and destroyed Baghdad's vital irrigation system. The city started to recover in the twentieth century as the capital of Iraq; beginning in the 1970s oil revenues financed extensive building and industrial and business development. Baghdad was hit on and off by Iranian missiles and bombs during the Iran-Iraq war of the 1980s and suffered extensive damage from allied bombing during the Gulf War of 1991.

Barak, Ehud (1942–)

Prime minister of Israel, 1999–2000. Barak was elected Israel's prime minister in 1999, decisively defeating incumbent Benjamin Netanyahu. Barak's background reflects much of the pain and struggle embedded in the creation and building of Israel. Most of his mother's family died during the Holocaust at Treblinka, one of the Nazi extermination camps. His father was orphaned when his family was murdered in an anti-Jewish riot in his native Lithuania. Barak was born and raised on a kibbutz near the Lebanese border his parents helped found. He spent most of his adult life in the military, eventually becoming the Israel's most decorated soldier. He rose to chief of staff of the Israeli army.

Barak entered politics after retiring from military service in 1995. In the 1999 election campaign, he pledged to do more than Netanyahu to further the peace process with the Palestinians. At the same time, he stressed that he would not compromise Israel's security needs. In 1999 he negotiated the Sharm al-Sheikh agreement with Yasir Arafat. Considered Yitzhak Rabin's political heir, Barak has a bachelor's degree in physics and mathematics from the Hebrew University in Jerusalem, a master's degree in systems analysis from Stanford University in California, and is an accomplished classical pianist. Barak's political fortunes declined after mid-2000 when American-sponsored Israel-Palestinian peace talks failed. Barak had offered the Palestinians unprecedented concessions that most Israelis considered excessive, but Palestinian leader Yasir Arafat nonetheless turned them down. This seriously undermined Barak's standing at home. In February 2001 he was defeated in his reelection bid by Ariel Sharon.

Begin, Menachem (1913–1992)

Prime minister of Israel, 1977–83. Born in Poland, Begin commanded the underground Irgun guerrilla organization that fought both the British and Arabs between 1943 and 1948 when Israel became independent. After years as the leader of the opposition, he finally became prime minister in 1973. Known for his hard-line views toward the Arabs, Begin surprised many observers when he responded to Egyptian president Anwar Sadat's peace initiative in 1977. With American help, the two leaders negotiated the Camp David Accords in 1978 and the Egyptian-Israeli peace treaty in 1979. They also shared the 1978 Nobel Peace Prize. Begin resigned as prime minister in August 1983, depressed over growing Israeli casualties in Lebanon, where he had sent the army to destroy PLO bases in 1982.

Beirut

Lebanon's capital and major port stands where the foot of Mount Lebanon reaches the Mediterranean Sea. Its history goes back to the more than 3,000 years to when it was a Phoenician port. The city remained an important port and cultural center under Greek, Roman, and Byzantine rule, but declined after the sixth century. Its revival began as European influence in the region grew in the 1860s; in 1920 the French made it the capital of their newly created expanded Lebanon. Beirut then prospered as the Middle East's financial center and a city whose lively and cosmopolitan cultural life and physical beauty led many people to call it the "Paris of the Middle East." The Lebanese civil war of 1975–90 left the city divided into Muslim West Beirut and Christian East Beirut and physically and economically devastated. Since the mid-1990s Beirut has been the

scene of major rebuilding, with the focus on restoring its business and commercial center, and with that the city's position of prominence in the region.

Ben-Gurion, David (1886–1963)

First prime minister of Israel. Ben-Gurion served as prime minister from 1948 to 1953 and again from 1955 to 1963. He also served as Israel's first minister of defense. Born in Poland, he arrived in what was then called Palestine in 1906 and spent several years as a farm worker. Ben-Gurion believed in socialist-Zionism, the dominant form of Zionism during his lifetime, which advocated building a Jewish state that would have a socialist economy. The outstanding Zionist and Israeli leader of his generation, Ben-Gurion supported compromise and acceptance of the UN-sponsored partition of Palestine in 1947. After retiring from politics, he lived on a kibbutz in the Negev Desert until his death.

Cairo

Cairo is Egypt's capital and its cultural, financial, and industrial center. More than sixteen million people live in greater Cairo, making it the largest urban center in the Middle East. Founded by the country's Fatamid rulers in A.D. 969, just a few miles north of Egypt's ancient capital of Memphis, Cairo means "the Victorious" in Arabic. Ibn Khaldun, the distinguished fourteenth-century Arab historian, called Cairo "the metropolis of the universe"; today's inhabitants, a bit more modestly, still call it the "Mother of the World." For most of its history Cairo has been the intellectual center of the Arab world. Since 970 it has been the home to the mosque and Islamic university of Al-Azhar, which continues to attract Muslim students from around the world. Many of Cairo's great monuments were built by the Egypt's Mamluke rulers beginning in the thirteenth century. Its modern center, however, is the huge square of Maydan at-Tahrir, which was laid out in 1865. Cairo's Egyptian Museum, built in 1902, contains the world's greatest collection of ancient Egyptian artifacts.

Ciller, Tansu (1946–)

Prime minister of Turkey, 1993–95, 1996. Ciller, who holds a doctorate in economics from the University of Connecticut, is the first and only woman to serve as Turkey's prime minister. She is a conservative who replaced Suleyman Demirel as prime minister when he became the country's president in 1993. Although Ciller once warned that Turkey's Islamic political movement would lead the country into "a thousand years of darkness,"[2] in 1996 she led her True Path Party into a coalition government with the Islamist Welfare Party.

Damascus

The capital of Syria, Damascus may be the oldest continuously inhabited city in the world. It has had the same name for more than 3,500 years. The city exists because of the Barada River, which rises in the Anti-Lebanon mountains and whose waters create an oasis in an otherwise barren region. It was ruled by various ancient conquerors, including the Egyptians and Hittites. Later, Damascus was an important urban center under the Persians, Greeks, and Romans. The apostle Paul was traveling to Damascus, at the time a major commercial center, when he underwent his dramatic conversion to Christianity. Damascus became a Muslim center when the Arab Umayyad dynasty made the city its capital. The Arabs took over the city's large Christian church originally built by the Roman Emperor Theodosius and rebuilt it as the Great Mosque. The mosque has survived several disasters, including a devastating fire in the nineteenth century, and remains one of the largest and most famous mosques in the Muslim world. Damascus remained an important city even after the Umayyads were succeeded by the Abbasids, who moved the Arab capital to Baghdad. But it declined, as did Baghdad, after being sacked by the Mongols, and remained a backwater until the 1940s, when it became

Syria's capital. Today a vastly expanded Damascus is Syria's cultural, financial, and industrial center.

Demirel, Suleyman (1924–)

President of Turkey, 1993–2001. Demirel's first career was as a successful engineer. He then turned to politics as a moderate conservative and served five terms as prime minister from the 1960s to the 1990s. After becoming president in 1993, the once-combative Demirel tried to take on the role of a statesman who avoids partisan political stands and serves as a unifying factor in Turkish life.

Doha

Doha, the capital of Qatar, was once a center of piracy, which led to its being razed in 1867. Prior to the oil boom it remained a village whose inhabitants earned their living by fishing and pearling. In recent decades oil money had turned Doha into a modern city with a deepwater port and international airport.

Ecevit, Bulent (1925–)

Prime minister of Turkey. Ecevit first served as Turkey's prime minister in 1974, and became a hero in Turkey when he ordered the invasion of Cyprus and occupation of 40 percent of the island to protect its Turkish minority. He became prime minister for the fifth time in 1999. In between, Ecevit was Turkey's most prominent left-of-center politician and a critic of the United States. He earned a reputation for financial honesty in a country where that quality is considered rare among politicians. He was imprisoned by the military in 1980 and, after his release, banned from political life while the military governed the country. He made a comeback in the 1990s, taking a hard line against Kurdish separatism and Islamic fundamentalism. Ecevit's nonpolitical interests include literature; he has translated T. S. Eliot's play, *The Cocktail Party*, into Turkish.

Erbakan, Necmettin (1926–)

Former Turkish prime minister, 1996–97. Trained as a mechanical engineer, Erbakan entered politics while in his early forties. His Islamist orientation got him into trouble with secular authorities in the early 1970s and with the military in 1980s, when he was banned from political life for five years. He led the Welfare Party to victory in 1995 and finally became prime minister in 1996. However, pressure from the military undermined his position, and he resigned in 1997. He remains Turkey's leading Islamist politician, but as of mid-2001 was facing a jail sentence for inflammatory remarks made during a political campaign. Many observers considered the matter a free speech issue and were warning that imprisoning Erbakan would hurt efforts to promote democracy in Turkey.

Fahd ibn Abdel Aziz al-Saud (1922–)

King of Saudi Arabia. The eleventh son of Saudi Arabia's founder Abdel Aziz al-Saud (Ibn Saud), Fahd became king at his half brother's death in 1982. He was at first a vigorous ruler, promoting economic development and, in 1981, suggesting the "Fahd Plan" for a peace settlement between the Arab world and Israel. However, his health deteriorated in the mid-1990s; since 1997 Fahd's half brother Abdullah has effectively been in charge of the country.

Gaza City

Gaza City is the capital of the Gaza Strip and the main base of the Palestinian Authority. Its roots date back to when it was an Egyptian garrison town 3,500 years ago. Later it was one of the main cities of the Philistines and, according to the Bible, the place where Samson destroyed one of their temples, killing himself as he brought destruction down on the enemies of the Israelites. Since then Gaza City has seen many conquerors. It became the capital of the Gaza Strip when that area fell under Egyptian control after the 1948–49 Arab-Israeli war and the home to many Arab refugees after that war.

Hussein ibn Talal (1935–1999)

King of Jordan, 1952–1999. Few people expected Hussein to have a long reign when as a teenager he became Jordan's king in 1952. Yet he survived numerous internal and external attempts to depose him and eventually took a leading role promoting peace between the Arab nations and Israel. Under Hussein, Jordan fought in the 1967 Six-Day War against Israel, losing control of the West Bank and eastern Jerusalem as a result. In

September 1970 the king defeated a Palestinian attempt to overthrow him in a short, fierce civil war. Thousands of Palestinians died during what they have since called "Black September."

A moderate in Arab politics and strongly pro-Western, Hussein held the first of many secret meetings with Israeli leaders in 1963. By the time Jordan and Israel finally signed a peace treaty in 1994, Hussein had warm friendships with many influential Israelis, including Yitzhak Rabin and

Shimon Peres. King Hussein's death from cancer in 1999 was widely mourned in the West, and especially in Israel, where he was trusted and respected.

Hussein, Saddam (1937–)

President of Iraq. Born into a landless peasant family, Saddam Hussein has been the unchallenged dictator of Iraq since 1979. He has used purges and murder to retain power, and has led Iraq into two disastrous wars: the eight-year war with Iran (1980–88) and the 1991 Gulf War, which pitted Iraq against a broad coalition of nations led by the United States. Hussein has spent billions of dollars to acquire biological, chemical, and nuclear weapons and appears to have successfully hidden equipment and materials to build these weapons from UN inspectors in the years since the Gulf War. His ruthless repression has enabled him to keep a tight grip on power despite American efforts to undermine his rule.

Islamic Fundamentalism

No development in the Middle East in the past two decades is more important than the resurgence of Islamic fundamentalism. This movement is a reaction to Western influences that have been growing since the early nineteenth century. Islamic fundamentalism rejects all Western secular ideas and values as decadent and destructive to Muslim civilization. It maintains that to combat Western influences, Muslim societies must reassert their Islamic heritage. This requires overthrowing all secular or insufficiently Islamic regimes and replacing them with regimes based strictly on Islamic teachings and on the Sharia, or Islamic law.

The most successful Islamic fundamentalists are in Iran, where they came to power in a revolution led by the Ayatollah Khomeini in 1979. However, Islamic movements are growing in influence in almost every Arab country in the Middle East, from Egypt to Jordan to Saudi Arabia, which has a fundamentalist regime, but one that is not strict enough for certain Islamic groups. In many Arab countries they are the main threat to the existing government. They frequently resort to terrorism and assassination against the regimes they are trying to overthrow. Aside from opposing Western influences in all their forms, Islamic fundamentalist organizations such as the Palestinian group Hamas have taken an uncompromising stand against all peaceful attempts to resolve the Arab-Israeli conflict. They continue to assert that Israel has no right to exist. Islamic fundamentalist groups also have attacked U.S. targets, including the World Trade Center in New York City and the Pentagon in Washington, D.C. The combined death toll of the 2001 attack was over 5,000.

Istanbul

Although Ankara is Turkey's political capital, Istanbul is its industrial, commercial, and cultural center. For 1,600 years before its name was officially changed in 1930, Istanbul was Constantinople, one of the world's great historic cities. Constantinople was founded in A.D. 330 at Europe's eastern rim on the site of the city of Byzantium by the Roman emperor Constantine, who made it the capital of the empire. The city was built on both sides of the Golden Horn, an inlet of the Bosporus, one of the two straits (the other is the Dardanelles) that separate Europe from Asia.

After the collapse of the western part of the Roman empire, Constantinople survived as the capital of the Byzantine Empire. In the sixth century the Byzantine emperor Justinian built the Hagia Sophia, considered the architectural wonder of its day and for 1,000 years the largest church in the Christian world.

The Ottoman Turks turned the Hagia Sophia into a mosque after they conquered Constantinople in 1453; in 1930 Turkish president Mustafa Kemal Ataturk made the building a museum.

Constantinople was by far Europe's largest and richest city during the Middle Ages. Even after it began to decline it remained the center of Orthodox Eastern Christianity until it fell to the Turks. The city enjoyed a building boom and golden age during the sixteenth and seventeenth centuries, when the Ottoman Empire and Turkish culture reached their heights. The majority of Istanbul's most beautiful mosques date from that period. As the city grew it expanded to the Asiatic side of the Bosporus. It experienced explosive growth in the 1970s and 1980s, when it tripled in size. In 1973, the Bosporus Bridge, one of the world's longest suspension bridges, finally linked the two parts of the city. The Second Bosporus Bridge was completed in 1988. In August 1999 Istanbul was among the cities battered by the devastating earthquake that struck northwestern Turkey, killing thousands of people. However, the city's major monuments, including the Hagia Sophia, Topkapi Palace, and the Blue Mosque, escaped severe damage.

Jerusalem

Jerusalem, the capital of Israel, has been at the center of Jewish identity and spiritual life since King David made it the capital of the ancient Israelite kingdom more than 3,000 years ago. Not only specific religious sites, but the city itself is sacred to people of the Jewish faith, who for centuries, when they lived outside the city, have regularly turned to face it in prayer. With a brief interlude in the sixth century B.C. when the Jews were exiled to Babylon, Jerusalem remained the capital of a Jewish state for more than nine hundred years, until the mighty Roman Empire put an end to Jewish independence. It became the capital of an independent Jewish state again in 1949, a year after the establishment of the modern state of Israel.

Jerusalem also has deep religious significance to Christians and Muslims. Christians revere the sites associated with the preaching and crucifixion of Jesus, while Muslims hold sacred the place where they believe the prophet Mohammad rose to heaven.

Jerusalem, whose name means "City of Peace," has known both glory and tragedy in its long and tumultuous history. The Jewish First Temple, built by David's son Solomon, was destroyed by the conquering Babylonians in 586 B.C. The Second Temple, completed about seventy years later, was leveled along with much of the city itself by the Romans in A.D. 70. The Temple's only remnant, known as the Western Wall, is the Jewish people's most important religious shrine. After Roman times Jerusalem passed through the hands of many foreign conquerors, including the Byzantines, Arabs, Christian Crusaders, Egyptian Mamlukes, and Turks. Christians and Muslims both built religious shrines in the city. In the fourth century the Roman emperor Constantine built the Church of the Holy Sepulchre at the site where it is believed Jesus was placed in his tomb after he was crucified. In the late seventh century the Arabs, who often built mosques on the holy sites of conquered non-Muslims, built a mosque called the Dome of the Rock on the vast elevated plaza called the Temple Mount where the two ancient Jewish temples once stood. They later built a second mosque, Al-Aksa, on the Temple Mount.

The Arab-Israeli war of 1948–49 left Jerusalem divided between Jordan and Israel. Jordan controlled the eastern part of the city, including the Old City where the Western Wall is located and which is surrounded by a wall built by the Turks. The Jordanians expelled all Jews from the Old City, destroyed or desecrated its Jewish holy places, and banned Jews from praying at the Western Wall. Christians faced constant discrimination, and eastern Jerusalem's Christian population dropped by more than half under Jordanian rule. Israel controlled the western and newer part of the city, which grew rapidly during the next two decades.

Jerusalem was reunited under Israeli control as a result of the 1967 Arab-Israeli war. Since then access to religious sites has been guaranteed by Israeli law. The appropriate religious authorities, whether Jewish, Christian, or Muslim, have jurisdiction over the city's religious sites. The city, however, remains a point of intense controversy between Israelis and Arabs. The Palestinian Authority claims the eastern part of the city, which it wants as the capital of a future Palestinian state. Israel, however, considers Jerusalem its permanent capital, and most Israelis insist they will never permit the city to be divided.

Kalthoum, Umm (1908–1975)

Egyptian singer and actress. Born in a peasant village, Umm Kalthoum moved to Cairo in the 1920s and in the years that followed became famous throughout the Arab world. Her fans traveled to Cairo from all over the Middle East on the first Thursday of every month just to hear her concerts, which usually consisted of one traditional song lasting for hours. Later, in the 1960s, Egyptians paused each night to listen to their beloved "Star of the East" perform on the radio. She was for many years the most popular singer in the Arab world. People packed Cairo's concert halls to see her in person and flocked to movie theaters throughout the Arab would to watch her films. In her later years Kalthoum stressed her attachment to the people and values of Egypt's traditional villages. She rejected modern music and always sang classical Arab melodies. When Umm Kalthoum died in 1975, leaders from across the Arab world attended her funeral, along with movie stars, literary figures, businesspeople, and thousands of ordinary Egyptians.

Even though Kalthoum has been dead for a quarter of a century, her songs are still heard throughout Egypt, much as the Beatles remain popular in the West. Egyptians have a saying that two things in their country never change, "the pyramids and the voice of Umm Kalthoum."

Katsav, Moshe (1945–)

President of Israel. Although Israel's presidency is mainly a ceremonial post with little power, Moshe Katsev's election to the post by parliament in July 2000 was a landmark because he was the first Sephardic Jew to hold that position. Born in Iran and the oldest of ten children, Katsav immigrated to Israel with his family in 1951 and grew up in a tent camp in the southern part of the country. The camp eventually developed into a small working-class town populated mainly by poor Jews who had immigrated from Middle Eastern countries. As a boy Katsav learned to speak Arabic from Jewish children who were immigrants from Arab countries. He became the first child from his town to attend a university and continued to live there with his wife and five children even as he rose through the Israel's political ranks and became a government minister. After his election, Katsav said he intended to represent all Israelis—religious and secular Jews, Sephardic and Ashkenazic Jews, and Israel's Arab citizens—and hoped they would all see him as their president.

al-Khalifa, Sheikh Hamad bin Isa (1950–)

Emir (ruler) of Bahrain. Sheikh Hamad came to power in 1999 at the death of his father, who had ruled as Bahrain's emir since 1961. Sheikh Hamad is a graduate of a British military academy and an experienced military commander. Bahrain's crown prince since 1964, he was in charge of building its military strength. He supports Bahrain's growing cooperation with Western powers in the Persian Gulf region.

Khamenei, Ayatollah Ali Hussein (1939–)

Supreme leader of Iran. Iran's president from 1981 to 1989 and a former student of the Ayatollah Khomeini, Khamenei succeeded his teacher as Iran's supreme religious leader when Khomeini died in 1989. Khamenei had remained in Iran during Khomeini's period of exile and was arrested six times. He also spent two years exiled to a remote Iranian province. After 1979 he served in several important posts before becoming the country's president. Although more moderate than his predecessor on issues such as economic reform, Khamenei remains bitterly anti-Western and uncompromisingly opposed to Israel's right to exist. In 1999 his regime used violence and threats of severe punishment to disperse and silence student protesters demanding democratic reforms.

Khatami, Sayed Mohammad (1943–)

President of Iran. Born into a highly religious family, Khatami earned a degree in theology and also studied philosophy. He later studied abroad and served as the head of the Islamic Center of Iran in Hamburg, Germany. After Iran's Islamic Revolution, he served for ten years as minister of education and Islamic instruction until conservative clerics forced his resignation in 1992. He later served as adviser to President Ali-Akbar Rafsanjani and taught political theory at the University of Tehran. In 1997, despite opposition from conservative religious leaders, Khatami ran for president as a reform candidate and was elected

with 69 percent of the vote. However, his limited powers prevented him from delivering any substantial reforms. The lack of change provoked student riots in 1999. Although the students constantly repeated their support for Khatami, he was forced to bow to pressure from supreme leader Ayatollah Khamenei and other conservative clerics and to repudiate the demonstrators even as he continued to advocate reform. In June 2001 Khatami was reelected to a second term with 77 percent of the vote. Unlike the Ayatollah Khamenei and many other Iranian leaders, Khatami is at ease among ordinary Iranians and appears responsive to their right to ask questions and expect answers.

Khomeini, Ayatollah Ruhollah (1902–1989)

Founder of Iran's Islamic Republic and its supreme leader, 1979–89. Khomeini was only five months old when his father, an Islamic clergyman, was murdered. By the age of six, he reportedly knew the Koran by heart. Trained as an Islamic cleric, he bitterly opposed the secularist policies of Mohammad Reza Shah Pahlavi and was forced into exile in 1963. Khomeini continued his campaign from exile, returning to Iran in triumph in February 1979 following the shah's overthrow. Khomeini then ruthlessly eliminated all opposition to the new Islamic republic and held ultimate authority as Iran's supreme religious leader until his death.

Kuwait City

Kuwait's capital was founded in 1710. In 1776 the British East India Company established a base there as a stopover point along the route from Britain to India. The city sustained severe damage during the Iraqi occupation of Kuwait in 1990–91, but that has since been repaired. Its main landmark is Kuwait Towers, a Swedish-designed structure made up of three towers, the tallest of which stands 613 feet (187 meters) high. Kuwait City's port area contains shipyards and oil refineries. Although Kuwait City is in the desert, Kuwait's desalinization plants provide water for parks and trees that line many of its streets.

Lahoud, Emile (1936–)

President of Lebanon. Lahoud was Syria's choice to become Lebanon's president when the parliament elected him in 1999. Prior to becoming president Lahoud served as the commander of Lebanon's army for nine years. He has studied military science in Britain and speaks English fluently.

Mahfouz, Naguib (1911–)

Egyptian novelist, short story writer, and screenwriter. Mahfouz, winner of the Nobel Prize in Literature in 1988, is widely considered the twentieth century's outstanding Arabic writer. His writing presents realistic portrayals of Egyptian social and political life and deals with issues such as the condition of political prisoners and women. A major theme in his work is that private morality cannot be separated from social morality. Mahfouz is most famous for his "Cairo Trilogy," the novels *Palace Walk*, *Palace of Desire*, and *Sugar Street* (1956–57). His novel *Children of Gebelawi* (1959) aroused controversy in Egypt because it put

Islam, Christianity, and Judaism on the same level, rather than presenting the latter two religions as inferior to Islam. Mahfouz strongly supported Anwar Sadat's policy of peace with Israel and has continued to advocate peace with Israel since Sadat's death. Because of that stand his books are not available in some Arab countries. In December 1988, the month Mahfouz was awarded the Nobel Prize, religious authorities in Egypt blocked the newspaper serialization of one of his books because it allegedly was destructive of Islamic values. In 1994 Mahfouz was stabbed in the neck in an assassination attempt by an Islamic fundamentalist. Mahfouz's wounds from that attack still affect his neck and arms and impair his physical ability to write.

Manama

Bahrain's capital and commercial center. Founded about 650 years ago, Manama was under Portuguese control for about 80 years before 1602 and under Persian rule from 1602 until 1783. The city is divided into a new area of gleaming modern hotels and office buildings constructed on reclaimed land and older sections that look much like they did a half century ago. Manama has a shipyard for building dhows, the traditional Arab boats of the Persian Gulf.

Manco, Baris (1943–1999)

Turkish musician and cultural figure. For decades Baris Manco was one of Turkey's most famous and beloved cultural figures. His more than two hundred recordings were enormously popular in remote rural areas as well as in Turkey's cities. Manco dressed ostentatiously in clothes he designed himself and wore his hair shoulder length. In the 1970s he was offered a television show on Turkey's only station, which was state controlled, if he would cut his long hair. When he refused, the normally uncompromising authorities gave in and Manco became the first countercultural figure to appear on Turkish television. His show ran for almost ten years and was the longest running in the country's history. Manco tried to educate his audience. The first half of the show was aimed at children, and a generation grew up singing "My Friend the Donkey" and other Manco songs. The second half featured documentaries about foreign countries and cultures. Manco's music was popular throughout the Balkans, Central Asia, and in many Arab countries. He took great pride in his first name, which means "peace" in Turkish. Thousands of people turned out for Manco's funeral, which was broadcast on national television.

Mecca

Mecca, the birthplace of the Prophet Mohammad in A.D. 570, is Islam's holiest city. All Muslims who are able to are expected to make the hajj, or pilgrimage, to Mecca once in their lifetimes, and about one million do so each year. Muslims all over the world say their daily prayers facing Mecca. The Great Mosque stands at Mecca's center; inside the Mosque is the Kaaba, a cube-shaped shrine covered by a black cloth that houses the holy Black Stone. The Black Stone, which may be a meteor, has been an object of worship since pre-Islamic times. The touches and kisses of uncounted pilgrims over many centuries have worn it smooth.

The hajj has not been without problems, especially in recent years. In 1979 more than 100 people died when Muslim fundamentalists seized the Grand Mosque and held it for two weeks. In 1987, more than 400 people died during a confrontation between Iranian pilgrims and Saudi authorities. In 1990, a stampede in a tunnel near the pilgrimage sites caused the deaths of more than 1,400 pilgrims.

Prior to Mohammad's birth Mecca was a commercial and religious center for pagan Arab tribes. The city has changed hands numerous times in its long history, most recently in 1924 when Abdel Aziz al-Saud seized it from the Hashemite clan as he completed his unification of Saudi Arabia.

Meir, Golda (1898–1978)

Israeli prime minister, 1969–1974. Meir was born in Russia but raised and educated in the United States from the age of eight before immigrating to what was then called Palestine in 1921. She was Israel's first ambassador to the Soviet Union and served as minister of labor and foreign minister before becoming prime minister in 1969. Meir was Israel's first (and up to now only) woman prime minister and the first woman to head a government in the Middle East. She led Israel through the 1973 Yom Kippur War, but resigned in 1974 in the wake of a special commission's report that criticized her government for being unprepared when Egypt and Syria attacked Israel.

Mubarak, Hosni (1928–)

President of Egypt. Mubarak became president of Egypt after Anwar Sadat's assassination in 1981. He was trained as an air force pilot and commanded the Egyptian Air Force in the 1973 war with Israel. In 1975 he was appointed Egypt's vice president. Unlike Nasser and Sadat, his two charismatic predecessors, Mubarak has an unemotional and unideological approach to politics. His policies, both at home and abroad, stress pragmatism and moderation. Mubarak is popular in Egypt, but his government also faces significant opposition, particularly from Islamic fundamentalists. He has maintained strong ties with the United States, being especially helpful in mobilizing Arab support for the Gulf War. A consistent supporter of the Israeli-Palestinian peace process, Mubarak at the same time has done little to encourage Egyptian-Israeli ties beyond the formal peace that exists between the two countries.

Muscat

Capital of Oman. A port city surrounded by mountains, Muscat's history as a center for trade with East Africa dates from the thirteenth century. The Portuguese held the port from 1508 until 1648 and it was briefly under Persian control in the early 1740s. Two sixteenth-century Portuguese forts still overlook the entrance to Muscat and the city's royal palace. The city's long-standing trade ties with Asia, Africa, and Europe give it a cosmopolitan atmosphere unmatched in the Persian Gulf region.

al-Nahyan, Sheikh Zayed bin Sultan (1918–)

President of the United Arab Emirates. Sheikh Zayed has been the emir of Abu Dhabi since 1966 and the president of the UAE since its founding in 1971. He came to power in Abu Dhabi via

a coup against his elder brother, who had opposed using oil revenue to promote economic development. Sheikh Zayed has been trying to strengthen the UAE's federal government in order to promote greater unity against the resistance of several of the small emirates, especially Dubai.

Nasser, Gamal Abdel (1918–1970)

President of Egypt, 1954–70. The son of a postal clerk, Nasser led the revolt that ended the Egyptian monarchy in 1952 and soon ruled Egypt with dictatorial powers. His militant Arab nationalism and personal charisma helped make him the symbol of Arab revival throughout the Middle East. Nasser's ideas—sometimes called Arab socialism—combined elements of anticolonialism, socialism, social reform, economic modernization, a commitment to Arab unity, and traditional Islamic ideas. He was anti-Western and committed to the destruction of Israel. His immense popularity in the Arab world survived the military defeats at the hands of Britain, France, and Israel in 1956 and in the Six-Day War against Israel in 1967. Nasser also was considered one of the outstanding leaders among nonaligned nations of Asia and Africa during the Cold War era. His stature in the Arab world has not been matched by that of any subsequent leader.

Netanyahu, Benjamin (1949–)

Prime Minister of Israel, 1996–99. Netanyahu was the first Israeli prime minister chosen directly by the voters rather than by parliament, defeating Shimon Peres in an election held in 1996. He also was the first prime minister born after the state of Israel's founding. Prior to becoming prime minister, Netanyahu served as Israel's ambassador to the United Nations

and as deputy foreign minister. Netanyahu was critical of the Oslo Accords, but pledged to implement them as prime minister. However, he insisted that additional Israeli concessions would depend upon the Palestinian Authority complying more fully with its commitments to Israel and doing more to combat terrorism. Nonetheless, in 1997 the Netanyahu government withdrew Israeli forces from most of the city of Hebron. In 1998 Netanyahu negotiated the Wye River Memorandum calling for further Israeli withdrawals from the West Bank, but carried out only one of three called-for withdrawals because he maintained the Palestinians were not meeting all their obligations under the agreement. Netanyahu left office after being defeated by Ehud Barak in elections held in May 1999.

Nuclear and Other Nonconventional Weapons

There are three types of nonconventional weapons: nuclear, chemical, biological. Because of their great killing power, they are also known as weapons of mass destruction. Several nations in the Middle East have at least one of these three types of weapons.

Israel is the only nuclear power in the Middle East. It has never officially admitted having nuclear weapons, but probably developed its first nuclear bomb in the late 1960s. Today it may have as many as one hundred nuclear bombs. Israel also has developed guided missiles and is one of a handful of nations that has used its own rocket to put a satellite into orbit. Israel never has used its nonconventional weapons.

Iraq has had a nuclear program since the 1970s, but its effort to build a nuclear bomb was set back in 1981 when Israeli jets destroyed its French-built nuclear reactor just before it was about to be loaded with nuclear fuel. In the aftermath of the Gulf War United Nations inspectors discovered that since that incident Iraq had put together an ambitious program to build a nuclear bomb. The UN destroyed the facilities it found in Iraq, but Iraq is widely believed to have the capability to restart its program in the future. Iraq also had a large stockpile of chemical weapons, which it made use of on the battlefield against Iran and against Kurdish civilians inside Iraq. UN inspectors also found proof that Iraq had developed biological weapons.

Iran is attempting to build nuclear weapons and the missiles to deliver them, as well as chemical and biological weapons. It has received technical help from Russia in developing both nuclear weapons and long-range guided missiles. Iran also has hired Russian scientists privately, taking advantage of Russia's hard economic times in the last ten years, which has left many of its scientists unable to make a living at home. Those scientists are helping Iran develop all three types of nonconventional weapons. The United States, deeply worried that Iran might develop weapons of mass destruction, has pressured the Russians to stop helping Iran build nuclear weapons and missiles, but is not satisfied that the assistance has been stopped.

Egypt has had chemical weapons for more than thirty years, and used them when it intervened in Yemen's civil war in the 1960s. Syria also has chemical weapons and missiles with ranges up to 300 miles (500 kilometers) to deliver them. Libya also probably has the ability to build chemical weapons. The United States government is especially concerned about nonconventional weapons in Iranian, Syrian, and Libyan hands because all three nations have been linked to international terrorism. Saudi Arabia, which reportedly has helped finance Pakistan's nuclear program, is also believed to be interested in acquiring a nuclear military capability.

Oil, OPEC, OAPEC

The Middle East has almost 700 billion barrels of oil reserves, about two-thirds of the world's total. Most of that is located in five countries: Saudi Arabia, Iraq, Kuwait, the United Arab Emirates, and Iran. Saudi Arabia alone has a quarter of the world's oil reserves. These states are the main powers in the Organization of Petroleum Exporting Countries (OPEC), a cartel established in 1960 that includes oil producing countries from outside the Middle East. OPEC's main goal is to control production so that oil prices remain high, but not so high that oil consumers will seek alternative forms of energy. In 1979 OPEC nations profited enormously when disorder caused by Iran's Islamic Revolution cut that country's production drastically, and world oil prices skyrocketed. From the mid-1980s until 1999, however, OPEC was unable to control production, and therefore prices, in large part because some members with large populations needed to sell as much oil as possible. The result was lower oil prices for importing nations such as the United States. That changed in early 1999, when OPEC and nonmember producing countries such as Russia, Mexico, and Norway agreed to cut production by two million barrels per day. When the countries involved actually adhered to their assigned cuts, oil prices doubled within six months.

The Organization of Arab Petroleum Exporting Countries (OAPEC) includes most Arab oil-producing nations, but has been much less active than OPEC. Its most significant act was to proclaim an oil boycott during the Yom Kippur War in October 1973 against Western countries until Israel withdrew from all territories it occupied in 1967. The United States remained subject to the oil boycott for six months, until March 1974. The Arab oil boycott cost the U.S. 500,000 jobs.

Oz, Amos (1939–)

Israeli writer. Amos Oz is Israel's best known contemporary writer. His novels, including *My Michael*, are internationally known and have been translated into twenty-eight languages. Oz for many years lived on a kibbutz in Israel and served in the Israeli army in the 1967 and 1973 wars. He was strongly influenced by the ideas of socialist-Zionism, which gave rise to the kibbutz movement. Among the themes in Oz's later fiction are the moral dilemmas Israel faced in controlling a large Palestinian population on the West Bank and Gaza in the decades after the 1967 war. He has long been an active supporter of reconciliation between Israelis and Palestinians.

Pahlavi, Mohammad Reza Shah (1919–1980)

Shah of Iran, 1941–79. Mohammad Reza Shah Pahlavi came to the throne after Britain and the Soviet Union deposed his father, who was sympathetic to Nazi Germany. In 1953, after

Pahlavi was forced to flee the country by radical nationalists, the United States intervened to restore him to power. With American support, he launched his "White Revolution" of social reform and modernization. The reforms, which included emancipation of women, angered Islamic traditionalists. The shah's dictatorial methods made him additional enemies. Although he was America's closest ally in the Persian Gulf region, the United States could do little to help him when opposition mounted in 1979. The shah, already ill with cancer, fled Iran in 1979 and died a year later.

Palestine

Palestine's boundaries have shifted over the centuries, although at a minimum they have included the territory between the Mediterranean Sea and the Jordan River. The region has had many different names. It was called Canaan in ancient times prior to the arrival of the Israelites. After the Israelites established themselves in the region, they briefly united most of it under their kings David and Solomon (usually called the Kingdom of David and Solomon). In the tenth century B.C. that kingdom split into two independent states: Judea in the south and Israel in the north. Although Israel disappeared after its conquest by the Assyrians in the seventh century B.C., Judea survived until Roman times.

"Palestine," which means "Land of the Philistines," has no historic link with any of the current inhabitants of the region, whether Jewish or Arab. It was the name given to the region by the Romans after they suppressed the second Jewish revolt against their rule in A.D. 135. The Romans chose that name to replace Judea in order to blot out any identification of the country with the Jews. "Palestine" had nothing to do with anyone living there at the time: The actual Philistines, who had lived along the region's Mediterranean coast beginning in about 1200 B.C., had long disappeared as an identifiable people.

Between Roman times and the twentieth century, the region again had a variety of names, depending on who was in control. In 1099 the Crusaders conquered the city of Jerusalem. They briefly united as the Latin Kingdom of Jerusalem an area that included most of present-day Israel, the West Bank, Gaza, western Jordan, and southern Lebanon. The Ottomans, who controlled the region from 1518 until 1917, divided it into three different administrative units, none of which was called Palestine. After World War I the British received a mandate from the League of Nations to govern what the League called Palestine. The mandate, which called for the establishment of a Jewish national home, initially extended eastward to include what today is Jordan. The British severed all territory west of the Jordan River—about three-quarters of the original mandate—from Palestine in 1923 to create the Kingdom of Transjordan. The majority of the region known as Palestine from the early 1920s until 1948 is occupied by the state of Israel. The rest consists of the West Bank and Gaza Strip, where Israel and the Palestinian Authority respectively exercise varying degrees of control.

Palestinian Organizations

By far the most important of the dozens of organizations formed by Palestinian Arabs is the Palestine Liberation Organization (PLO). It was founded in 1964, when Jordan controlled the West Bank and eastern Jerusalem and Egypt controlled the Gaza Strip. Since then it has served as the umbrella organization bringing together many independent groups, often with sharply conflicting views. The PLO was initially set up by the Arab League and was not really controlled by Palestinians themselves for about five years. Its founding covenant—adopted in 1964 and amended in 1968—repeatedly denied Israel's right to exist and called for its destruction. The PLO Covenant therefore was a stumbling block in the Israeli-Palestinian peace process until it was amended in 1999. Yasir Arafat became the PLO's chairman in 1969 and proved to be an effective leader. His achievements included winning observer status for the PLO at the United Nations in 1974 and, by the late 1970s, diplomatic recognition from more than one hundred countries. The funds for the PLO's $500 million budget came mainly from the oil-rich Arab states.

The largest and most powerful PLO member is al-Fatah ("Conquest" in Arabic), co-founded by Arafat in 1958. Arafat built al-Fatah into the most powerful Palestinian guerrilla group, and it has dominated the PLO since 1969. A large part of its reputation came from terrorist attacks against Israel, but it also made Americans a target, including two diplomats murdered in 1973 in Khartoum, capital of Sudan. At its peak in the 1970s al-Fatah had an armed force of 6,000 to 10,000 fighters.

Other PLO groups generally were even more militant than the Fatah in rejecting any political solution to the Arab-Israeli conflict. They also carried out terrorist acts against Israel. The largest was the Popular Front for the Liberation of Palestine (PFLP), led by Dr. George Habash, which combined Arab nationalism with Marxist-Leninist ideology. It carried out several airline hijackings and in 1972 murdered 27 passengers at Israel's main airport. A smaller but equally militant group was the Democratic Front for the Liberation of Palestine (DFLP), led by a Jordanian named Naif Hawatma. The DFLP is best known for murdering twenty-two Israeli schoolchildren and wounding more than one hundred in the small town of Ma'alot. Both the PFLP and DFLP, along with others both inside and outside the PLO, opposed the Oslo Accords and all peace negotiations Arafat conducted with Israel.

Perhaps the most radical of all Palestinian groups was the Fatah Revolutionary Council, better known, after its leader, as the Abu Nidel group. Abu Nidel was a renegade within the Palestinian movement who in the 1970s was condemned to death by Fatah for planning to assassinate Yasir Arafat. At various times his organization was based in Iraq, Syria, and Libya. The United States at one point considered him the most dangerous terrorist in the world, and in 1991 blamed him for more than one hundred terrorist attacks since 1974.

In the 1980s Palestinians began forming groups with Islamic fundamentalist beliefs. The largest and best known is Hamas (Movement of Islamic Resistance), led by Sheikh Ahmad Yasin. Yasin and several other Islamic leaders founded Hamas in 1987. The organization opposes any peace with Israel and has carried out suicide bombings inside Israel in an attempt to stop the peace process. It wants to see Israel replaced by an Arab Islamic state. Another important fundamentalist group is Islamic Jihad, founded in the mid-1980s, which also has opposed the peace process with suicide bombing attacks against Israeli civilians.

Peres, Shimon (1923–)

Prime minister of Israel, 1984–86, 1995–96. Peres was born in Poland, arriving with his family in what was then called Palestine in 1934. Under David Ben-Gurion, Peres played a major role in building Israel's military capabilities, including its program to develop nuclear weapons. From the 1970s until the 1990s he and Yitzhak Rabin struggled for leadership of Israel's Labor Party. Peres began the peace negotiations

that led to the 1993 Oslo Accords while serving as Israel's foreign minister under Rabin. Peres became prime minister for the second time in 1995 when Rabin was assassinated, but lost to Benjamin Netanyahu in the 1996 elections.

Qaddafi, Muammar (1942–)

Dictator of Libya. Even though he holds no official government post, Muammar Qaddafi dominates Libya today as he has for three decades. His ruthlessness is matched only by his grand visions and vast ambitions. These range from uniting the Arab world under his leadership, to uniting Africa, to relieving Libya's water shortage with his "Great Man-Made River" project. His other passionately held goal is the destruction of Israel.

Qaddafi also bitterly detests the United States. He has supported terrorist organizations both in the Middle East and in Europe, which is why the United States bombed his capital of Tripoli in 1986. In 1999 there were widespread reports that Qaddafi had been seriously injured in an assassination attempt. These reports appeared to be confirmed when he was interviewed by a Western news organization sitting in a wheelchair and looking pale and weak. Opposition to his regime appears to be growing, but reports about attempted coups and Qaddafi's declining health only add to the mysteries surrounding one of the most durable and charismatic leaders in the Middle East.

Rabin, Yitzhak (1922–1995)

Prime minister of Israel, 1974–77, 1992–96. Rabin fought in Israel's War of Independence of 1948–49 and rose to become the Israeli army's chief of staff. He became a hero when he led the army to victory over Egypt, Syria, and Jordan in the 1967 Six-Day War. He joined the Labor Party after retiring from the army. During his second term as prime minister, Rabin presided over secret talks with the Palestine Liberation Organization that led to the Oslo Agreement in September 1993. The next year Rabin's government negotiated a peace treaty with Jordan. Rabin's peace policies, which included turning land over to Palestinian control,

were bitterly opposed by right-wing Israeli extremists, and he was assassinated by a religious fanatic on November 4, 1995

Riyadh

The capital of Saudi Arabia. Riyadh in the early nineteenth century became the center of the Wahhabi fundamentalist religious movement that today dominates Saudi Arabia. It also was the base from which Abdel Aziz al-Saud (Ibn Saud) began his conquest of that country. Riyadh is an oasis town about 240 miles (390 kilometers) inland from the Persian Gulf. In recent decades it has grown from a medieval town into a modern city. It is Saudi Arabia's business, industrial, educational, and administrative center and the largest city on the Arabian Peninsula.

al Sabah, Sheikh Jaber al-Ahmad (1920–)

Emir (ruler) of Kuwait. Sheikh Jaber has ruled Kuwait since 1977. He restored Kuwait's parliament, suspended a year before he came to the throne, in 1980, but suspended it again in 1986. He survived a Shiite assassination attempt in 1985. Sheikh Jaber fled Kuwait when Iraq invaded in 1990 and established a govern-

ment in exile in Saudi Arabia. After the American-led coalition liberated Kuwait, Sheikh Jaber, under Western pressure, restored Kuwait's parliament. He caused an enormous stir among his conservative subjects in 1999 when he issued a decree giving Kuwaiti women the right to vote. However, Kuwait's parliament voted against the decree, and as of mid-2001 it had yet to become law.

Sadat, Anwar (1918–1981)

President of Egypt, 1970–1981. After a career spent in the shadow of Gamal Abdel Nasser, Sadat became president of Egypt on Nasser's death and emerged as one of the outstanding statesmen of the modern Middle East. Like Nasser, he governed with dictatorial powers. His first dramatic move was to shift Egypt from a pro-Soviet to a pro-American stance. After launching the Yom Kippur War against Israel in 1973, Sadat became a peacemaker. His peace initiative of 1977 won him a share (with Israeli prime minister Menachem Begin) of the 1978 Nobel Peace Prize. In 1979 he came to Washington to sign the Israeli-Egyptian peace treaty. The treaty earned Sadat great respect in Israel and the West, but bitter hatred in most of the Arab world. He was assassinated in 1981 by Islamic fundamentalists opposed to peace with Israel.

al Said, Qaboos ibn Said (1940–)

Sultan (ruler) of Oman. Qaboos came to power in 1970 by overthrowing his father, an archconservative opposed to any reform. As Oman's sultan, Qaboos promoted economic and social development. He distinguished himself by following a foreign policy that broke with Arab rejection of Israel's right to exist. Under Qaboos, Oman was the only Arab country that openly supported Anwar Sadat's peace with Israel. After the Israeli-Palestinian

Oslo Agreement, Qaboos fostered ties between Oman and Israel and hosted visits to Oman by two Israeli prime ministers, Yitzhak Rabin in 1994 and Shimon Peres in 1996. Qaboos also has strongly supported United States policies in the Persian Gulf region.

Saleh, Ali Abdullah (1942–)

President of Yemen. Saleh was president of North Yemen from 1978 to 1990 before becoming president of a united Yemen in 1990. In reality, he rules Yemen as the head of a military dictatorship. He angered Saudi Arabia by remaining neutral in the Gulf War crisis of 1990–91, and the Saudis retaliated by supporting a secessionist movement in Yemen in 1994. Saleh's success in defeating that movement boosted his standing in Yemen.

Sanaa

Capital of Yemen. Sanaa stands on a high plateau in the interior of Yemen more than a mile above sea level. Founded in the second century A.D., its name means "fortified city," and much of its ancient city wall still stands. Muslim conquerors in the seventh century destroyed most important pre-Islamic struc-

tures and replaced them with mosques. Over the centuries Sanaa was the scene of many battles and its fortunes rose and fell according to shifting balances of power in the region. Sanaa became the capital of the Kingdom of Yemen (North Yemen) in 1918, but lost that status between 1948 and 1962. It became a capital again in 1962 with the founding of the Yemen Arab Republic, and in 1990 became the capital of a united Yemen. Sanaa's population has mushroomed from 34,000 in 1962 to almost one million today. Its Muslim university and other centers of learning make it a center of Islamic culture.

Sharon, Ariel (1928–)

Prime minister of Israel. Born in a small Jewish cooperative agricultural village, Ariel Sharon joined the Hagana, the Jewish self-defense organization during the era of the British mandate in Palestine, at the age of fourteen. He remained a soldier and became one of Israel's most brilliant and daring army commanders in a military career that lasted until 1973. Sharon commanded an infantry company during Israel's War of Independence in 1948–49. After the war he organized and commanded the special "101" commando unit whose job it was to retaliate for Arab terrorist attacks against Israeli civilians launched from the Egyptian-controlled Gaza Strip and the Jordanian-controlled West Bank. Sharon commanded a parachute brigade that fought one of the key battles of the 1956 Suez war, the armored division that seized control of the Sinai Peninsula in the 1967 Six-Day War, and an armored division during the 1973 Yom Kippur War. Having led his division across the Suez Canal and encircled the Egyptian army, Sharon, who even before 1973 was considered one of Israel's legendary soldiers, emerged from the Yom Kippur War as a national hero.

Sharon then entered politics and was minister of defense when Israel invaded Lebanon in June of 1982 to drive the PLO from that country and end its attacks against Israeli territory and civilians. In September, when the fighting was almost over and the Israeli army had surrounded Beirut, Lebanese Christian militiamen entered two refugee camps near the city and murdered hundreds of Palestinian civilians. Although Israeli troops were not involved, the incident shocked the Israeli public, and a special government commission found Sharon indirectly responsible because he had not anticipated what the Lebanese Christians might do and stopped them from entering the refugee camps. He was forced to resign, but remained active in politics and held several ministerial posts in various Israeli governments in the 1980s and 1990s. In February 2001 he was elected prime minister in a landslide victory.

Shemer, Naomi (1931–)

Israeli songwriter and composer. Shemer is known as the "First Lady of Israeli Song." Her most famous song is "Jerusalem of Gold." She wrote it in 1967 just before the Six-Day War and then revised it with the addition of a new stanza to reflect the reunification of the city that took place after the war. The song eloquently expressed the Israeli emotions about Jerusalem and almost took on the status of an unofficial national anthem. In 1998 it was chosen in a national survey as the "Song of the Jubilee," the most popular song in Israel's first fifty years. Another enormously popular Naomi Shemer song is "Lu Yehi" ("Let It Be"), which is about the 1973 war. The song began as a translation of the Beatles' song of the same name, but Shemer then changed it into an original composition. Naomi Shemer's enormous contributions to Israeli music won her the prestigious Israel Prize in 1983.

Tarkan (1972–)

Turkish pop music star. Tarkan actually is an international pop music star with millions of fans in both Western Europe and Turkey. He was born in Germany and raised there until his family returned to Turkey when he was thirteen. Tarkan's music combines Western and Turkish sounds. In 1999, along with several other male Turkish pop singers, Tarkan found himself in trouble with Turkish authorities because he had

not served eighteen months of military service, which is required of all Turkish males when they reach the age of eighteen. Tarkan, who calls himself the "Prince of the Bosporus," has refused to return to Turkey in order to avoid arrest and faces the loss of his Turkish citizenship.

Tehran

Capital of Iran. Tehran has a long history of settlement, but remained a minor town until chosen as Persia's capital in the late eighteenth century. In 1943 it was the site of the first World War II meeting between U.S. president Franklin Roosevelt, Britain's prime minister Churchill, and Soviet leader Joseph Stalin. After the war the city grew rapidly and underwent modernization under Mohammad Reza Shah Pahlavi, leaving little of significance that is more than a half century old. Today Tehran is Iran's industrial center, but also a sprawling, overcrowded metropolis with severe pollution problems and teeming slums. The population has fallen slightly in recent years as people who fled the fighting of the Iran-Iraq war have begun returning to their native towns and villages.

Tel Aviv

Tel Aviv was founded on sand dunes in 1909, a few miles north of the ancient port of Jaffa. Since then, enveloping Jaffa in the process, Tel Aviv, which means "hill of spring," has grown into Israel's center of business, culture, and commerce and is considered one of the liveliest cities in the world. Although Tel Aviv proper is smaller than Jerusalem, it is the core of Israel's largest metropolitan region. If Jerusalem is known for its history and religious shrines, Tel Aviv is known for its thriving commercial activity, beachside hotels, and nightlife that runs until dawn. It was in Tel Aviv on May 14, 1948, that David Ben-Gurion proclaimed the independence of the state of Israel.

Terrorism

Terrorism is the systematic organized use of extreme violence against civilians to achieve political ends. While terrorism is an old tactic, it did not become a significant political weapon until the 1960s. This occurred in large part because modern electronic media, especially television, spread the news and the frightening reality of terrorism to hundreds of millions of people, and therefore exponentially increased the impact of any given act. Modern terrorism includes acts such as bombings, hijacking and skyjacking, and assassinations. Most terrorist acts are committed by independent organizations, but often they act as proxies of governments. As of 2001 the United States State Department listed seven countries that sponsored terrorist groups. Four of them—Iran, Iraq, Libya, and Syria—are Middle Eastern Arab states. The fifth, Sudan, has an Islamic fundamentalist regime. The two remaining countries, Cuba and North Korea, are Communist states.

The most frequent target of terrorism in the Middle East has been Israel. Terrorism against Israel has been carried out by a variety of Palestinian and Islamic organizations. While most of the Palestinian groups joined the PLO, they continued to operate independently. These organizations turned to terror after Arab states failed to defeat Israel on the battlefield in 1948–49 and again in 1967. Among their more notorious actions was the murder of thirteen Israel athletes at the 1972 Olympic Games by Yasir Arafat's Fatah group; the murder of twenty-two schoolchildren in the Israeli town of Ma'alot by the Democratic Front for the Liberation of Palestine (DFLP) in 1974; and al-Fatah's 1978 hijacking of an Israeli bus on the Haifa–Tel Aviv highway, which ended with thirty-four Israeli dead. Sometimes terrorist actions did not target Israel itself but were designed to take hostages, including Israelis, who could be used for political purposes. Examples are the hijacking of four European and American airliners in September 1970 by the Popular Front for the Liberation of Palestine (PFLP) and the hijacking of a French airliner to Entebbe, Uganda, by Palestinian and German terrorists in July 1976. That episode ended with almost one hundred Israeli and Jewish hostages being rescued in a daring raid by the Israeli army.

In the 1980s and 1990s, Islamic fundamentalist groups opposed to an Israeli-Palestinian peace tried to derail the peace process with suicide bombings inside Israel. The most deadly attacks were carried out by two groups, Hamas and Islamic Jihad. They were responsible for a series of attacks that killed more than 60 Israelis in just two months in 1996. Between the signing of the Oslo Accords in September 1993 and September 2000, more than 250 Israelis were killed in terrorist attacks.

Middle Eastern terrorism has not been used only against Israel. Radical groups have murdered moderate Palestinian officials who favored negotiations with Israel. That was the fate of PLO moderate Issam Sartawi in 1983 (murdered by a group commanded by archterrorist Abu Nidal), and two moderate West Bank mayors, Aziz Shehadeh of Ramallah and Zafir al-Masri of Nablus, both assassinated by the PFLP. Nor is Middle

Eastern terrorism always linked to the Arab-Israeli conflict. Syria has used terrorism against both moderate Palestinians and Jordanians for its own purposes, some of which have little or nothing to do with Israel. Libya and Iraq have followed similar courses of action.

The United States also has become a target of Islamic and Arab terrorists for several reasons. Libya's planting of the bomb that destroyed an airborne American airliner in 1988, killing 270 people, grew out of a number of U.S.-Libyan confrontations. U.S. support of Israel and the Israeli-Palestinian peace process has angered Arab and Islamic extremists. On a deeper level, Islamic fundamentalists consider Western and American values, and therefore American influence in the Middle East, as a threat to the Islamic way of life. They believe they must end Western and U.S. influence in the Middle East to achieve their goal of establishing strict Islamic regimes everywhere in the religion. The 1983 suicide truck bomb attack by an Iranian-backed group that killed 241 U.S. marines in Lebanon was an effort to drive Western peacekeeping forces from that country. The bombing of the World Trade Center in New York City in 1993, which killed six people and injured 1,000, was carried out by an extremist Islamic group whose goal was to overthrow the secular Egyptian government of President Hosni Mubarak, a government the United States strongly supports. In 1996, Islamic fundamentalists backed by Iran bombed the Khobar Towers, a U.S. military residence in Saudi Arabia, killing nineteen U.S. airmen, while in 1998 terrorists controlled by Saudi exile Osama bin Laden bombed two American embassies in Africa. Those bombings killed 244 people, including twelve Americans, and wounded more that 4,600. In September 2001, in the worst terrorist act in history, terrorists loyal to bin Laden destroyed the World Trade Center in New York City and damaged the Pentagon in Washington, D.C., killing well over 5,000 people.

al-Thani, Hamad bin Khalifa (1950–)

Emir (ruler) of Qatar. Sheikh Hamad came to power in 1995 after engineering a bloodless coup against his conservative father. Like several other Persian Gulf rulers, he graduated from a British military academy and held military and defense positions before becoming emir. He became crown prince in 1977 and accumulated considerable political power by the early 1990s prior to deposing his father. Sheikh Hamad, one of the most reform-minded Arab monarchs, is best known for his support of the Al Jazeera television station, the only station in the Arab world permitted to broadcast free of government censorship or bias.

Tripoli

Libya's capital was founded as a Phoenician colony and port more than 2,600 years ago. For centuries a terminal point for several trans-Sahara caravan routes, it currently is an important Libyan transportation, commercial, and industrial center. In 1986 the United States bombed Tripoli in retaliation for Libyan-sponsored terrorism attacks in Europe in which several Americans were killed. Since 1996 the city has benefited from Muammar Qaddafi's "Great Man-Made River" project, which is being built to transport water from aquifers deep in the Sahara desert to the parched Libyan Mediterranean coast. People in Tripoli no longer have to drink brackish local groundwater. As one shopkeeper exulted, "What used to be salty is now as sweet as can be.[3]

Notes

Chapter Two

1. Quoted in Martin Gilbert, *Israel: A History* (New York: William Morrow and Company, 1998), p. 487.
2. *The New York Times*, April 1, 1999.
3. *The New York Times*, November 3, 1999.
4. *Ibid*.
5. *Boston Globe*, May 8, 1999.

Chapter Three

1. *The Illustrated Jerusalem Bible*, English translation, edited by M. Friedlander. (Jerusalem, London, New York: Jerusalem Bible Publishing Co., 1958), p. 1525.
2. Quoted in Abba Eban, *My Country: The Story of Modern Israel* (New York: Random House, 1972), p. 48.
3. Quoted in Martin Gilbert, *The Arab-Israeli Conflict: Its History in Maps* (London: Weidenfield and Nicolson, 1974), p. 68.
4. Quoted in Howard M. Sachar, *A History of Israel: From the Rise of Zionism to Our Time* (New York: Knopf, 1976), p. 673.
5. Quoted in the preface to *The Rabin Memoirs*, 2nd ed, (Bnei Brak, Israel: Steimatsky Ltd., 1994), pp. v-vi.
6. Quoted in Robert Slater, *Rabin of Israel: Warrior for Peace* (New York: Harper Collins, 1996), p. 583.
7. U.S. State Department Daily Press Briefing, Thursday, January 22, 1999.
8. *The New York Times*, July 7, 1999.
9. *The New York Times*, April 4, 2001.

10. *The New York Times*, November 25, 1998.
11. *The Jerusalem Post*, December 15, 2000.
12. *The New York Times*, February 8, 1999.

Chapter Four

1. Quoted in Avraham Sela, editor, *Political Encyclopedia of the Middle East* (Jerusalem: The Jerusalem Publishing House, 1999), p. 710.
2. *The New York Times*, May 9, 1999.
3. *Ibid*.
4. Quoted in Howard M. Sachar, *A History of Israel: From the Rise of Zionism to Our Time*, Second Edition, Revised and Updated (New York: Alfred A. Knopf, 1996), p.879.
5. *The New York Times*, January 27, 1999.
6. *The New York Times*, February 18, 2001.
7. *The New York Times*, December 23, 1998.

Chapter Five

1. *The New York Times*, May 26, 1999.
2. *The New York Times*, July 4, 1999.
3. *The Boston Globe*, January 18, 1999.
4. *The New York Times*, May 3, 1999.
5. *The New York Times*, May 3, 1999.
6. *The New York Times*, May 4, 1999.
7. *The New York Times*, April 17, 1999.

8. *The New York Times*, April 30, 1999.
9. *The New York Times*, May 11, 1999.
10. *The New York Times*, June 30, 1999.
11. *National Geographic*, vol. 196, no. 1 (July 1999), p. 14.
12. *National Geographic*, vol. 196, no. 1 (July 1999), p. 6.
13. *The New York Times Magazine*, November 1, 1998, p. 53.
14. *Ibid*.
15. *The New York Times*, July 19, 1999.
16. *Ibid*.
17. *The New York Times*, February 4, 1999.
18. *Ibid*.
19. *The New York Times*, July 15, 1999.

Chapter Six

1. *The New York Times*, January 16, 1999.
2. *The New York Times*, May 24, 1999.
3. *The New York Times*, January 16, 1999.
4. *The New York Times*, July 4, 1999.
5. *Ibid*.
6. *The New York Times*, September 19, 1999.
7. *Ibid*.

Encyclopedia

1. *The New York Times*, March 28, 2001.
2. *The New York Times*, January 15, 1999.
3. *The New York Times*, October 3, 1998.

Index

Page numbers in *italics* refer to illustrations.

Abbasid dynasty, 123, 253, 254
Abdel Aziz al-Saud (Ibn Saud),
    191–192, 194, 195, 261, 272, 282
Abdullah Ibn Abdel Aziz al-Saud,
    185, 192, 198, *245*, 261
  profile of, 245
Abdullah ibn Hussein, 98–99
Abdullah ibn Hussein, II, 102–103,
    246
  profile of, 245–246
Abu Dhabi, United Arab Emirates,
    207, 208, *246*
  profile of, 246
Abu Nidal, 288
Aegean Sea, 10, 140, 154
Agriculture
  in Egypt, 28–29
  in Iran, 165
  in Iraq, 126
  in Israel, 59–61
  in Jordan, 96
  in Lebanon, 107
  in Saudi Arabia, 190
  in Syria, 116
  in Turkey, 143
  in Yemen, 217

Ahmed Fuad, King of Egypt, 32–33
Akhenaton, 9, 27, 30
al-Assad, Bashar, 118, 121–122, *252*,
    253
  profile of, 252
al-Assad, Hafez, 118–122, *253*
  profile of, 252–253
al-Assad, Rifaat, 121, 253
Alawite sect, 117–119, 122, 144, 252
Al-Azhar Mosque, Cairo, 22, 31
Al-Daklah oasis, 25
Alexander the Great, 16, 30–31, 162,
    184, 247
Alexandria, Egypt, 23, 31
  profile of, 247
al-Fatah ("Conquest") guerrilla orga-
    nization, 79, 86, 87, 91, 251,
    252, 288
Al-Fayyum oasis, 25, 26
Algeria, 5, 48, 49
al-Jihad ("Holy War"), 38, 40, 42, 45
al-Khalifa, Hamad bin Isa, 205, 206
  profile of, 268
al-Khalifa, Isa bin Sulman, 205
al-Nahyan, Zayed bin Sultan, 208, 209
  profile of, 273–274

al Sabah, Jaber al-Ahmad, 203
  profile of, 282–283
al Said, Qaboos ibn Said, 212, 214, 215
  profile of, 283–284
al Said, Said ibn Taimur, 212
al-Thani, Hamad bin Khalifa, 211
  profile of, 289–290
al-Thani, Khalifa bin Hamad, 211
Amenemhet I, 25
Amman, Jordan, 95
  profile of, 247–248
Anatolia (Asia Minor), 13, 16, 139–142, 146, 148
Animals, 25, 27, 59, 62, 106
Ankara, Turkey, 142, 149
  profile of, 247
Anti-Lebanon Mountains, 115, 116, 258
Aouzou strip, 54
Arabian-American Oil Company (Aramco), 189
Arabian Desert, 12, 25
Arabian Peninsula, 10, 12–14, 17, 18, 22, 184–185, 216 (*see also* specific countries)
Arabian Sea, 10, 184, 216
Arabic language, 14, 31
Arab-Israeli conflict, 19
  Camp David Accords, 37–38, 78, 249
  Egyptian-Israeli peace treaty of 1979, 78, 249, 283
  Lebanese civil war (1975-1990), 78–79, 255
  Lebanon War (1982), 248
  peace negotiations (*see* Israeli-Palestinian peace negotiations)
  profile of, 248–250
  Six-Day War (1967), 34–35, 74–75, 99, 100, 118, 248, 249, 266, 274, 282, 285
  Suez War (1956), 72, 74, 248, 285
  War of Attrition (1969-1970), 248
  War of Independence (1948-1949), 71–72, 76, 99, 118, 128, 248, 266
  Yom Kippur War (1973), 36, 76, 100, 119, 189, 195, 248, 272, 277, 285
Arab League (League of Arab States), 37, 42, 71, 74, 76, 101, 112, 202, 279
  profile of, 250–251

Arab nationalism, 22
Arabs, 9, 13–14, 17, 19–20, 62, 65–68 (*see also* Arab-Israeli conflict, Israeli-Palestinian peace negotiations)
Arab socialism, 34, 274
Arafat, Yasir, 67, 76, 83, 85, 86, 88, 91–95, *251*, 254, 279, 280, 288
  profile of, 251–252
Aramaic language, 14
Arava Valley, 59
Armenian deportation, 147–148
Aryans, 161
Ashkenazic Jews, 63–64, 72
Assyrians, 16, 30, 278
Aswan, Egypt, 24, 26
Aswan High Dam, 26, 28, 34, 35
Ataturk, Mustafa Kemal, 147–150, 166, 247, *253*, 264
  profile of, 253
Ayyubid dynasty, 1

Baathists, 118, 119, 129
Bab al-Mandab strait, 216
Babylonians, 16, 69
Baghdad, Iraq, 123, 125, *127*, 258
  profile of, 253–254
Baha'i faith, 9, 166
Bahrain, 6, 9, 185, 268
  capital of, 204, 271
  economy of, 205
  flag of, 229
  geography of, 204
  oil resources in, 205
  politics in, 205, 206
  population of, 204
Balfour Declaration, 69–70
Balkan Peninsula, 18
Bani-Sadr, Abolhassan, 172
Barada River, 258
Barak, Ehud, 83–85, 87, 95, 252, *254*, 275
  profile of, 254–255
Barbary pirates, 50
Basra, Iraq, 124
Bayar, Celal, 151
Bedouin, 97
Beersheba, Israel, 59
Begin, Menachem, *37*, 77–79, *255*, 283
  profile of, 255
Beirut, Lebanon, 105, 109–110, *256*
  profile of, 255–256
Bekáa Valley, 105, 106, 109, 120

Benghazi, Libya, 49
Ben-Gurion, David, 70, 71, 74, 77,
    256, 280, 287
    profile of, 256
Berbers, 15, 49
Bethlehem, Israel, 67
bin Laden, Osama, 197, 219, 289
Biological weapons (*see* Weapons of
    mass destruction)
Birket Qarun, 25
Black Sea, 10, 13, 140–142, 150
Black September, 100, 262
Blue Nile, 11
Bosporus, 13, 139, 142, 148, 263, 264
Boutros-Ghali, Boutros, 43
Bush, George W., 54
Butler, Richard, 135
Byzantine Empire (Eastern Roman),
    16–17, 31, 140, 146, 263
Byzantines, 14, 139, 162, 265

Cairo, Egypt, 23, 31, 42, *257*
    profile of, 257
Cairo Agreement of 1994, 81, 249
Camel races, *207*
Camp David Accords, 37–39, 78, 249
Canal Zone, 34
Carter, Jimmy, 37, *37*, 38, 78, 85, 172
Caspian Sea, 10, 163, 165
Castro, Fidel, 48
Catal Huyuk, Turkey, 7
Caucasus Mountains, 10
Cedars of Lebanon, *106*
Chad, 48, 54
Chemical weapons, 276 (*see also*
    Nuclear weapons)
Child labor, 29
Christianity, 9, 16–18, 29, 31, 56
Ciller, Tansu, 152, *258*
    profile of, 258
Climate, 10–13
    of Bahrain, 204
    of Egypt, 24
    of Iran, 163–164
    of Israel, 59
    of Kuwait, 199
    of Lebanon, 105
    of Libya, 48
    of Oman, 213
    of Saudi Arabia, 187
    of Turkey, 142
    of United Arab Emirates, 207
    of Yemen, 216

Clinton, Bill, 83, 85, 103
Cold War, 20, 33, 150, 168, 274
Constantinople, Turkey, 17, 31, 140,
    146, 148, 149, 263–264
Coptic Christians, 15, 29, 31, 40–41
Crusaders, 18, 31, 32, 95, 108, 139,
    265, 278
Cyprus, 5, 154, 155, 260
Cyrenaica, 48, 49
Cyrus the Great, 161, 170

Damascus, Syria, *115*, 258–259, *259*
Dardanelles, 13, 139, 140, 147, 148,
    263
Dayan, Moshe, 75
Dead Sea, 7, 10, 58–59, 61, 95
Declaration of Principles of 1993
    (*see* Oslo Accords)
Demirel, Suleyman, 151, 152, 258,
    259
    profile of, 259
Democratic Front for the Liberation
    of Palestine (DFLP), 280, 288
Deserts, 11, 12, *12*, 24–26, 59, 163,
    187, *213*, 216
Dhimmi (inferiors), 17
Doha, Qatar, profile of, 259–260
Druze Christians, 15, 62, 67,
    108–111, 117, 118
Dubai, United Arab Emirates, 207,
    208
Dulles, John Foster, 5

Earthquakes, 159–160, 164
Ecevit, Bulent, 151, 152, 155–156,
    161, *260*
    profile of, 260
Economy, 9
    of Bahrain, 205
    of Egypt, 22, 29, 33, 34, 36, 38, 39
    of Iran, 164–165, 168, 171, 175
    of Iraq, 125–126, 135
    of Israel, 60–61
    of Jordan, 96, 98, 100, 103
    of Kuwait, 199–202
    of Lebanon, 107
    of Libya, 49
    of Oman, 214
    of Palestinian Authority (PA),
        91–92, 94
    of Qatar, 210
    of Saudi Arabia, 186, 188–191
    of Syria, 116–117, 122

of Turkey, 142–144, 149–150, 160
of United Arab Emirates, 209
of Yemen, 217
Egypt, 5, 6, 8, 9, 11, 12, 15, 16,
    21–47, 273, 274, 283 (see also
    Arab-Israeli conflict)
    agriculture in, 28–29
    Arab League membership and, 37,
      42, 250
    capital of, 23, 31, 42, 257, 257
    chemical weapons and, 276
    climate of, 24
    cultural life in, 46–47
    economy of, 22, 29, 33, 34, 36, 38,
      39
    flag of, 226
    geography of, 23–29
    history of, 30–44
    Islamic fundamentalism in, 38–42
    law in, 45–46
    leadership in Arab world, 21–23
    oil resources in, 29
    politics in, 44–45
    population of, 21, 22, 29–30
    press in, 45
    women's rights in, 33, 45–46
El Alamein, battle of, 19
Elat, Israel, 35
Elburz Mountains, 163
Empty Quarter desert, 187, 216
Erbakan, Necmettin, 152, 153, 155
    profile of, 260
Eshkol, Levi, 76
Ethiopia, 5, 63, 64
Euphrates River, 8, 11, 13, 30, 116,
    117, 123–125, 141, 143, 144

Fahd ibn Abdel Aziz al-Saud, King of
    Saudi Arabia, 131, 192, 195,
    197, 198, 245
    profile of, 261
Faisal, King of Saudi Arabia, 192, 195
Faisal ibn Hussein, King of Iraq, 128
Faisal II, King of Iraq, 128
Farouk, King of Egypt, 33
Fatah Revolutionary Council, 280
Fatamids, 31, 215, 247, 257
Fertile Crescent, 6, 13, 16, 18, 22, 59,
    184
Fezzan, 48, 49
Ford, Gerald, 38
Fossil water, 12, 190
Fuda, Faraj, 40

Galilee, 58
Gallipolli, 147
Gama'a al-Islamiya ("Islamic
    Group"), 41, 42, 45
Gaza City, 89
    profile of, 261
Gaza Strip, 34, 57, 71, 75, 77–81, 85,
    86, 89–91, 94, 95, 249, 251, 261,
    278, 279
Giza, Egypt, 23
Giza plateau, 23
Golan Heights, 57, 58, 75–78, 100,
    115, 118–120
Great Mosque, Damascus, 258
Great Pyramid of Khufu, 23
Great Rift Valley, 58, 116
Great Salt Desert, 11
Great Sphinx, 23–24, 30
Greeks, 14, 16
Groundwater, 11–12, 205
Gulf Cooperation Council (GCC),
    185
Gulf of Aden, 10, 184, 216
Gulf of Aqaba, 35, 57–58, 95, 186
Gulf of Elat, 58
Gulf of Oman, 10, 163, 184
Gulf of Sidra, 49, 53
Gulf of Suez, 25
Gulf War (1991), 6, 22, 39, 43, 78–80,
    96, 101–102, 120, 123, 124, 126,
    131–132, 196–197, 199, 201, 203,
    250, 262

Hagia Sophia, 146, 263, 264
Haifa, Israel, 58
Hajj (pilgrimage), 187, 196, 272
Hamas (Movement of Islamic Resis-
    tance), 79, 86, 88, 93, 95, 103,
    263, 280, 289
Hamito-Semitic languages, 30
Hammurabi, King of Babylon, 123
Harawi, Elias, 112
Hasbash, George, 279
Hashemites, 97, 98, 128, 194, 272
Hassan, Crown Prince of Jordan,
    102, 245
Hatshepsut, 27
Hawatma, Naif, 280
Hebrew language, 14, 56, 66
Hebron, 82, 91, 275
Hebron Protocol of 1997, 82,
    249–250
Hejaz, 187

Herodotus, 25, 26
Herzl, Theodor, 69
Hezbollah (Lebanon), 84, 112
Hezbollah (Turkey), 160–161
Hieroglyphics, 32
Hittites, 16, 139
Holocaust, 62, 70, 254
Hussein, Qusai, 137
Hussein, Saddam, 101, 123, 124,
    126, 129–137, *136*, 172, 173,
    196, 197, 250–251, *262*
  profile of, 262
Hussein, Udai, 133, 137
Hussein Ibn Ali, 194
Hussein ibn Talal, King of Jordan,
    83, 99, 103, 110, 245, 262
  profile of, 261–262

Ibn Khaldun, 257
Idris I, King of Libya, 48, 50
Inonu, Ismet, 150
Intifada, 79, 86, 88, 94
Iran, 5, 6, 9–12, 14, 15, 20, 161–183,
    268–269, 277–278 (*see also* Arab-
    Israeli conflict)
  agriculture in, 165
  ancient history of, 161–162
  capital of, 163, 287
  economy of, 164–165, 168, 171,
    175
  flag of, 227
  geography of, 163–164
  -Iraq War of 1979-1988, 42, 53,
    119, 123, 124, 130, 172–173,
    191, 196, 203, 254, 262
  Islamic Revolution in, 138,
    170–174, 196, 199, 248, 276
  land reform in, 168
  law in, 167
  modern history of, 166–170
  natural resources in, 164
  nuclear and biological weapons
    and, 176–177, 276
  oil resources in, 169, 276
  population of, 165–166
  post-Khomeini generation in,
    177–182
  religion in, 166, 167, 171
  U.S. hostage crisis (1979), 172
  White Revolution in, 168, 278
  women's rights in, 167, 168, 171,
    179
Iranian language, 14–15

Iraq, 5, 6, 10, 11, 13, 15, 18, 20, 22,
    38, 63, 95, 123–137 (*see also*
    Arab-Israeli conflict)
  agriculture in, 126
  Arab League membership and, 250
  capital of, 125, 253–254
  economy of, 125–126, 135
  flag of, 228
  geography of, 123–125
  Gulf War and, 78–80, 101–102,
    123, 124, 126, 131–132, 196–197,
    199, 201, 203
  history of modern, 128–137
  Iran-Iraq War of 1979-1988, 42,
    53, 119, 123, 124, 130, 172–173,
    191, 196, 203, 254, 262
  nuclear and biological weapons
    and, 78, 126, 130–131, 133–135,
    275
  oil resources in, 276
  population of, 126–128
Irrigation, 60, 143
Islam, 9, 14, 15, 17–18, 31, 33, 184,
    192–193
Islamic fundamentalism, 22–23, 29,
    38–42, 93, 101–103, 118–120,
    144, 150, 152, 160, 191–192,
    253, 263
  profile of, 262–263
Islamic Jihad, 79, 86, 93, 280, 289
Islamic Revolution, 138, 170 174,
    196, 199, 248, 276
Israel, 5, 6, 9, 11–13, 15, 18, 19, 33,
    34, 55–89, 253–256, 267–268,
    272, 274–275, 280–282, 285–286
    (*see also* Arab-Israeli conflict)
  agriculture in, 59–61
  capital of, 265–266
  economy of, 60–61
  flag of, 226
  geography of, 56–59
  history of modern, 69–89
  industry in, 61–62, 88
  natural resources in, 61
  nuclear program of, 275
  peace negotiations (*see* Israeli-
    Palestinian peace negotiations)
  politics in, 68–69, 77, 79, 82
  population of, 62–68
  religion in, 64–65
  women's rights in, 66
Israeli-Palestinian peace negotia-
    tions, 288–289

Cairo Agreement of 1994, 249
Camp David negotiations of 2000,
    85–86, 94
Hebron Protocol of 1997, 82,
    249–250
Israeli-Jordanian peace treaty of
    1994, 249
Oslo Accords, 43, 80–81, 90, 249,
    251–252, 275, 281, 282
Sharm al-Sheikh agreement of
    1999, 84, 91, 94, 250, 254
Taba Agreement (Oslo II), 81, 93,
    249
Wye River Memorandum of 1998,
    83, 84, 91, 93, 250, 275
Israelite kingdom, 16, 55, 162, 265,
    278
Istanbul, Turkey, 139, 140, 142, 149,
    264
    profile of, 263–264
Izmit earthquake, 159–160

Jaffa, Israel, 287
Jebel an-Nusariyah mountain range,
    115
Jefferson, Thomas, 50
Jericho, 7, 80, 90
Jerusalem, 31, 57, 58, 71–72, 75, 77,
    85, 86, 90, 92, 99, 100, *266*
    profile of, 265–266
Jews, 15, 17, 34, 55–56, 62–64, 70,
    128, 265, 266, 278 (*see also* Israel)
Jezreel Valley (Valley of Israel), 58
Jiddah, Saudi Arabia, 187, *188*
Jihad (holy war), 17, 251
Jordan, 6, 11, 12, 15, 18, 35, 42, 58,
    71, 95–103, 245–246, 261–262,
    266, 278, 279 (*see also* Arab-
    Israeli conflict)
    agriculture in, 96
    capital of, 95, 247–248
    economy of, 96, 98, 100, 103
    flag of, 227
    geography of, 95–96
    history of modern, 98–103
    politics in, 101
    population of, 97–98
    women's rights in, 101
Jordan River, 11, 58, 60, 95, 99, 100,
    105, 278
Jordan Valley, 58, 77, 96
Judaism, 9, 55–56
Judea, 56, 89, 278

Kaffiyeh (headcloth), 13
Kalthoum, Vmm, profile of, 267
Karnak, 27
Karun River, 163, 165
Kassem, Abdul Karim, 128, 129
Katsav, Moshe, *267*
    profile of, 267–268
Kavakci, Merve, 156–157
Khalid, King of Saudi Arabia, 192, 195
Khamenei, Ayatollah Ali Hussein,
    174, 176, 181–183, *268*, 269
    profile of, 268
Khatami, Sayed Mohammad,
    175–176, 179–183, *269*
    profile of, 268–269
Khomeini, Ayatollah Ruhollah,
    168–174, 182, 263, 268, *269*
    profile of, 269
Khudaibiya treaty, 251
Kibbutz, 60
Kizil Irmak, 141
Koran, 17, 40, 45
Koroglu Mountains, 140
Kurdistan, 15, 145
Kurds, 15, 117, 125–128, 132, 144–
    145, 155, 157–161, 165, 260, 275
Kuris, Konca, 160
Kush, 30
Kuwait, 6, 9, 282–283
    capital of, 200, 270
    economy of, 199–202, 205
    flag of, 229
    geography of, 199
    Gulf War and, 79, 123, 124,
        131–132, 197, 199, 201, 203
    modern history of, 202–204
    oil resources in, 185, 187,
        199–202, 205, 276
    politics in, 203–204, 205
    population of, 185, 200–201
    women's rights in, 203–204, 206,
        283
Kuwait City, Kuwait, 200, 202
    profile of, 270

Lahoud, Emile, 112
    profile of, 270
Lake Nasser, 26, 28
Languages, 14–15
Latakia, Syria, 115
Law
    in Egypt, 45–46
    in Iran, 167

Sharia (Muslim religious law), 23,
  45, 171, 193, 203, 209, 263
  in Turkey, 147, 149
League of Nations, 18, 69–70, 109,
  114, 128, 278–279
Lebanon, 5, 6, 9, 11, 13, 15, 18, 58,
  104–114, 270, 278 (*see also* Arab-
  Israeli conflict)
  agriculture in, 107
  Arab League membership and, 250
  capital of, 105, 255–256
  civil war (1975-1990), 78–79, 104,
    107, 111–114, 255
  economy of, 107
  flag of, 227
  geography of, 105–106
  Palestine Liberation Organization
    in, 110, 111
  politics in, 109–111
  population of, 107–108
  religion in, 108
  Syria and, 104–105, 112–114, 117,
    120
Lebanon War (1982), 248, 285–286
Libya, 5, 6, 9, 10, *12*, 12, 15, 23, 38,
  47–56, 281, 288, 289 (*see also*
  Arab-Israeli conflict)
  capital of, 290
  chemical weapons and, 276
  climate of, 48
  economy of, 49
  flag of, 226
  geography of, 48–49
  history of, 50
  oil resources in, 49, 51
  politics in, 51–52
  population of, 49
  under Qaddafi, 50–54
Luxor, 27, 41

Maghreb, 49
Mahan, Alfred Thayer, 6
Mahfouz, Naguib, 22, 40
  profile of, 270–272
Mamlukes, 32, 95, 257, 265
Manama, Bahrain, 204
  profile of, 271
Manco, Baris, profile of, 271
Maronite Catholics, 108–112
Marsh Arabs, 124
Mecca, Saudi Arabia, 173, 187, 193,
  195, *196*
  profile of, 272

Medina, Saudi Arabia, 187, 193
Mediterranean Sea, 7, 10, 13, 18, 23,
  27, 28, 48, 55, 56, 140, 255, 278
Meir, Golda, 61, 76, 99, *272*
  profile of, 272
Menderes, Adnan, 151
Mesopotamia, 8, 11, 16, 123, 128
Middle East (*see also* specific coun-
  tries)
  climate, 10–11
  as cradle of civilization, 7–8
  definition of countries in, 5, 6
  first use of term, 6
  geographic setting, 7, 10–13
  historical overview, 16–20
  peoples of, 13–15
  population of, 10
Mohajerani, Ayatollah, 183
Mohammad, Prophet, 17, 92, 187,
  195, 251, 272
Mohammad Ali, 32
Mongols, 32, 123, 139, 146, 162, 254,
  258
Monotheism, 8–9, 16, 56
Morocco, 5, 49, 63
Moshav, 60–61
Mossadegh, Mohammad, 167–168
Mount Ararat, 141, *141*
Mount Catherine, 26
Mount Hermon, 58, 106, 115
Mount Lebanon, 105, 106, 255
Mount Sinai, 26
Mubarak, Hosni, 38–44, 289
  profile of, 273
Muscat, Oman, 213
  profile of, 273
Muslim Brotherhood, 34, 41–42, 45,
  118, 119, 253
Muslims (*see* Islam)

Nabavi, Ibrahim, 182
Nagib, Mohammad, 33
Nasser, Gamal Abdel, 22, 33–36, 44,
  50, *51*, 74, 129, 283
  profile of, 274
Nasser, Khaled Abdel, 45
Natural resources (*see also* Oil
  resources)
  in Iran, 164
  in Israel, 61
  in Syria, 116
  in Turkey, 143
Nazareth, Israel, 67

Negev Desert, 12, 59, 256
Netanyahu, Benjamin, 43, 82, 83,
    254, 281
  profile of, 274–275
Nile River, 8, *8*, 11, 13, 21, 23, 26–27
Nile Valley, 23, 25–27
Nixon, Richard, 38
North Africa, 5, 6, 9, 14
Nouri, Abdullah, 181
Nubia, 29, 30
Nuclear Non-Proliferation Treaty
    (NPT), 43
Nuclear weapons, 6, 20, 43, 78, 126,
    130–131, 133–135, 176–177
  profile of, 275–276

Oases, 25
Ocalan, Abdullah, 156–159
Oil resources, 6, 9, 10, 13, 19, 20, 29
  in Bahrain, 205
  in Egypt, 29
  in Iran, 164, 169
  in Iraq, 125–126
  in Kuwait, 185, 187, 199–202, 276
  in Libya, 49, 51
  in Oman, 214
  profile of, 276–277
  in Qatar, 210
  in Saudi Arabia, 185, 187–190
  in United Arab Emirates, 185, 199,
    207, 209, 276
  in Yemen, 217
Olympic Games (1972), 76, 288
Oman, 6, 11, 185, 283–284
  capital of, 213, 273
  economy of, 214
  flag of, 229
  geography of, 212–213
  oil resources in, 214
  politics in, 214, 215
  population of, 214
Operation Desert Storm, 131–132
Operation Moses, 64
Operation Solomon, 64
Organization of Arab Petroleum
    Exporting Countries (OAPEC),
    277
Organization of Petroleum Export-
    ing Countries (OPEC), 186, 189,
    276–277
Orontes River, 105, 116
Oslo Accords, 43, 80–81, 90, 249,
    251–252, 275, 281, 282

Ottoman Empire, 14, 18, 22, 32, 69,
    95, 98, 109, 114, 128, 144,
    146–148, 184, 194, 202, 247,
    263, 264, 278
Oz, Amos, 88
  profile of, 277
Özal, Turgut, 151

Pahlavi, Mohammad Reza Shah,
    167–170, 269, 287
  profile of, 277–278
Pahlavi, Reza Shah, 162, 166–167
Palestine, 18, 69–71, 248
  profile of, 278–279
Palestine Liberation Organization
    (PLO), 42, 194–195, 197, 248,
    251, 288
  establishment of, 76, 100
  profile of, 279
  recognition of, 101, 279
Palestinian Authority (PA), 6, 18,
    89–95, 266
  economy in, 91–92, 94
  establishment of, 90, 249
  flag of, 226
  geography of, 89
  peace negotiations (*see* Israeli-
    Palestinian peace negotiations)
  population of, 89
Palestinian Council, 81, 83, 91
Pan American Flight 103, 53, 54
Papyrus, 27
Peres, Shimon, 43, 77, 79, 82, 87,
    211, 214, 262, 274, 284
  profile of, 280–281
Persia, 9, 18, 287
Persian Empire, 16–17, 184
Persian Gulf, 6, 10, 11, 13, 19, 20,
    123, 124, 163, 184
Persian language, 165, 167
Persians, 14, 16, 25, 30, 31, 161–162
Pharoahs, 30
Politics, 9
  in Bahrain, 205, 206
  in Egypt, 44–45
  in Iran, 172, 174–175, 182–183
  in Israel, 68–69, 77, 79, 82
  in Jordan, 101
  in Kuwait, 203–204
  in Lebanon, 109–111
  in Libya, 51–52
  in Oman, 214, 215
  in Qatar, 211

in Saudi Arabia, 186, 191–193, 198
in Syria, 118
in Turkey, 151–156
in United Arab Emirates, 208
in Yemen, 219–220
Pontic Mountains, 140
Popular Front for the Liberation of
    Palestine (PFLP), 279–280, 288
Population, 10
    of Egypt, 21, 22, 29–30
    of Iran, 165–166
    of Iraq, 126–128
    of Israel, 62–68
    of Jordan, 97–98
    of Kuwait, 185, 200–201
    of Lebanon, 107–108
    of Libya, 49
    of Oman, 214
    of Palestinian Authority (PA), 89
    of Qatar, 185, 210
    of Syria, 117–118
    of Turkey, 144–145
    of United Arab Emirates, 185, 208
    of Yemen, 215–217
Ptolemaic dynasty, 31, 32, 247
Pyramid of Khafre, 23
Pyramids, 23–24, 24, 30

Qaddafi, Muammar, 48, 50–54, 51,
    290
    profile of, 281
Qatar, 6, 204, 289–290
    capital of, 259–260
    economy of, 210
    flag of, 229
    geography of, 210
    oil resources in, 210
    politics in, 211
    population of, 185, 210
    television station in, 211–212
Qattara Depression, 25

Rabin, Yitzhak, 42, 43, 76–77, 80–82,
    84, 102, 214, 251, 254, 262, 280,
    281, 284
    profile of, 281–282
Rafsanjani, Ali Akbar Hashemi,
    174–175
Rahman, Omar Abdel, 41
Rainfall, 11–13, 24 (see also Climate)
Ramadan War (see Yom Kippur War)
Ramses II, 27, 30
Reagan, Ronald, 172

Red Sea, 18, 23, 25, 74, 184, 186,
    187, 216
Religion, 8–10, 15–18 (see also spe-
    cific religions)
    in Iran, 166, 167, 171
    in Israel, 64–65
    in Lebanon, 108
    in Saudi Arabia, 186, 192
    in Turkey, 144, 149
Riyadh, Saudi Arabia, 187
    profile of, 282
Romans, 14, 16, 31, 56, 184
Rosetta Stone, 32

Sadat, Anwar, 36–39, 37, 41, 42, 44,
    53, 78, 101, 119, 174, 249, 271,
    273
    profile of, 283
Safavid dynasty, 162
Sahara Desert, 12, 12, 13, 24, 49
Saladin, 31
Saleh, Ali Abdullah, 218–220
    profile of, 284
Samaria, 89
Sanaa, Yemen, 216, 284
    profile of, 284–285
Sand Sea, 25
Sanskrit, 14
Sargon, King of Akkad, 8, 16, 123
Sartawi, Issam, 288
Saud, King of Saudi Arabia, 192, 195
Saudi Arabia, 5, 6, 9–11, 22, 35, 95,
    176, 245, 261 (see also Arab-
    Israeli conflict)
    Arab League membership and, 250
    capital of, 187, 282
    economy of, 186, 188–191
    flag of, 228
    geography of, 186–187
    Gulf War and, 131, 196–197
    modern history of, 194–198
    oil resources in, 185, 187–190, 276
    politics in, 186, 191–193, 198
    religion in, 186, 192
    women's rights in, 193
Sea of Galilee (Lake Tiberias), 58, 60
Sea of Marmara, 13, 140
Seljuk Turks, 18, 123, 139, 162
Sephardic Jews, 63–64, 72, 77
Sezer, Ahmet Secdet, 161
Shamir, Yitzhak, 79
Sharia (Muslim religious law), 23,
    45, 171, 193, 203, 209, 263

Sharm al-Sheikh agreement of 1999, 84, 91, 94, 250, 254
Sharon, Ariel, 86–88, 255
  profile of, 285–286
Shatt-al-Arab, 123–124, 130, 172–173, 199
Shemer, Naomi, profile of, 286
Shiite Muslims, 15, 108, 109, 111, 112, 117, 126–128, 132, 144, 166, 171, 191, 198, 204, 206, 215, 217
Sinai Peninsula, 23, 25–26, 29, 34–36, 74–78
Siwah oasis, 25
Six-Day War (1967), 34–35, 74–75, 99, 100, 118, 248, 249, 266, 274, 282, 285
Socialist-Zionism, 256
Strait of Hormuz, 163, 207, 213
Strait of Tiran, 35, 74
Sudan, 5, 11, 23, 28, 43, 48, 288
Suez Canal, 18, 19, 19, 29, 32, 34
Suez War (1956), 72, 74, 248, 285
Suleyman the Magnificent, 146–147
Sumerians, 8, 16, 123
Sunni Muslims, 15, 18, 49, 97, 108, 109, 111, 112, 117, 119, 122, 126–128, 144, 166, 191, 195, 198, 204, 215, 217, 252
Syria, 5, 6, 9–11, 13, 15, 18, 32, 35, 36, 38, 58, 95, 119–122, 252–253, 288
  (see also Arab-Israeli conflict)
  agriculture in, 116
  Arab League membership and, 250
  capital of, 115, 115, 258–259, 259
  chemical weapons and, 276
  economy of, 116–117, 122
  flag of, 227
  geography of, 114–116
  Gulf War and, 120
  Islamic fundamentalism in, 118–120, 253
  Lebanon and, 104–105, 112–114, 117, 120
  modern history of, 118–122
  natural resources in, 116
  politics in, 118
  population of, 117–118
Syrian Desert, 116

Taba Agreement (Oslo II), 81, 93, 249
Tabaqa Dam, 117

Taif Agreement of 1989, 112
Tamerlane, 146, 247
Tarif, Saleh, 87
Tarkan, 286
  profile of, 286–287
Taurus Mountains, 140
Tehran, Iran, 163
  profile of, 287
Tehran Conference (1943), 287
Tel al-Amarna, 27
Tel Aviv, Israel, 58
  profile of, 287
Terrorism, 10, 38–42, 53–54, 76, 77, 79, 82–84, 86, 88, 93, 120, 198, 219, 251, 263, 279–281
  profile of, 287–288
Thebes, Egypt, 27
Tigris River, 8, 11, 13, 123–125, 141, 143, 254
Tourism, 29, 61, 67, 142
Transjordan, 98, 128, 250, 279
Tripoli, Libya, 49, 50, 281
  profile of, 290
Tripolitania, 48, 49
Truman Doctrine, 150
Tunisia, 5, 38, 46, 48, 49
Turkey, 5–7, 9, 11, 13–15, 138–161, 148–151, 155–156, 253, 258–260
  agriculture in, 143
  Ataturk and, 148–150
  capital of, 142, 149, 247
  economy of, 142–144, 149–150, 160
  flag of, 228
  geography of, 139–142
  Islamic fundamentalism in, 144, 150, 152, 160
  Kurds in, 144–145, 155, 157–161
  law in, 147, 149
  natural resources in, 143
  Ottoman era, 146–148
  politics in, 151–156
  population of, 144–145
  postwar era in, 150–160
  religion in, 144, 149
  women's rights in, 149, 156–157
Tutankhamen, 27

Umayyad dynasty, 258
Unemployment, 39, 92, 94, 96, 122
United Arab Emirates, 6, 176, 204, 273–274
  capital of, 208, 246, 246

economy of, 209
flag of, 228
geography of, 207
oil resources in, 185, 199, 207, 209, 276
politics in, 208
population of, 185, 208
United Arab Republic, 35
United Nations, 34, 35, 38, 131, 133–135, 248–249
U.S.S. *Cole*, 219
U.S.S. *Enterprise*, *19*

Valley of the Kings, 27

Wahhabi sect, 191, 192
Wahiba Sands, Oman, *213*
War of Attrition (1969-1970), 248
War of Independence (1948-1949), 71–72, 76, 99, 118, 128, 248, 266, 281, 285
Water, 10–12, 27–28, 125, 143–144
Weapons of mass destruction, 6, 20 (*see also* Nuclear weapons)
profile of, 275–276
West Bank, 57, 71, 75, 77–83, 85, 86, 89–92, 94, 95, 98–101, 249, 275, 278, 279
Western (Libyan) Desert, 24–25, 29
White Nile, 11
White Revolution, 168, 278
Women's rights
in Bahrain, 206
in Egypt, 33, 45–46

in Iran, 167, 168, 171, 179
in Israel, 66
in Jordan, 101
in Kuwait, 203–204, 206, 283
in Saudi Arabia, 193
in Turkey, 149, 156–157
in Yemen, 219
World Trade Center bombing, 41, 219, 263, 289
Writing, 8, 32
Wye River Memorandum of 1998, 83, 84, 91, 93, 250, 275

Yasin, Ahmad, 280
Yemen, 6, 9, 11, 35, 63, 185, 276, 284
agriculture in, 217
Arab League membership and, 250
capital of, 216, *284*, 284–285
economy of, 217
flag of, 229
geography of, 216
oil resources in, 217
politics in, 219–220
population of, 215–217
women's rights in, 219
Yom Kippur War (1973), 36, 76, 100, 119, 189, 195, 248, 272, 277, 285

Zagros Mountains, 163, 165
Zeid, Nasr Abiu, 40
Zionism, 69, 92, 99, 256
Zoroastrianism, 9, 17, 162
Zuckerman, Pinchas, 88